D0553857

The Caddos, the Wichitas, and the United States

NUMBER SIXTY-FOUR:
*The Centennial Series
of the Association of Former Students,
Texas A&M University*

THE CADDOS, THE WICHITAS, AND THE UNITED STATES, 1846-1901

F. Todd Smith

Texas A&M University Press
College Station

Copyright © 1996 by F. Todd Smith
Manufactured in the United States of America
All rights reserved

03 02 01 00 99 98 97 96   5 4 3 2 1

The paper used in this book meets the minimum requirements
of the American National Standard for Permanence
of Paper for Printed Library Materials, Z39.48-1984.
Binding materials have been chosen for durability.

Library of Congress Cataloging-in-Publication Data

Smith, F. Todd (Foster Todd), 1957–
    The Caddos, the Wichitas, and the United States, 1846–1901 / F. Todd Smith.
      p.   cm. — (The centennial series of the Association of Former Students,
Texas A&M University ; no. 64)
    Includes bibliographical references and index.
    ISBN 0-89096-708-3
    1. Caddo Indians—History—19th century. 2. Caddo Indians—Government
relations. 3. Caddo Indians—Ethnic identity. 4. Wichita Indians—History—19th
century. 5. Wichita Indians—Government relations. 6. Wichita Indians—Ethnic
identity. 7. Indian reservations—United States—History—19th century. 8. United
States—Race relations. I. Title. II. Series.
E99.C12S66   1996
305.8´00973—dc20   96-26186
          CIP

For Sophie

Contents

Illustrations

Maps

Table

Acknowledgments

This book is the sequel to my first book, *The Caddo Indians: Tribes at the Convergence of Empires, 1542–1854,* which was an extension of my dissertation completed at Tulane University in 1989. In my first book I did not have the opportunity to acknowledge all those people who assisted in its preparation. Thus, I will take the space offered me here to give a joint thank you for the help I have received in producing both books.

I must first thank my family for providing constant support during and after the long years of graduate work. While at Tulane University I received much needed guidance from Richard Greenleaf, Munro Edmunson, and, particularly, Richard Latner, who painstakingly went through draft after draft of my dissertation and helped me achieve a semblance of coherence out of a jumble of confusion. Paul Dosal, Richmond Brown, John Nolan, and Katherine West also gave assistance—not all of it scholarly—during this formative period.

The process of turning my dissertation into a publishable manuscript began in Austin in 1990–91 with those die-hard Texans, *la famille Burton,* who made my stay there particularly enjoyable. Brian Belanger—who has since become Brother Timothy—proofread every chapter and gave instructive advice, particularly on matters concerning the Spanish and the Franciscans, long after he had tired of the entire procedure. Among those who read parts of the manuscript and forced me to go back to correct my mistakes were David Weber, Gilbert Din, Light

Cummins, Timothy Perttula, Daniel Usner, Robert Jackson, and Jim Norris. Following eight years of research and writing, my first book was finally published in 1995 by the Texas A&M University Press.

Work on this second book has gone more quickly and smoothly. While researching the first book, I found great quantities of material for the second; therefore, only a little more research was needed before I was ready to begin the writing phase of this manuscript. I must thank the staff at the Eugene C. Barker Center for American History at the University of Texas in Austin as well as the staff of the Oklahoma Historical Society in Oklahoma City, particularly Joe Todd. Through Xavier University in New Orleans I won a scholar-in-residence fellowship at New York University, where for a full month in the summer of 1994 I was able to devote all my time to writing. Gary Donaldson, fellow professor in the history department at Xavier University, read every chapter to make sure they were understandable. Xavier professors Shamsul Huda, Jonathan Rotondo-McCord, and Father Earl Niehaus also gave unflagging support.

Mainly, I must offer a million thanks to Sophie Burton, who has helped immensely with the research, the writing, and, most importantly, the living.

Introduction

For most of the two centuries of its existence, the United States government's Indian policy had rested on the belief that Euro-American and Native American cultures were so completely at odds with one another that there could be no accommodation between the two. Policy makers were certain that Euro-American culture was superior, and thus it was only a matter of time before the Indians' way of life would be destroyed by it. Therefore, if the Indians were to have any hopes of survival, they would need to abandon their doomed culture and adopt the ways of the civilized white man. The federal government's humanitarian duty then was to familiarize the Indians with the "arts of civilization," using force if necessary, in an effort to mold a new human: an individual, devoid of tribal ties, ready to assimilate as a citizen into the Christian, English-speaking culture of the United States.[1]

This belief has also been reflected in many of the past century's historical studies of Indians and their interaction with Euro-Americans. Prior to the 1970s most historians focused on the period before the various tribes were all settled on reservations, with emphasis on the inevitable destruction of the tribes and their cultures by the overwhelming force of the United States. According to this idea, once the Indians were placed on reservations they ceased to be Indians and thus were of little interest to historians or anyone else. The tribesmen were expected to "vanish" either by extinction or through their evolution into second-rate white men. What little focus there was on the reservation period was placed on those tribes, such as the nomadic, buffalo-hunting Sioux, who desperately resisted the federal government by adopting an apocalyptic version of the Ghost Dance ritual, resulting in their massacre at Wounded Knee in 1890. Most histories of the Sioux, or any other tribe, ended with the tribe's acceptance of a defeated life on the reservation.[2]

The strength and the resilience of Native Americans, however, have forced historians—much as Indians themselves were forced—to adopt new points of view. For Native Americans utlimately did not vanish, but instead their numbers grew from the nadir reached in 1900. Not only do they still exist, but most, while adapting themselves to the new order, have proudly retained their Native American identity. Therefore, recent historians have begun to view the interaction of Native Americans and Euro-Americans not as one of mutual exclusivity but as one of great interaction and accommodation. Right from the beginning both groups regarded the other with interest—sometimes guarded, sometimes not—in an attempt to discern what items these people had in their cultures that might be beneficial to their own. Native Americans did not lose their "Indianness" when they adopted horses—in fact, most Euro-Americans continue to associate a "traditional" Indian as being one on horseback—any more than white men broke with their European heritage when they began to raise corn or potatoes. Native Americans actively took the items they desired from the Euro-American intruders, whether it was material goods such as metal tools and weapons or spiritual aids such as Christianity. The best, new studies of interaction have demonstrated that the Native Americans and Euro-Americans (as well as African Americans) created a genuine "new" world for all those involved.[3]

Although all of the Indian tribes of North America were utlimately overwhelmed by the United States and placed on reservations, even there they continued to resist the policy of complete assimilation as best they could. Many were willing to adapt to the new way of life on the reservation, but few had any desire to denounce their "Indianness" and become white men. Even after the federal government legally dissolved the tribes and broke up the reservations through allotment, Native Americans persistently hung on to their identities. To some extent, their tenacity paid off, for in the 1930s the United States radically shifted its Indian policy and initiated a program—however limited and imperfect—designed to recognize and preserve Native American culture and identity.

Historians, however, have hesitated to study the reservation period and the twentieth century with the same intensity as the colonial and national periods of interaction. The historiography of the Wichita and Caddo Indians reflects this trend. In the first place, few scholars have studied these tribes during any period, because of their having been located within the neglected French and Spanish empires of North America instead of the well-surveyed English colonies. The few historical studies of these tribes focus mainly on the colonial period, with little discussion of the American period and almost nothing about their lives on the reservation. Two recent excellent studies of the Caddos, written by Caddo tribal members themselves, have lightly touched upon the tribe's experience in the twentieth century.[4]

I am also guilty of neglecting the reservation period and beyond. My first book on the Caddo Indians deals with the tribe from first contact with Euro-Americans until they settled on a reservation.[5] As I did my research, however, I realized that the tribe did not cease to exist on the reservation but continued despite many travails. This knowledge spurred me to do even further research, which is intended to be the first in-depth history of the reservation experience of the Caddos and their linguistic relatives, the Wichitas.

In this work, I have tried to demonstrate how individual members of both tribes sought to adapt to their new, constricted life on the reservation while at the same time struggling to hold on to their tribal indentities. This adaptation was nothing new for the Wichitas and Caddos, for both tribes had been very receptive to innovations in their own cultures ever since their first contact with Euro-Americans in the mid-sixteenth century. This study intends to demonstrate the strategies each tribe adopted to make a successful life for themselves on the reservation while resisting the federal government's efforts to break tribal ties and force individual assimilation.

This study also seeks to show the fallacy behind the rhetoric of federal Indian policy in the reservation period. The Wichitas and Caddos both seemed to be prime candidates for accomplishing the goals set at this time by the United States government. Both tribes had been sedentary agriculturalists long before the Euro-American intrusion; thus the goal of turning the Indians into farmers had already been accomplished. Both tribes settled near their homes on reservation land that they were very familiar with, so they did not have to endure a particularly traumatic relocation experience. In addition, both tribes actually sought to settle down on the reservation in hopes of escaping pressures from white incursions onto their lands in Texas as well as attacks from other Indians. Therefore, the Wichitas and the Caddos did not have to be forced to accept life on the reservation.

Nonetheless, the reservation experience of the Wichitas and the Caddos was a miserable one. Not only did they fail to receive even a modicum of paternal protection from the federal government, but they were also treated callously and forced to relinquish land promised to them, first to tribes they had helped the United States defeat and then to land-hungry white settlers. All tribal individuals suffered great neglect while at the same time feeling the constant pressure to dissolve their tribal ties and assimilate into white society. That they did not succumb and that the Wichita and Caddo tribes exist to this day are testaments to their strength and their desires to retain their "Indianness." That the United States broke every promise they ever made to the Wichitas and Caddos on the reservation demonstrates that land, rather than assimilation, was the true goal of federal Indian policy during this period.

This work mainly seeks to provide an outline of what occurred between the United States and the Wichitas and Caddos during this period in which the reservation experiment was implemented. Although this study is not written in the manner of "new" Indian history—it is most definitely not an ethnohistory—it is different than "old" Indian history in that it does not take the point of view of the United States government. It seeks rather to understand the Indians' actions on their own terms and not through the lens that sees "backward savages" resisting "inevitable progress." This work has attempted to achieve a middle ground. Certainly this work is not meant to be the final word on the subject of the Caddos and Wichitas; perhaps it will spur further studies which focus especially upon the Native American responses— in particular, the cultural adaptations the Indians made—to the dramatic changes that were forced upon them. It is also hoped that historians (including Native American scholars) will begin to give as much attention to the reservation period and the twentieth century as they have given to the sixteenth through eighteenth centuries and thus produce a fuller understanding of the five hundred years of interaction between Euro-Americans and Native Americans, an interaction that continues to exist today.

The Caddos, the Wichitas, and the United States

Chapter One

Through the Treaty of Council Springs

In early May, 1846, representatives of the various Indian tribes of Texas gathered at the trading post that John F. Torrey and his brothers had established three years earlier on Tehuacana Creek, two miles above its confluence with the Brazos River. Torrey's Trading Post (which stood seven miles east of present Waco) had been chosen by the Indians in March as the site of their treaty negotiations with representatives of the United States, which had annexed Texas in December, 1845.[1]

Two of the tribes assembled at Tehuacana Creek had had relations with various groups of Euro-Americans dating back to the earliest Spanish *entradas* into North America. Francisco Vásquez de Coronado and a party of thirty visited the Wichita Indians in their villages, located near the great bend of the Arkansas River, in July, 1541. Eleven months later Luis de Moscoso led the remnants of the Hernando de Soto expedition to the Red River where they encountered the Caddo Indians.[2] Although neither Spanish party tarried long among the two tribes, both the Caddos and the Wichitas would feel the effects of the Euro-American intrusion into their world for three centuries before they began to deal solely with the United States in 1846.

Actual Euro-American occupation of the Caddo and Wichita country did not occur until the late seventeenth century, nearly 150 years after the appearance of the first Spaniards. By this time the Caddos had organized themselves into three confederacies.[3] The Kadohadacho confederacy was located around the bend of the Red River near the present Arkansas, Texas, and Oklahoma border. Thirty-five hundred Kadohadachos lived in four tribes, while the two thousand members of the three Natchitoches tribes lived farther downstream near the modern town of the same name. To the west, along the upper reaches of the Neches and Angelina Rivers in East Texas, were the nine principal tribes of the Hasinai confederacy, which consisted of forty-five hundred people.[4]

Although they enjoyed close relations and shared the same culture, each of the Caddo confederacies was a separate and independent political entity, and each was treated as such by both Euro-Americans and other Indians. At the head of each confederacy was a religious leader, the *xinesi*. He provided blessings for the planting of crops and construction of houses and presided over various feasts and ceremonies. As with all aspects of their society, the religion of the Caddos was well-defined. The supreme deity was called Ahahayo, which means the "Father above." The Caddos believed that he was the creator of everything and that he rewarded good and punished evil. Communication between Ahahayo and the tribe was carried out by the xinesi. A more numerous, lesser class of priests or shamans, called *connas,* existed below the xinesi. They were medicine men, charged with healing the sick, and they performed many other religious duties, such as presiding over burials. The Caddos believed that a dead person's soul went up into the sky and entered the House of Death which was presided over by Ahahayo. Here all were required to wait until all the Caddo souls had been gathered together, at which time the whole tribe would "enter another world to live anew." All the Caddo people were entitled to enter the House of Death "where everyone is happy and there is no hunger, sickness, or suffering."[5]

Although the xinesi was recognized as the head of each confederacy, actual political power was exercised at the individual tribal level. The highest political office of each tribe was that of the *caddi,* which, like the xinesi, was a hereditary position. The caddi presided over a well-defined chain of command consisting of four to eight principal aides called *canahas,* who in turn had a number of assistants called *chayas.* The clearly defined lines of authority allowed the tribal government of the Caddos to function smoothly.[6]

The highly organized Caddos were also prosperous agriculturalists who lived in fixed, permanent villages in the southwestern edge of the Eastern Woodlands. In addition to raising corn, beans, and squash, the Caddo men—who worked in the fields alongside the women—also hunted deer, bear, and turkey. After they obtained horses indirectly from the Spanish in the mid-seventeenth century, the Caddos began traveling west to the plains each winter to hunt buffalo.[7]

Agriculture, however, determined the way the Caddos arranged their living quarters. They lived in scattered dwellings in the midst of their fields, grouped around a central village where their chief officials lived. The heavily wooded country with few clearings lent itself to spread-out communities, described by one observer as being "twenty leagues long, not that it is constantly inhabited, but in hamlets of ten or twelve cabins." The Caddo "cabins" were well-constructed dwellings made of grass and reeds "in the shape of a beehive, or a rick of hay." Several families, three or four at most, occupied each house. The Caddos were, for the most part, monogamous, although marriages were very loose, and couples rarely stayed together for life. The Caddos were matrilineal, thus the children remained with their mother in case of divorce, and the maternal uncle was the most important adult male figure.[8]

The Caddos were very concerned about their appearance and wore clothes the women made from deerskin. Both sexes adorned their bodies with jewelry made from shells, while women were often tattooed. The men kept their hair short except for a thin braid which grew from the middle of the head "like a Chinaman." The women, on the other hand, always wore their hair long. The Euro-Americans who first encountered the Caddos considered them to be very attractive, claiming that they were "well built and robust" with "good features and thin faces."[9]

Although war played a role in Caddo society, it was not central to their culture. Traditional Caddo warfare was not economically motivated but provided an opportunity for lesser tribal members to demonstrate valor and enhance their social status. Battle usually consisted of hit-and-run raids on an enemy in which an attempt was made to capture a foe. The unfortunate captive was returned to the Caddo village where the entire tribe, including the women, would participate in an extended torture session which served as a bonding mechanism for the tribe.[10]

The central nature that war played in Wichita society is only one of many differences between their culture and that of the Caddos.[11] Despite the divergence in life-styles, the two tribes had maintained close ties since long before the arrival of Euro-Americans. Although their languages were mutually unintelligible, they were linguistically related, both being of Caddoan stock, as were the Arikaras and the Pawnees. These two latter tribes, along with the Wichitas, separated from the Caddos about 1500 B.C.[12]

While the Arikaras and the Pawnees eventually migrated north to the valleys of the Missouri and Platte Rivers, respectively, the Wichitas settled on the eastern edge of the Great Plains in the Arkansas River Valley. Their location on the prairie rather than in the forest is the main cause for the cultural differences between the Wichitas and Caddos, for the Wichitas relied upon buffalo hunting much more than their linguistic kin to the east. Although the Wichitas were also horticulturists, their dependence on the buffalo was only reinforced by the adoption of the horse—also obtained indirectly from the Spanish—in the seventeenth century.[13]

To facilitate the hunt, the Wichitas lived in about twenty autonomous villages, each containing about one thousand people. Each village was headed by a principal chief and a subordinate, both chosen by the warriors—unlike the Caddos who had a hereditary elite—on the basis of physical prowess and leadership abilities. War was very important to the Wichitas, and it was the only way that a man could gain power and prestige. The power of the chiefs, however, was restricted by the warriors, who also played a significant role in the decision-making process. A warrior council dealt with matters of importance, and problems were solved by consensus; dissenters were free to join other villages rather than adhere to decisions they opposed. The relatively independent, egalitarian nature of the Wichita political system stands in marked contrast to the hierarchical system of the Caddos.[14]

The Wichita religious system also differed from the Caddos' in that it did not revolve around an authority figure such as the xinesi. Instead, various shamanistic societies, open to anyone who cared to join, paid homage to the important deities who controlled tribal welfare by performing certain ceremonies and dances. The Wichitas believed in a pantheon of gods, led by a supreme creator, Kinnikasus, meaning "man-never-known-on-earth." Below him was a hierarchy of deities divided into those of the sky (represented by male gods) and the earth (represented by female goddesses). Individual Wichitas could also appeal to personal guardian spirits—revealed in dreams—that inhabited all objects, including various animals.[15]

Like the Caddos, the Wichitas raised corn, beans, and squash during the spring and summer in fields located near their villages. However, unlike the Caddos, the Wichitas considered agriculture solely a female task. The men were free to make war and hunt near the village until fall, when the entire group would pick up and head west for the annual buffalo hunt. On the hunt, the women would skin the buffalo and smoke the meat; upon returning to the village in the spring, they tanned the hides and fashioned them into blankets and robes. Women also made pots and other cooking utensils as well as deerskin and wolfskin pouches for storage.[16]

Although the Wichitas hunted buffalo, they did not live in portable tepees like those tribes which depended solely on the chase and did not engage in agriculture. Rather, the Wichitas lived in grass lodges like the Caddos, each house containing between ten and twenty occupants. Wichita marriage customs resembled the Caddos in that they were generally monogamous, and separation and divorce were common. Both tribes were matrilineal.[17]

Physically, the Wichitas were short, stocky, and dark-skinned—so dark the Siouan tribes called them Paniwasaba, or Black Pawnee. The feature noted by all observers of the Wichitas was their elaborate tattoos: the men, particularly around the eyes—therefore, they called themselves "raccoon eyes"—the women, mainly on the arms and breasts. For this reason, the French called the tribe the Panis Piques, or Pricked Pawnees. Men and women both had long hair, wore deerskin clothing, and ornamented themselves with shell jewelry.[18]

Thus, the Caddos and Wichitas had developed successful, satisfactory ways of life long before the arrival of the Spaniards. However, both tribes eagerly accepted Euro-Americans into their world in the early eighteenth century, for they hoped to acquire the metal goods and weapons that their enemies, namely the Athapaskan-speaking Lipan Apaches to the west and the Siouan Osages to the northeast, had already obtained. By the 1720s the Spanish and French were well established in Texas and Louisiana, respectively, the borders of the two empires converging in the midst of Caddo country. The Caddos allowed the French to set up three trading posts along the Red River among the Kado-

hadacho and Natchitoches confederacies. The Hasinais tolerated the
Spanish presence in their country only because it consisted of just one
Franciscan mission run by a single priest. However, they refused to ac-
cept Christianity and maintained their traditional religious beliefs.[19]

In order to escape Osage attacks and gain greater access to the French
traders, the Wichitas began migrating southward from the Arkansas
basin in the 1740s. By this time, the Wichita population had declined,
because of disease and warfare, to perhaps fifteen thousand people, and
the tribe began gathering together in larger villages for protection. Two
distinct Wichita divisions emerged at this point: the Tawakonis and
the Taovayas. The Tawakonis (along with their subgroup, the Iscanis)
were the first of the Wichita tribes to move south, and they settled in
the area between the Sabine and the Brazos Rivers. Another group of
Caddoan-speakers, the Kichais, already lived in the region. Although
their language was intermediate between Caddo and Pawnee and unintelligible to the Wichitas, the Kichais shared the same culture as the
Tawakonis and welcomed them to their country. Over time, the Kichais
would become amalgamated with the Wichitas and be considered a
part of the overall confederacy.[20]

In 1757 the Taovayas (along with their associates, the Wichita proper)
established one of the landmark villages of the southern plains on the
Red River at the juncture of the Great Plains and the Western Cross
Timbers—the farthest extension of the Eastern Woodlands. The location was strategic, for it placed the Taovayas at the easternmost edge of
the range of the Comanches—plains buffalo-hunting Shoshonean
speakers who had recently migrated from the north—and the wes-
ternmost point frequented by French traders. The Taovayas took advantage of their position as middlemen to open up a very profitable
trade in which they exchanged their own agricultural products and
French trade goods with the Comanches in return for buffalo hides.[21]

The French goods which flowed freely into the villages of all the
Caddo and Wichita tribes caused great changes in their material cultures.
By the mid-eighteenth century they had almost completely forsaken
the traditional crafts they had produced in favor of European-manufac-
tured goods. In return for buffalo skins, deer chamois, and bear fat, the
Wichitas and Caddos received guns, powder, and balls as well as steel
hatchets, tomahawks, and knives. These items not only allowed the
tribesmen to hunt more efficiently, but they enhanced military profi-

ciency as well. With the acquisition of these tools of war, the two tribes turned away from the traditional bow and arrow and became dependent upon European firearms.[22]

The Wichitas and Caddos also became dependent on European shirts, cloth, and blankets. Tools such as scissors, awls, screws, and flints for fire became necessities. Cosmetic goods were greatly desired by the tribes as well. Beads, combs, vermilion, mirrors, copper bracelets, and strips of scarlet were all vanity items that the French readily kept on hand to supply their customers. By the middle of the eighteenth century, life without European goods had become incomprehensible to the tribes.[23]

The Wichitas and Caddos clearly recognized their dependence upon their French allies for weapons and were willing to take up arms against anyone, including the Spanish, who threatened to disrupt the trade. In 1731 the Caddos rushed to the aid of the French soldiers at the trading post of Natchitoches when it was besieged by hostile Natchez warriors. Halfhearted attempts by the Spanish in 1750 and 1752 to halt the flow of French trade into Texas were thwarted by the bold, aggressive stance adopted by the Caddo tribes. In 1758 Caddo warriors joined a group of two thousand Wichitas and Comanches—more than half of whom carried French weapons—in an attack upon the mission the Spanish had set up for the enemy Apaches on the San Saba River in central Texas. Eight Spaniards were killed, and the mission buildings were burned down. A Spanish punitive expedition was aimed at the Wichitas the following year, but it was rebuffed by the Taovayas at their fortified village—over which flew a French flag—on the north bank of the Red River.[24]

Three years later, following the disastrous Seven Years' War, the French abandoned North America and their Indian allies and turned Louisiana over to Spain. The Caddo tribes quickly made peace with the Spanish—who began supplying them with trade goods just as the French had—and then helped negotiate a treaty between the Spanish and the Wichitas. Just as it seemed that the consequences of the French withdrawal might be overcome, the Caddos were struck by a disastrous epidemic disease in 1777–78.[25]

Disease was nothing new to either the Caddos or the Wichitas; in fact, they had both been struck by an epidemic that killed three thousand tribesmen less than a year after the Franciscans' first attempt to establish a mission among the Hasinais in 1690. Epidemics continued to occur about every generation after that, in addition to annual outbreaks of colds, fever, measles, and smallpox. These were especially damaging to the Caddos, who lived in closer proximity to the Euro-Americans than the Wichitas. The Caddos overcame the problem, however, by consolidating the tribes within each confederacy and by discontinuing the office of their religious leader, the xinesi.[26]

The epidemic of 1777–78, which killed about eight hundred (or one-third) of the remaining Caddos, came at a time when the tribe could least afford it. The weakening Spanish could no longer provide the Caddos or the Wichitas—ravaged by epidemics of their own in 1788 and later in 1801—with weapons or protection from the Osages, who bore down upon both tribes during the last quarter of the eighteenth century. When the United States obtained Louisiana in 1803, the Red River Caddos eagerly became allies with the young republic in order to receive the abundant trade goods it had to offer. The Kadohadacho caddi, Dehahuit, led these negotiations and also acted as intermediary between the United States and the Wichitas. Although the Caddos experienced a temporary renascence from their association with the Americans, the Wichitas failed to establish close ties with the United States at this time. The inability to obtain trade goods, coupled with the political confusion caused by disease, forced the one thousand remaining Taovayas to abandon their strategic village site on the Red River and scatter across the southern plains along with the fifteen hundred Kichais and Tawakonis.[27]

Following the War of 1812 the Caddos and Wichitas were faced with new pressures which forced them to move even farther west. Anglo-American settlers flooded into the Red River Valley and beyond into Texas (controlled by Mexico after 1821). Not only did these settlers encroach upon the Indians' land, they also seriously depleted the game and introduced the tribes to the vice of alcohol. In addition to the white settlers, emigrant Indian tribes from the east began settling on land that had once been considered the domain of the Caddos and Wichitas. Delawares, Shawnees, Kickapoos, and Cherokees, among others, moved to East Texas and by 1830 outnumbered the helpless Caddos. In 1835 the five hundred or so remaining Kadohadachos—who by now included the shattered remnants of the Natchitoches confederacy—were forced by the United States to sell their land in Louisiana for eighty thousand dollars in the expectation that they would move to Mexican Texas to join their Hasinai kinsmen. By this time the Hasinai confederacy had been reduced to two independent tribes, the Nadacos and the Hainais, each numbering about three hundred tribesmen.[28]

The Wichita tribes moved their villages westward on their own, without the prodding of the United States government. The Taovayas, who had been wandering since 1811, settled in villages near the Wichita Mountains north of the Red River. The Tawakonis and the Wacos—which now emerged as an independent Wichita tribe—who lived in neighboring villages on the Brazos (near the present town of Waco), moved up the river in the early 1830s and occupied various village sites on both sides of the Red during the next decade. The Kichais also traveled westward, moving their villages farther up the Trinity River almost to its source. From their new homes, all the Wichita tribes carried out incessant raids upon the livestock of the Anglo-American settlers in Texas as well as the eastern emigrant tribes. The Wichitas found a ready market for the stolen horses, mules, and cattle at posts set up by unscrupulous traders north of the Red River.[29]

Although the Wichitas were able to overcome the encroachment on their lands by moving west, the federal government's policy of settling eastern tribes on land north of the Red River in the so-called Indian Territory posed a far more serious long-term danger. In the two decades following the War of 1812 the United States set aside land between the Red and the Canadian Rivers for the Muskoghean Choctaws and Chickasaws without regard for the Wichita claim to the area. In an effort to make sure warfare did not occur between the intruders and the Wichitas or the Comanches, in 1834 the federal government sent troops west of the Cross Timbers to arrange a council. The following year, on the Canadian River near the mouth of Choteau Creek, Taovaya headmen (along with a small group of Wacos) and Comanche chiefs entered into an agreement with United States treaty commissioners and representatives of various eastern tribes being settled in the Indian Territory. The Treaty of Camp Holmes—the first agreement of any kind the Wichitas or the Comanches made with the United States—called for pledges of perpetual peace and friendship among all signatories as well as recognition of the right of all parties to hunt west of the Cross

Timbers. Importantly, neither the Taovayas nor the Comanches explicitly recognized the sovereignty of the United States nor did they relinquish any possessory rights to the territory.[30]

The separate agreements made between the United States and the Kadohadachos and Taovayas in the summer of 1835 were seriously affected by the unsettled condition of Texas, which revolted against the Mexican government later in the year. Although Texas quickly gained its independence and the first president of the republic, Sam Houston, had peaceful intentions towards the Texas Indians, his successor, Mirabeau Buonaparte Lamar, embarked on a policy of extermination. As a result, the Nadacos, Hainais, and Kadohadachos—of which only two-thirds had moved to Texas since 1835—were driven north by Texas troops in 1839 to the Indian Territory, where they took refuge on the Washita River. The two hundred Kadohadachos who had remained in Louisiana moved to the Indian Territory the following year; this group, known as the Whitebead Caddos established a village on the Kiamichi River near Fort Towson. The Whitebeads would continue to remain aloof from the rest of the Caddo tribes for the next two decades.[31]

The Wichitas—already considered hostile by the Texans because of their constant raiding—were also ravaged by Lamar's troops. In 1841 Texas Rangers attacked the Waco settlement on Village Creek (in present Tarrant County) and destroyed it the following year. Many Wacos and Tawakonis, who were forced to abandon their village on the West Fork of the Trinity River, moved either west to the Wichita River or north to join the Taovayas in the Indian Territory. A few Kichais also sought refuge with the Taovayas; most of the three hundred tribesmen, however, settled in a village on the Brazos River, fifteen miles below the mouth of the Clear Fork. For the next decade, the Kichai village (in present Palo Pinto County) would serve as a great meeting place for all the Wichita tribes, as well as for the Caddos and Penateka Comanches.[32]

Relations with the Texans took a positive turn during Sam Houston's second term as president of the republic. Following his inauguration in December, 1841, President Houston once again called for a peaceful relationship with the Indians and sent commissioners out to the prairies to "treat with any and all Indians on the frontiers of Texas." The Caddos on the Washita were the first to respond to Houston's entreaties, and they agreed to be peace emissaries and visit with the other tribes to invite them to meet with the Texas commissioners at Torrey's Trading Post on Tehuacana Creek.[33]

After various delays, the treaty council was held in March, 1843, even though the Caddos were unsuccessful in getting any representatives of the powerful, hostile Penateka Comanches to attend. Of the Wichita tribes, only Acaquash (Short Tail), second chief of the Wacos, appeared. The Delawares and Shawnees were the only tribes other than the Caddos to attend in full. On March 31, 1843, an agreement was signed by all parties in which it was "solemnly agreed that the war . . . should cease." The tribes were invited to trade with the Texans and to plant corn anywhere above Torrey's Trading Post. Because of the absence of the Comanches and Wichitas, the council could not be considered a complete success; however, it did begin the process of ending the hostilities between the Texans and the Indians.[34]

Following the treaty at Tehuacana Creek most of the Caddos moved south of the Red River. Only the two hundred Whitebead Caddos stayed in the Indian Territory; they did, however, move their village from the Kiamichi River westward to Caddo Creek (in present Carter County), a tributary of the Washita.[35] By early 1844 the other three Caddo tribes had settled in one contiguous village located on the Brazos River about forty-five miles above Torrey's Trading Post and twenty-five miles below Comanche Peak. Most white observers agreed that the Caddos had made a fine choice for their village site; one commented that a "more suitable and pleasant place could not have been selected" by the tribe. The village lay "in the center of a plain two miles long," bordered by hills "covered with horses, they being . . . fine for grazing, present[ing] a lively green as far as the eyes could reach." Flowing diagonally through the plain was a "beautiful, clear creek" on the banks of which stood, "in picturesque disorder," the Caddos' traditional grass houses. Adjoining each abode were the Caddo fields; one Texan Indian agent felt that the tribe had "about 150 acres of the finest corn" he had ever seen, in addition to "innumerable" peas, beans, and pumpkins.[36]

Among the three Caddo tribes, the Nadacos began to emerge as the most influential. This was the result, in part, of the stability of their population, which remained at about two hundred fifty throughout the period after the Texas Revolution. This number stood in marked contrast to the Hainais, whose numbers fell from about three hundred at the beginning of the Texas Revolution to half that by 1845. So many

Traditional Wichita grass house, 1870s. The Caddos also lived in houses much like this one. Courtesy William S. Nye Collection

Hainai leaders had died that the tribe was without a caddi until Toweash came of age in 1845. Before that time, a headman named Bedi had acted in his place.[37]

Another reason for the Nadacos' prominence was their political stability; unlike the Kadohadachos, who were torn in half by the Texas Revolution, the Nadacos held tightly together behind the leadership of Iesh, one of the most impressive chiefs in Caddo history. Born in 1806, Iesh was called José María by the whites. Although he was small in stature, Iesh had an indomitable spirit that would allow him to keep the Caddo tribes together during the desperate decades to come. His influence was so great that the leaderless Hainais attached themselves to the Nadacos, and Toweash was considered to be Iesh's "second chief" when he finally took charge of his tribe.[38]

The two hundred and fifty or so Kadohadachos also had a young caddi, Bintah, who did not assume his position until 1843. Often Bintah looked to a leading Kadohadacho headman named Red Bear for guidance. However, following Red Bear's death in the winter of 1846, Bintah increasingly followed the lead of Iesh. The Kadohadachos' dependence upon the Nadaco caddi was reinforced by Bintah's death the following year and his successor's demise in 1853. By 1855, when the three Caddo tribes finally were able to settle on land reserved for them, it was clear that Iesh was their leader and that the Nadacos were the dominant tribe.[39]

A group of about one hundred Delawares settled near the Caddos on the Brazos. This Algonquian tribe had been in contact with Euro-Americans since their arrival on the Atlantic Coast in the early seventeenth century. Over the years remnants of the shattered tribe wandered westward; the Texas group had arrived around 1820 and was dominated by members of white and native ancestry. Such "mixed bloods" as John Conner, Jim Shaw, and Jim Ned filled important roles as intermediaries and interpreters between Texas officials and the native tribes of the area; they were also employed as scouts for numerous United States Army exploratory expeditions.[40]

Along with the Caddos, the Delawares tirelessly campaigned to effect a peace between the Texans and the hostile Penatekas and Wichitas. They were assisted in their efforts by Acaquash, who convinced a few more Wichita headmen—most importantly, Kechikaroqua (Stubborn), the Tawakoni chief—to enter into a peace treaty with Texas representatives at a council held in September, 1843, at Bird's Fort on the Trinity. During the following year, Acaquash and Kechikaroqua were successful in persuading the Kichai chief, Anohetchtowey (White Feather), and the main chief of the Wacos, Narhashtowey (Lame Arm), also to make peace with the Texans.[41]

By this time, most of the two hundred fifty Tawakonis had been led by Kechikaroqua back to their village on the West Fork of the Trinity River. The Tawakoni village was situated on a hill overlooking one hundred acres of corn, beans, melons, and pumpkins planted along the river. Most of Narhashtowey's two hundred fifty Wacos resided in a village fifteen miles to the west. Despite making peace with the Texans, renegade Tawakonis, Wacos, and Kichais continued to raid their settlements. The democratic nature of the Wichita political system made it very hard for the chiefs to control warriors who were inclined to lead a war party against the Texans.[42]

Often these raids were led by warriors from the Taovaya village, tucked safely away north of the Red River at the eastern edge of the Wichita Mountains. The six hundred or so Taovayas, led by Tosaquash, had lived in their village since the mid-1830s. According to one observer, the Taovayas had "exhibited much taste and judgement in the selection of the site for their town," for it was situated on a plateau that offered it a "commanding position . . . well secured against surprise." Beneath the village was Cache Creek, which provided water for fertile soil that produced enormous yields of corn. In addition, there was an adequate supply of timber.[43]

The Taovaya warriors raided the Texas settlements not only out of hostility but increasingly out of economic necessity. For as the whites continued their westward migration, the number of buffalo began to dwindle. Not only were there fewer buffalo, but their range became restricted to the high plains west of the Wichita country. This area was jealously guarded by the fierce Northern Comanches—mainly, the Nokoni, Tenawa, Kotsoteka, and Yamparika tribes—and the Kiowas, who considered Wichita hunters to be intruders. Increasingly cut off from the buffalo country, the Taovayas (and the renegade Wacos, Tawakonis, and Kichais) were forced to plunder the Texas settlements for cattle, horses, and mules to sell in the illegal market of the Indian Territory.[44]

But the southernmost Comanche tribe, the Penatekas, pressured the Taovayas to make peace with the Texans. Of all the Indian tribes of Texas, the Penatekas, about fifteen hundred in number, had engaged in the bloodiest war with the Republic of Texas. Finally, in October, 1844, the Penatekas agreed to give up the fight. The Penateka chiefs— Mopechucope (Old Owl), Pahayuco (Amorous Man), Santa Anna, and Buffalo Hump—were dedicated to maintaining the friendship of the Texans and considered the Taovaya raids on the whites to be threatening to their own peace. Although the Penatekas also depended upon plunder for a living, they turned their attacks toward the Mexicans south of the Rio Grande instead of the Texans.[45]

Penateka pressure, as well as the persuasions of their fellow Wichita tribesmen, ultimately convinced the Taovayas to make peace with the Republic of Texas. In November, 1845, Tosaquash sent a warrior named Saatzarwaritz to Torrey's Trading Post where he entered into an agreement with Texas treaty commissioners. Thus, by the time the United

States annexed Texas the following month, all the Wichitas were legally, at least, at peace with the new state.[46]

The United States quickly took steps to assume its constitutional duty of supervising relations with the Indian tribes of Texas. In fact, even prior to the annexation of Texas, the War Department had commissioned Cherokee Agent Pierce M. Butler and M. G. Lewis to negotiate a treaty with the Texas Indians. On January 8, 1846, the commissioners, along with a party of about fifty people—including representatives from the Cherokee, Seminole, Choctaw, and Chickasaw tribes—left the Indian Territory and crossed the Red River into Texas. A few days later, Butler and Lewis (through the Delaware interpreter, Jim Shaw) hired a group of Kickapoos to notify the various Texas tribes to meet them at Comanche Peak on the Brazos River, about seventy miles above Torrey's Trading Post. In a comic turn of events, it took the commissioners a full month to finally locate the assigned meeting place.[47]

Butler and Lewis spent nearly all of March at Comanche Peak holding friendly talks with the Texas Indian tribes, including the Tonkawas, Lipan Apaches, and Caddos. The most important meeting took place on March 7 when Buffalo Hump and Mopechucope decided that they could not speak for the entire Penateka Comanche tribe, making it necessary to meet again in May at Torrey's Trading Post to conclude the treaty.[48]

Four days later Butler held a talk with a group of Wichitas including Tawakoni chief Kechikaroqua, Waco chief Narhashtowey, and a Taovaya warrior named Kosharokah. Tensions arose when Butler inquired about some stolen horses and the Waco and Tawakoni chiefs refused to deliver any until they were given beeves and presents. Butler informed them that they had received enough and that he would send soldiers, if necessary, to retrieve the stolen horses. Not until Butler broke down and gave the Wichitas twenty beeves did they finally agree to accompany all the other Texas Indians to Tehuacana Creek in May to conclude the treaty with the United States.[49]

Despite all the troubles Butler and Lewis encountered in the early part of 1846, the treaty council at Torrey's Trading Post went smoothly. The meeting got under way on May 12, and an agreement was reached three days later between the United States and the Penateka Comanche, Hainai, Nadaco, Kadohadacho, Lipan Apache, Tonkawa, Kichai, Tawakoni, Taovaya, and Waco tribes. The Indians "acknowledged themselves to be under the protection of the United States," and perpetual peace was pledged between the two parties. The Indians agreed to surrender stolen property and prisoners and trade only with licensed traders. In turn, the federal government pledged to keep trespassers off tribal land and promised to provide the tribes with blacksmiths, teachers, and "preachers of the gospel." The United States also agreed to set up official trading posts for the Indians and present them with an undetermined amount of gifts in the fall of 1846. Twenty-eight Wichitas—including Tosaquash, the Taovaya chief—and five Caddos affixed their mark to the treaty.[50]

Thus, in 1846 the Caddos and Wichitas entered into an agreement with yet another Euro-American power. From this point on, however, both tribes' options would dwindle as the increasing power of the United States gradually swept over them. In the future, the fate of the Caddos and Wichitas would be decided not by themselves but by the whim of the federal government.

Chapter Two

Searching for a Home, 1846-53

I need a home for me and my people. The buffalo are gone and but few deer are left and the white people have most of them, and I want to raise cows and hogs to supply their place. I went to Washington City and saw what the white people are and I know it is folly to fight them. Give me a spot for my people, and my white brother can pass around and go (pointed to the sunset).

—Nadaco caddi Iesh,
September 15, 1853

Despite being concluded in May, 1846, the Treaty of Council Springs was not ratified by the United States Senate until the following February and President James K. Polk finally signed it into law on March 8, 1847. Although the United States was now ready to assume responsibility for the Indian tribes, the unique circumstances of Texas' entrance into the Union hampered the federal government's efforts. Unlike the other states, Texas retained complete control of its public lands upon joining the Union. This presented a complex legal problem, for the land occupied by the Texas tribes was not the domain of the United States, thus the federal government's Indian laws were rendered inapplicable. For this reason, the Senate removed provisions from the treaty which extended the federal trade and intercourse laws over the Texas Indians and protected them from trespassers. To make matters more difficult, the laws of Texas did not acknowledge that the Indians had any right to the land.[1]

Commissioner of Indian Affairs William Medill spelled out the problem in March, 1847, to Maj. Robert S. Neighbors upon Neighbors's official appointment as special agent to manage Indian affairs in Texas. Medill stated "it is difficult if not impossible to determine at present how far the department has the power and jurisdiction with respect to the Indian country in Texas."[2] Since the trade and intercourse laws, as well as other laws for the regulation of Indian affairs, could not be applied to Texas, the federal government was almost powerless to deal effectively with the Indians, illegal traders, or encroaching Texans.

To add to the problem, the state of Texas, upon turning over responsibility of the Indians to the federal government, became hostile to the tribes' interests. In the latter years of the Texas republic, the government had been forced to adopt an Indian peace policy and had pledged paternal protection over the tribes. Now, however, the Texans washed their hands of the Indian problem and gave almost no assistance to the helpless Indian agents of the federal government. As time wore on, the Texas government's Indian policy harkened back to that of President Lamar. Matters were made worse by the fact that the United States was presently at war with Mexico, and all federal troops were routed there. Thus, the only soldiers the federal Indian agents could turn to for assistance were the Texas Rangers, who were controlled by the state governor.

This tenuous state of affairs was made more dangerous by the Taovaya warriors' refusal (as well as the refusal by renegades from the other Wichita tribes) to cease their raids upon the Texan settlements, despite the stipulations of the Treaty of Council Springs. Their continued attacks increased the ire of the Texans toward all Indians, including the peaceful Caddos and Wichitas settled along the Brazos River. The federal government's inability to protect the tribes from white encroachment left the Indians at the mercy of the Texas government, which continually opposed any attempts to set aside reservations for the tribes. The situation was a dynamite keg ready to explode; when it finally did, the Caddos and Wichitas would be made to suffer the most.

Following the signing of the treaty, Commissioners Butler and Lewis prevailed upon a number of chiefs to visit Washington in an attempt to "impress" them with the strength and resources of the United States.

Between forty and fifty Indian headmen made the trip, including Iesh, Tosaquash, Acaquash, and Kechikaroqua. On July 25 the party traveled to the White House to meet with President Polk, who presented Iesh with a testimonial of friendship. Although the chiefs were quartered in the outskirts to give them more room and freedom from the crowds, a few became ill, and the entire party returned to Texas soon after the interview with Polk. Despite the brevity of their stay in Washington, most of the chiefs were impressed. Acaquash told the president that he would return home and advise his people not to wage war. Iesh later remarked that he had observed the ways of the white people and knew it was "folly to fight them." For the rest of their lives, both men would maintain a policy of peace and cooperation with the whites, for they realized their tribes had no viable alternative. Acaquash, however, was not completely sold on everything the whites had to offer; he later commented that he could not understand "how the white men ever thought he wanted a steamboat, a railroad, a ship, and all the machinery that he had seen. It did not seem . . . so wonderful to make all those things as it did to conceive the idea that man should stand in need of them."[3]

Despite the signing of the Treaty of Council Springs, Wichita warriors resumed their horse stealing in Texas even while their comrades were being overawed in Washington. In the summer of 1846 a party of Taovayas and Wacos stole several horses from the Texas Ranger encampment near Austin. Another band of Taovayas later raided through Fannin County. In retaliation Texas Ranger Capt. Thomas Smith led a troop, accompanied by Indian allies, across the Red River where they engaged the Taovayas at their village near the Wichita Mountains. Although several Taovaya warriors were killed in the fight, they continued to raid into Texas throughout the rest of the year.[4]

By January, 1847, when Major Neighbors, acting United States Indian Agent, held a council for the Texas tribes at Tehuacana Creek, a portion of the Wacos, Tawakonis, and Taovayas were said to have "declared themselves hostile." Neighbors believed that it would be useless to attempt to induce them to come in for a council. Acaquash stated that the Taovayas would "steal horses till they are exterminated." The Waco chief, along with the Penateka Comanche headmen, offered his assistance to Neighbors if troops were sent to punish the warriors.[5]

Part of the reason the large group of Wichitas refused to cease their raiding was because of the U.S. Senate's failure to ratify promptly the Treaty of Council Springs, and the Indians had not received the presents that had been promised by Butler and Lewis. In an attempt to quiet the tribes, Commissioner Medill directed Major Neighbors to distribute more than seven thousand dollars worth of goods on credit to the Texas tribes at Tehuacana Creek. At the council Neighbors explained that the federal government would fulfill its obligation to them as soon as the treaty was ratified. Neighbors claimed that the council was successful, for it "resulted in establishing that good understanding which had heretofore existed with these tribes, and remov[ed] anything like disaffection."[6]

Finally, President Polk signed the ratified treaty in March, 1847, and the United States assumed responsibility for the Indians of Texas. The complex legal problems that would hinder the federal government's actions, however, did not immediately come to the fore. Instead, Major Neighbors quickly won the admiration and respect of the friendly tribes by demonstrating his willingness to assist them in whatever problems might arise. This acceptance was made clear in his first tour of the Indian country in the late spring of 1847. On May 30 Neighbors arrived at the Caddo villages and found "everything perfectly quiet . . . and the Indians satisfied and friendly." The only complaint that the Caddos had was with the Wichitas, who continued to steal horses from them and the Texans. This conflict had led to a skirmish between the Caddos and the Wacos in which two Wacos were killed, one of them a headman who had visited Washington the previous summer.[7]

Major Neighbors decided to travel up the Brazos to the Kichai village, where many Wichitas were gathered, to end the hostilities between the tribes and to urge the Wichitas to desist in their horse raiding. When Texas Ranger Captain Howe refused Neighbors's request for an escort—on the grounds "that he had no orders to send troops to the Indian country"—the federal Indian agent asked Iesh for assistance. The Nadaco caddi, however, had been thrown from his horse and could not travel. As his replacement, Iesh sent his second chief, Toweash, the Hainai caddi, along with six warriors. Six Delawares, led by John Conner, also accompanied Neighbors. The party arrived at the Kichai village on June 10. Having won the confidence of the Caddos and Delawares, Neighbors adopted a bold stance with the Wichitas, believing "that the friendly Indians would sustain me in any measure I might adopt towards them." In the face of the major's assertiveness, the Kichais immediately delivered seven horses, while the Taovayas promised to bring in a stolen herd that had been driven to the Big Wichita River. The Wacos and Caddos also "settled the matter to the satisfaction of both parties."[8]

Not all the Wacos, however, had decided to be friendly. On July 13, 1847, Waco warriors attacked and killed four men who were surveying land on the San Saba River for a group of Germans who had recently immigrated to Texas.[9] In response to the killings and the turmoil they caused throughout the state—white settlers organized a militia to attack the Penatekas, who were at first thought to be the culprits—Major Neighbors decided to tour the Indian country once again in the late summer.

On August 28 he met with the Caddo headmen and "found them all perfectly peaceable and friendly." However, their corn crop had been destroyed by the excessive dryness of the summer, inaugurating a trend in which many Caddo corn crops failed in the dry climate of their new plains homeland. Iesh also complained to Neighbors that his people found it difficult to obtain food and that they scattered in pursuit of game. Unfortunately, this search for food did not alleviate the problem since the increase in white settlements had caused the buffalo and other game to "almost entirely disappear" from the eastern prairies of Texas. Relatively large numbers of buffalo still roamed the high plains of West Texas, but the fierce Comanches jealously guarded these hunting grounds. Problems of subsistence, rarely an issue in their traditional eastern homelands, continually haunted the Caddos in the drier lands of the west.[10]

Neighbors then traveled up the Brazos to the Kichai village and found them and their fellow Wichitas to be willing to abide by the "friendly arrangements" made two months before. Because the Indian agent could not trace any act of hostility or theft to this group of Wichitas, the attack on the surveyors must have been carried out by Wacos living north of the Red River. Although the Taovayas had yet to return the stolen herd they had promised in June, Neighbors thought it best not to push the matter, "provided they do not commit some other act of hostility." A group of Penateka Comanches, led by Mopechucope, showed up at the Kichai village, and on September 6 Neighbors assembled all the tribes in council to inform them that the presents which had been promised in the Treaty of Council Springs had finally arrived at Torrey's Trading Post. The tribes eagerly agreed to meet there later in the month for a grand council.[11]

Neighbors counted twenty-two hundred Indians—most from the Caddo, Wichita, and Penateka Comanche tribes—in assembly when the council began on September 27, 1847. In view of the federal government's helplessness concerning the disposition of public lands, Neighbors "avoided as much as possible any discussion of land matters, or questions of boundary." However, Texas governor J. Pinckney Henderson chose to assist the federal agent, and he and the tribes reached an agreement which held that a "temporary line"—twenty miles below Torrey's and thirty miles from the nearest white settlements—would serve as the boundary between the races. The "temporary line" satisfied the tribes, and each principal chief pledged to assist Major Neighbors in "carrying into full effect the several stipulations" of the Treaty of Council Springs. The "friendly dispositions" of the Indians convinced Neighbors that they were "sincere in their many professions of friendship for the government and citizens of the United States." The agent informed Commissioner Medill that he felt "fully assured that, unless the Indians are improperly interfered with, we have nothing to fear for the future."[12]

Although the Indians of Texas had established a trusting friendship with Neighbors, it soon became apparent how limited the federal Indian agent's powers were in two vital areas: preventing illegal traders from introducing alcohol into the Indian country and protecting the tribes from encroaching white settlers. The former issue caused the Caddos and Wichitas only temporary problems. Both tribes had successfully avoided alcohol for awhile before 1846 when members of the settled tribes of the Indian Territory began crossing the Red River with large quantities of liquor. In August, 1847, Agent Neighbors visited the Nadaco village and found the tribe "in some degree disorganized" as a result of a recent shipment of whiskey. In early September, while Neighbors was at the Kichai village, a party of traders—two whites and four Indians—from the Indian Territory arrived with forty gallons of whiskey. The agent was powerless to arrest them, but "by threatening to induce the Indians to seize their goods and put them to death," Neighbors forced the traders to retreat without making a sale. On September 11 Neighbors met a party of Cherokees on their way to the Caddo villages with thirty gallons of whiskey, which he seized and destroyed. He immediately informed Commissioner Medill of his actions and stated that "in the absence of all law regulating intercourse" with the Indians, he was "confined . . . to the destruction of the spirits."[13]

The traders from the Indian Territory were back in Texas the following year. They opened a trading post at the Kichai village in June, 1848, and were "supplying as much whiskey" as they could sell. The whiskey traders arrived at the Kadohadacho village two months later with eleven barrels of liquor, which the Indians were reported to be "drinking in great excess." Major Neighbors informed Medill that he was helpless to interfere because of "the present indefinite position of our Indian affairs . . . having no authority or force to employ for its destruction." Soon after, however, the Wichita and Caddo tribes successfully policed themselves and prevented the introduction of whiskey into their villages despite the helplessness of the federal government.[14]

The Wichitas and Caddos were less successful in overcoming the federal government's impotence in protecting them from white encroachment. Almost as soon as the council of September, 1847, had ended, white settlers pushed beyond the "temporary line." A man named Spencer settled on the council grounds near Torrey's Trading Post and "threatened to shoot the first Indian that came on the land claimed by him." However, Major Neighbors, with the assistance of Governor Henderson and a troop of Texas Rangers, removed Spencer below the line in December, 1847. Following Spencer's removal, Neighbors traveled through western Texas for about a month. When the Indian agent returned in January, 1848, he found that the situation had radically changed for the worse. Spencer, along with a man named Moore, had returned to the council ground, and the Texas Rangers had abandoned the enforcement of the "temporary line" agreement. The Ranger captain informed Neighbors that he had been ordered to move the Ranger station fifteen miles above the council grounds and not "interfere or prevent any settlers from going above" Torrey's. As a result, white settlement had pushed ten miles above the trading post by March, 1848.[15]

The whites' westward advance reinforced the decision—which Neighbors had suggested the previous fall—made by most of the Caddo and Wichita tribesmen in Texas to settle together near the Kichai village. The Wacos, now led by Acaquash following Narhashtowey's recent death, along with the Tawakonis under Neshochilash (Traveler)—replacing the late Kechikaroqua—established a contiguous village on the north bank of the Brazos, six miles above the Kichais and nine miles below the mouth of the Clear Fork. The Kadohadachos, now led by Haddabah after Bintah's death over the winter, settled on the south bank of the Brazos, directly across the river from the Kichai village. Toweash's Hainais assembled thirteen miles below the Kadohadachos on the north bank of the Brazos. About one hundred fifty Delawares and Shawnees lived interspersed among the Caddos and Wichitas.[16]

Among the Caddo tribes, only the Nadacos under Iesh persistently refused to relocate, and they returned from their winter hunt to the old Caddo villages now only about thirty miles above the highest white settlements. Agent Neighbors met with the Nadaco caddi on February 27 and found him "perplexed." Iesh confessed that he was hesitant to settle and plant corn since the whites might drive his tribe off before harvest time. Neighbors, in an attempt to restore Iesh's confidence in the United States, advised him to remain where he was, for the federal government "would do him justice" even if the whites moved beyond his village. Major Neighbors, however, was not as confident in his report to Commissioner Medill on March 2, 1848. He stated that "a crisis has now arrived" and that the whites' insistence upon settling on Indian lands "regardless of the consequences . . . must necessarily and inevitably lead to serious difficulty."[17]

Major Neighbors's forecast of trouble soon proved correct, as violence broke out on the frontier and the animosity between the Texans and the Indians came to the surface. In late March, 1848, thirty-five to forty Taovaya and Waco warriors were camped on the Llano River when they were discovered by Capt. Samuel Highsmith's company of Texas Rangers. When the Wichitas tried to flee, Captain Highsmith ordered an attack and killed twenty-five. Two weeks later, the Taovayas retaliated by killing and scalping three surveyors of the Texas Emigration and Land Company near the headwaters of Aquilla Creek.[18]

The day after the murder of the surveyors, Capt. M. T. Johnston's troop of Texas Rangers traveled to the Aquilla to supervise the burial of the three men. One of the land company's wagons arrived on the scene, and the driver reported that he had encountered six Indians who had refused to answer his inquiries. The following morning, April 11, a small party commanded by a Lieutenant Smith started out in search of the Indians. Instead, they ran across a sixteen-year-old Kadohadacho boy who had become separated from his father, with whom he was hunting. The boy was frightened by the approach of the mounted Rangers and fled on foot, despite their orders for him to halt. One of the Rangers grabbed the boy's rifle to stop him, and the boy, feeling threatened, drew his knife in defense. A volley was fired by the other Rangers, and the boy was killed. The Rangers left him where he lay, and he was found the next day by a Kadohadacho search party.[19]

During the crisis that followed, Iesh clearly demonstrated that he had become the leader of the entire Caddo tribe, including the Kadohadachos. The murdered boy's brothers immediately flew to arms, resolving to seek vengeance for the murder. Despite the fact that Haddabah, the new Kadohadacho caddi, was the boy's uncle, Iesh took charge of the matter and was able to pacify the warriors "with great difficulty." On April 18 the Nadaco caddi met with local trader Charles Barnard and "promised to keep his people quiet" until the matter could be investigated. Iesh agreed to abide by the stipulations of the Treaty of Council Springs which stated that any citizen charged with the murder of an Indian would be tried and punished by the laws of the state. However, the Nadaco caddi insisted that the tribe "was determined to have satisfaction for this outrage." Now it was up to the commander of the Texas Rangers, Col. Peter H. Bell, to see that justice was carried out.[20]

In response to the Taovaya murders of the surveyors and the Kadohadachos' call for revenge, the whites on the frontier mobilized for war. Between two and three hundred Texas citizens organized an attack on the Indians to "drive them out of the country." The Texas Rangers, however, prevailed upon the settlers to "desist" in their planned attack. Nevertheless, in the face of this intense white hostility, Colonel Bell refused to arrest the soldiers responsible for the murder of the Kadohadacho boy.[21]

In mid-June, two months after the incident, Iesh and the boy's father protested the lack of progress in the matter to Major Neighbors. Although they agreed to wait, they told Neighbors that unless the murderers were brought to justice, "they will personally seek to take satisfaction out of the company that killed the boy." Neighbors informed Commissioner Medill that he fully believed that "unless the matter is properly noticed . . . it will lead to serious difficulties." Neighbors asked

Medill to use his influence to force Colonel Bell to investigate the matter since Bell seemed so unwilling.[22]

Prodded by his superiors, Colonel Bell finally took action and met with the Kadohadacho caddi, Haddabah, at Torrey's on July 29. Colonel Bell vowed to bring the men responsible for killing the boy to the trading post in September to settle the matter. Despite this promise, when the colonel and a number of Ranger officers arrived at Torrey's on September 10 to meet the principal chiefs of the entire Caddo tribe, Lieutenant Smith's men were not with them. The Caddos were very upset for they had come to "see punishment inflicted" upon the men. Major Neighbors, fearing "serious difficulties" if the issue was not definitely settled at this point, took action to resolve the matter. He used all the influence he "could possibly bring to bear to induce" the Caddos to accept an agreement, calling for the tribe to receive five hundred dollars in cash "and give up the idea of revenge." Colonel Bell also agreed to bring the matter before the grand jury at its next session that fall. It was obvious, however, that no Texas grand jury would bring charges against a Texas Ranger for killing an Indian.[23]

In the meantime, the Taovayas completely broke off contact with the whites and held "themselves aloof" from all councils. Neighbors reported that the Taovayas "occupy a very doubtful and threatening position" and were "making preparations to attack the frontier" as soon as their corn was harvested. The attack, in conjunction with the Wacos and Northern Comanches, came on August 1. The Taovayas and their allies stole fifty horses from two Ranger companies north of San Antonio. As they made their northward retreat, however, they passed through the Kichai village where friendly chiefs forced them to give up twenty-two of the stolen horses. Although the Taovayas were still hostile, they refrained from raiding the Texans throughout the rest of the year. The Wichitas on the Brazos River remained peaceful as well.[24]

For the time being, the arrangement with the Texans satisfied the Caddos, and Major Neighbors found "everything quiet and peaceable" in the Kadohadacho and Hainai villages when he visited them in October, 1848. Although a large part of the tribe had dispersed for the winter hunt, the agent found "nothing calculated to disturb our peaceful and friendly relations with them." The Nadacos, however, were frightened by the hostility of the white settlers and the Texas Rangers. Instead of returning to their old village in the spring of 1849, the Nadacos decided to move farther up the Brazos to join with the Kadohadachos and the Hainais. They quickly settled into their new home—directly across the Brazos from the Hainais—by constructing traditional grass houses and, with the other Caddo tribes, made "very creditable efforts" at raising corn, beans, pumpkins, and melons.[25]

Although there were no outbreaks of violence between the whites and the Indians in the winter of 1848–49, Major Neighbors realized that the quiet situation was temporary and that the tribes' position would continue to deteriorate unless bold steps were taken to resolve the Indian matter in Texas. On March 7, 1849, Neighbors put forth his solution to Maj. Gen. William J. Worth, commander of the United States' military forces that were now being deployed at a string of forts established on the Texas frontier following the end of the Mexican War. Neighbors called for a reservation system to be implemented in Texas in which the Indians would be placed under federal jurisdiction and separated from the whites. He proposed that the federal government acquire land from the state of Texas for the "permanent location and settlement of the Indians; said land to be divided among the several bands and tribes according to their numbers." The federal trade and intercourse laws would be extended over the Texas Indians, and agents would be provided for them. To protect the tribes on the reservation, Neighbors called for the federal government to establish military posts in the Indian country whose commanders would be in "full cooperation with the Indian agent in carrying into effect all laws or treaty stipulations." Although Neighbors was soon removed from his position as Texas agent by the newly installed Whig administration of President Zachary Taylor, the establishment of an Indian reservation in Texas soon became the federal government's goal.[26]

Unfortunately, the actual implementation of the policy did not come immediately, and the tribes' uneasiness continued. The new Indian agent, Judge John Rollins, was a political appointee who remained in Washington throughout the summer of 1849; this left the Indians of Texas without a representative of the federal government, which, in view of the state's hostile attitude, was their only ally. Without the steadying influence of Major Neighbors, the frontier erupted in flames, and, with the Taovayas leading the way, warriors from the Wichita, Penateka, Lipan, and Tonkawa tribes attacked the southern part of the state throughout the summer. At least 171 Texans were killed, 25 taken captive, and over a hundred thousand dollars' worth of property was stolen.[27]

The Caddos, however, resisted the attackers' invitations to join in their raids and followed Iesh's policy of friendship. The Caddos stayed at their villages all summer and fall, where they "made a very large crop." In fact, the Caddos saved the lives of two white men who were in their village when a group of Penateka Comanches arrived. The Penatekas had just been attacked by a party of Texans, and five of them had been killed. They sought revenge on the two white men, but the Caddos "manifested much firmness and friendship" and refused to cede them. The Caddos received nothing from the whites in return for earning the Comanches' enmity. Instead, eager surveyors arrived at the Nadaco village a few months later to mark off the land for future white settlement.[28]

The federal government, realizing that it had no power to enforce the boundary between whites and Indians, continued to push for the establishment of an Indian reservation. But despite the continued Indian attacks, the Texans refused to accede to the wishes of the United States. The February, 1850, session of the state legislature rejected a specific proposal to authorize the federal government to extend the trade and intercourse laws to the Indians of Texas. The situation became so desperate that President Millard Fillmore personally tried to persuade Texas to "assign a small portion of her vast domain for the provisional occupancy of the small remnants of tribes within her borders." Commissioner of Indian Affairs Luke Lea suggested the appointment of a commission to confer with Texas authorities "for the purpose of effecting the conventional arrangements indispensable to a satisfactory adjustment" of the state's Indian affairs. William M. Williams, chairman of the Texas House Committee on Indian Affairs, responded favorably to these entreaties. In August, 1850, he called upon his state to adopt the proposals of the federal government; yet once again the Texas legislature refused to comply.[29]

The Taovaya raids, which continued into 1850, left the members of the peaceful Wichita tribes on the Brazos in danger from retaliatory attacks from federal troops, Texas Rangers, and enraged white settlers. The Kichais complained that the actions of the Taovayas "gives them great uneasiness, thinking that the Texans might suppose that they were also engaged in stealing horses from them." To quiet their fears, most of the two hundred or so Kichais abandoned Texas and established a village in the Indian Territory on Choteau Creek, near its confluence with the Canadian River.[30]

On the other hand, most of the Wacos and Tawakonis remained on the Brazos, and Acaquash, the acknowledged leader of the Brazos Wichitas, campaigned to assure the whites of their friendly intentions. In June, 1850, the Waco chief returned two horses that had been stolen by Waco renegades to the commander of Fort Gates on the Leon River. Two months later, at the Kadohadacho village, Acaquash admitted to Capt. George Blake, in command of the U.S. Second Cavalry, that some of his young men had committed depredations and that he was unable to "prevent the commission of such acts." He returned one stolen horse to Captain Blake and offered to guide the troops to the Taovaya village, from where most of the raids took place. The captain declined because of the lack of provisions and the fatigued state of his own horses.[31]

Acaquash also gave his support to a peace proposal put forth in the fall of 1850 by Judge Rollins. On September 21 the federal Indian agent held a talk with the Waco chief and Penateka Comanche chief Buffalo Hump on the Clear Fork of the Brazos. The Penatekas, who had been devastated by an outbreak of cholera the previous year, agreed to attend a general council in December of all Texas Indians in an attempt to "honestly and faithfully try to adjust all differences" between the whites and the Indians. Although all the tribes were notified of the council, the Tonkawas, Kichais, and the Taovayas refused to attend the meeting, which was held on the San Saba in December. The Caddos, even though they had "expressed much anxiety about their situation and a determination to attend the treaty," sent only leading headmen to the council instead of their three chiefs.[32]

It is possible that the absences were the result of a general lack of faith in Judge Rollins, who proved his impotence by failing to accomplish anything lasting at the council. Rollins included the same items in the treaty document—known as the Treaty of Spring Creek—that had been struck by the Senate three years before from the Treaty of Council Springs. These items included an extension of the federal trade and intercourse laws over the Texas Indians and a promise to define a line between the tribes and the whites in the future. All the major headmen of the Wacos, Tawakonis, Penatekas, and Lipans signed the treaty. The U.S. Senate, however, never even bothered to ratify the treaty since the question of the federal government's lack of control over the public lands of Texas had yet to be resolved. By the summer of 1851 the Texas Indians, the United States, and the state of Texas were still without a solution to their problem.[33]

In June, 1851, two representatives of the federal government made separate visits to the Caddo and Wichita villages on the Brazos. Col. Samuel Cooper, with Maj. Henry H. Sibley and a company of the Second Cavalry, left Fort Graham on the Brazos on June 5 and spent a week among the various tribes. Almost as soon as Cooper left the villages, Special Indian Agent Jesse Stem arrived from Fort Martin Scott (Fredericksburg) on May 7. He was accompanied by Col. William J. Hardee and a cavalry troop. The previous September, Congress had provided for two subagents to assist Agent Rollins. Agent Stem had been assigned to the agricultural tribes of the Brazos (as well as the Tonkawas), while John Rogers was placed in charge of the Penateka Comanche and Lipan Apache tribes.[34]

Both Cooper and Stem held talks with the Caddo and Wichita headmen, and their reports were very similar. Both claimed that the tribesmen were "perfectly peaceable" and "professed the most cordial feelings towards our government and people." However, the tribes' leaders strongly desired that "a permanent boundary should be fixed, so that they might have a country where they could be secure from encroachments of the white settlements." Only then could they build up their villages and raise crops without fear of being "forced to abandon their homes, the fruits of their labor, and the graves of their kindred." Iesh— whom Stem felt was the "most influential chief on the Brazos"— complained to the agent that the boundary line was constantly being crossed by whites "who marked trees, surveyed lands in [the Indians'] hunting grounds, and near their villages . . . and this is not just."[35]

The Caddos and Wichitas also complained that the sparseness of game made it difficult to obtain enough to eat, and at times they were "in a starving condition." They "expressed a desire" to be provided with better farming implements, which had been promised in the Treaty of Council Springs, so that they might cultivate their crops "to better advantage and to greater extent." The headmen asked to be furnished with a few cows and hogs to compensate for the depletion of game.

Agent Stem arranged a conference to be held in the fall and promised to bring them hoes, plows, and harnesses. He also wanted to teach the tribes how to raise potatoes, which he felt would fare well in the dry country. Colonel Cooper recommended that the government should supply the tribes with these items which "would greatly contribute to their comfort, and might through their influence, effect a salutary change in the temper and feelings" of some of the hostile tribes.[36]

Stem took a census of the Brazos tribes and found that the uncertainty of their situation had caused many tribesmen to abandon Texas and join their kinsmen north of the Red River. Only thirty-eight Kichais, led by Chacheroqua, remained on the Brazos, the rest having fled to Choteau Creek. Nearly half of the Wacos had moved to the Indian Territory; Acaquash had only 114 people with him on the Brazos. Fewer Tawakonis had abandoned their new chief, Ocherash; Stem counted 141 among his tribe. The Caddos had fewer defectors than the Wichita tribes. There were 161 Kadohadachos, 202 Nadacos, and 113 Hainais remaining on the Brazos. About 100 Caddos had moved north of the Red and joined the Whitebeads on Caddo Creek near the newly established Fort Arbuckle.[37]

Most of the two hundred or so Wacos and Tawakonis who had abandoned the Brazos settled down with the six hundred Taovayas, still led by Tosaquash, in their new village (in present Grady County) on the headwaters of Rush Creek, a tributary of the Washita River. Because of the increased hostility between them and the Texans, as well as conflicts with the Kiowas and Northern Comanches, the Taovayas had left their village on Cache Creek in the Wichita Mountains and moved to the northeast. Once again, the Taovayas displayed a fine sense of knowing where to settle; the village on Rush Creek was situated about twenty miles west of the Western Cross Timbers and was described by one observer as being "situated in the rich and fertile valley of the creek, where they have cultivated corn, pumpkins, beans, peas, and melons." Although they lacked metal tools, the Taovayas were successful farmers for the "prolific soil gives them bountiful returns."[38]

Despite the reports of Stem and Cooper concerning the tenuous situation of the agricultural tribes of the Brazos, no action was taken by the federal government to protect them. In fact, matters were actually made worse by the establishment in the summer of 1851 of Fort Belknap on the Clear Fork of the Brazos (in present Young County). The post, located above the Caddo and Wichita villages, served as an invitation for the whites to stream into and beyond the Indian settlements.[39]

Following their annual winter hunt, the Nadacos and Hainais returned to their villages in early 1852 only to find the area surveyed and surrounded by white settlers. They were forced to move down the Brazos to an unoccupied tract of land near Comanche Peak. This land was of a lesser quality, and the corn crop of 1852 was "unusually small." Combined with their inability to construct adequate shelters, the Nadacos and Hainais "experienced an unusual amount of sickness and mortality" throughout the year. Agent Stem reported that their precarious situation had caused tribesmen to "have no courage for vigorous and hopeful effort." The Kadohadachos, on the other hand, moved their village upstream near Fort Belknap. Realizing the desperate situation of the tribe, Major Sibley purchased the land on which the Kadohadachos resided and gave them written permission to live on his property for five years. However, since the land was "previously uncultivated," the Kadohadachos were only able to "make but little" corn for the year.[40]

The encroachment of the white settlers forced almost all of the Wichitas on the Brazos to move north of the Red and join their kinsmen on Rush Creek. Only Acaquash and a small band of Wacos remained on the Brazos; for protection they eventually relocated near the post Agent Stem established on the Clear Fork of the Brazos at the crossing of the road between Fort Belknap and Fort Phantom Hill to the west.[41]

The hardship and hostility caused by these forced removals led the Wichitas north of the Red to resume their raids upon the Texans. In June, 1852, a group of Taovayas invaded Texas and robbed a wagon train of eight horses and mules. Agent Stem sent a member of Acaquash's band of Wacos to Rush Creek, where he was able to retrieve the stolen animals. Two months later a troop from Fort Belknap visited the Wichita encampment on Rush Creek and convinced them to give up six more stolen horses and mules. The visit of the soldiers quieted the Wichitas for the rest of the year.[42]

In January, 1853, however, the Wichitas began to make raids into Texas in earnest. By late February five separate parties had committed depredations in Texas, often using Acaquash's camp as a rendezvous

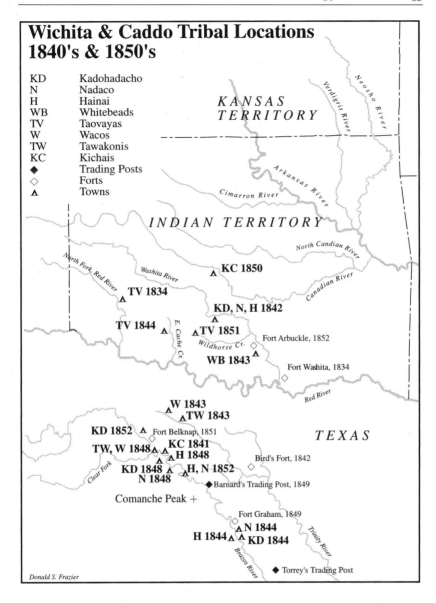

Wichita & Caddo Tribal Locations
1840's & 1850's

KD   Kadohadacho
N   Nadaco
H   Hainai
WB   Whitebeads
TV   Taovayas
W   Wacos
TW   Tawakonis
KC   Kichais
◆   Trading Posts
◇   Forts
▲   Towns

KANSAS TERRITORY

Neosho River
Verdigris River
Arkansas River
Cimarron River

INDIAN TERRITORY

North Canadian River
North Fork, Red River
Washita River
Canadian River

▲ KC 1850

▲ TV 1834

▲ KD, N, H 1842

▲ TV 1844   *E. Cache Cr.*
▲ TV 1851
Wildhorse Cr.
◇ Fort Arbuckle, 1852

WB 1843 ▲

◇ Fort Washita, 1834

Red River

W 1843 ▲
▲ TW 1843

KD 1852 ▲ ◇ Fort Belknap, 1851
TW, W 1848 ▲ ▲ KC 1841
▲ H 1848
KD 1848 ▲ ▲ H, N 1852   ◇
N 1848   ◆ Bird's Fort, 1842

TEXAS

◆ Barnard's Trading Post, 1849

Comanche Peak +

Clear Fork

◇ Fort Graham, 1849
▲ N 1844
H 1844 ▲ ▲ KD 1844

Trinity River
Brazos River

◆ Torrey's Trading Post

Donald S. Frazier

point. Agent Stem, with the assistance of a Penateka headman named Sanaco, captured two Waco men and four boys. Stem turned the boys over to Acaquash, but the men escaped from Sanaco's custody. The agent felt certain that Acaquash had concealed the two in his camp.[43]

The uneasiness between the Wichitas and the whites soon led to bloodshed. On February 22 a Taovaya headman named Koweaka led twenty-two warriors into Texas, purportedly to fight the Lipan Apaches. They visited Agent Stem, who accused them of committing "many depredations over the past year" and ordered them back across the Red River to obtain the stolen property. Koweaka did not deny the charges, and he and his party returned to Rush Creek. Koweaka recrossed the Red on March 23 with eight warriors and several women and children and returned fourteen stolen horses to Stem. Despite this demonstration of good faith, Stem and Major Sibley decided to detain Koweaka's party as hostages in an attempt to recover the large number of horses that had been stolen in the past month. Two of the Taovayas were sent back to retrieve the horses, and Koweaka and his party were disarmed and put under guard in their own camp. That night, Koweaka sacrificed himself and his family so that the rest of the Taovaya hostages could escape. He stabbed his wife and child in the heart and then rushed one of the guards with the knife and was killed. In the confusion the others slipped away.[44]

This shocking incident only raised the level of tension on the Brazos. A few days later Acaquash and his band of Wacos killed five head of Agent Stem's cattle with "no explanation or apology." Stem, accompanied by a troop of soldiers commanded by Major Sibley, visited the Waco camp and demanded three horses as payment. While Acaquash feigned compliance, the Waco men began driving their horses away to safety. When Major Sibley tried to stop them, shots were traded between the parties, and the Waco warriors were forced to retreat. The Waco women immediately decamped, burned the lodges, and all of Acaquash's band headed north to join their kinsmen. The last of the Wichitas had finally abandoned Texas.[45]

Although most of the Caddos remained south of the Red River, their situation was not much better than that of the Wichitas. The Kadohadachos' problems were exacerbated by the untimely death of their caddi, Haddabah, in the summer of 1853. George W. Hill, Stem's replacement, reported in August to Major Neighbors—appointed superintendent of Texas Indian affairs by the Democratic administration of President Franklin Pierce—that there was no clear successor to Haddabah's position and that the tribe was "much scattered and divided in sentiment." In their misery, the Indians had again taken up drinking whiskey, which they obtained from the soldiers at Fort Belknap. Hill told the old men of the tribe to gather the people and select a chief, and he promised to "remove as far as possible [the] evils" of liquor upon his return the following month.[46]

Before returning to the Kadohadacho village, Hill held a council on September 15 with most of the Hainai and the Nadaco warriors one hundred miles down the Brazos at the trading post that had been recently established by Charles Barnard. Iesh did most of the talking for both of the tribes and "urged with force the necessity" of the government procuring a home for him and his people, around which "his white brother could pass" to the west. He told Hill that "the buffalo was gone and but a few deer were left and the white people had most of them" and thus again asked to be provided with cattle and hogs. Agent Hill was forced to reply that he could not do anything for them until he received orders from the "white father."[47]

On September 26 Hill returned to the Kadohadacho village and met with the headmen, who "after much effort" had still been unable to choose a new leader. They requested that Hill "give them one," whom they promised to "hold up and make strong." Expecting this, Hill had gathered information about the various canahas and chose Tinah, "a sensible and good man," to be the new Kadohadacho chief. In a symbolic gesture, Hill delivered "the papers and principal effects of Haddabah" to Tinah. The canaha then promised to help his tribe refrain from drinking whiskey and requested that Hill give them a permanent home. Although the agent was unable to fulfill this request, he did travel with a group of Kadohadachos to Barnard's Trading Post and purchased "articles of necessity to enable them to make" their fall hunt.[48]

In late 1853, just in time to save the desperate Texas Indian tribes from further despair, the Texas government at last realized that something had to be done. In his message to the Texas legislature on November 9, 1853, Governor Bell—former commander of the Texas Rangers—recommended that the United States be given the authority to settle the Indians on a reservation to be located within the boundaries of the state. The Texas legislature followed the governor's advice and on February 6, 1854, passed an act giving the federal government jurisdiction over twelve leagues of the state's vacant land "for the use and benefit of the several tribes of Indians residing within the limits of Texas."[49] The reservation proposal of Major Neighbors was at last being put into effect, a full five years after it had first been suggested. With the federal government finally receiving the full authority to protect them, the Caddos and Wichitas hoped that they could settle down on the reservation and end the wandering and suffering they had been forced to endure since the 1830s.

Chapter Three

The Brazos Reserve, 1854-59

The Indians [Caddos, Wichitas, and Tonkawas] at the several villages have made very good crops of wheat and corn this season. . . . The Indians have generally made over an average crop, compared with the crops of the white citizens in this section. . . . All the Indians on this reserve are tillers of the soil, and their support is principally derived from its products. They have a fair stock of horses, cattle, and hogs, and are paying particular attention to stock raising; and I am satisfied that in a few years their condition will bear comparison with our frontier citizens.

—Shapley P. Ross,
Special Indian Agent,
Brazos Reserve, Texas, September 11, 1857

By the 1850s the Indian policy of the United States had evolved from simply removing the tribes from the path of the encroaching whites to the development of the reservation system. Small parcels of land were to be "reserved" out of the original holdings of the tribes or bands as an alternative to extinction. On these reserves—many of which were to be located near the white settlements—the federal government's trade and intercourse laws would be implemented, the Indians would be protected, and their country preserved from land-hungry whites. In return for agreeing to remove to the reservation, the tribes would be provided with weekly food rations as well as periodic distributions of presents, such as clothing and blankets.[1]

The ultimate goal of the reservation system, however, was not just to protect the Indians but also to transform them. The notions of Major Neighbors, who was placed in charge of the Texas reservations in

1854, neatly summarized the general policy of the federal government concerning the reservation system. Neighbors saw himself as a "civilizing agent" who would help the Indians convert to the ways of the white man. The Indians would be taught advanced agricultural techniques and the art of stock raising and would be provided with the tools necessary to implement these practices. English education would be provided for the children, and attempts would be made to convert the tribes to Christianity. Neighbors claimed that his efforts, as well as those of his subagents, would be "directed particularly to give individuality to the Indians, and to teach them the value of property . . . to encourage each head of a family to settle and cultivate his own farm."[2]

The Caddos, Wacos, and Tawakonis who settled on the Brazos Reserve seemed particularly well suited to proving that the reservation system could work. They were traditionally sedentary and agricultural, had given up any hopes of living independently of whites, and were particularly eager to obtain a parcel of land they could permanently call their own. The Caddos and Wichitas had painfully learned the lesson that the Texans were not to be deterred in their westward march, and the tribes realized they would need to adapt to the whites' ways if they wished to survive. Although not ready to give up their traditional way of life, the tribes saw nothing wrong with learning white ways— such as raising cattle or having their children attend school—which would profit them. The tribes' optimistic attitude toward reservation life went far in the success that they experienced in the four years they spent on the Brazos Reserve.

Unfortunately, the reservation experiment in Texas was not undertaken in a vacuum, and there were two mutually antagonistic groups who viciously opposed its success: hostile Northern Comanches and white settlers. From its opening in 1854, the Brazos Reserve was susceptible to attacks from both groups. Ultimately, the reserve was left in an untenable position, and once again the Caddos and Wichitas were forced to give up their lands and move into the Indian Territory—this time abandoning Texas for good.

Although legislation had been passed in February, 1854, for the establishment of reservations for the Indians of Texas, it took a full year before the tribes were actually able to settle there. All the Wichita tribes spent the entire year north of the Red River, either at the Kichai

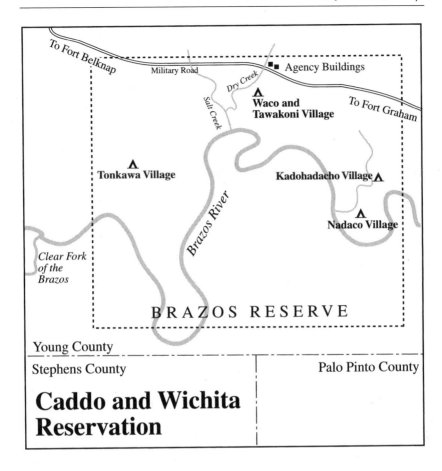

village on Choteau Creek or at the Taovaya settlement on Rush Creek. Following their winter hunt, large numbers of the three Caddo tribes also settled in the Indian Territory, where they joined the Whitebead village near Fort Arbuckle. By this time the Whitebeads were led by Showetat. They successfully raised their own crops and began making conscious attempts to adopt the whites' ways, as evinced by Showetat taking the name of George Washington.[3]

In the meantime the Caddos who did remain in Texas in 1854 had a particularly difficult year. Grasshoppers destroyed their first crop of corn in early spring, and torrential rains—combined with an extremely dry summer—injured their second crop. Their harvest was so small that it had been consumed by September. The men of the tribe tried to supplement their food supply through the chase but met with little success, as their hunting grounds had been severely reduced by the encroaching white settlements to the east and by the Northern Comanches who controlled the land to the west. To keep the Caddos from starving, Agent Hill was forced to distribute food to the tribes throughout the year.[4]

The three Caddo tribes were therefore very eager to settle down permanently, and on July 15, 1854, Iesh, representing both the Nadacos and the Hainais, and Tinah, chief of the Kadohadachos, met with Capt. Randolph B. Marcy and Major Neighbors to discuss the proposed reservation. Chiefs Acaquash and Ocherash also were present as representatives of the absent Wacos and Tawakonis. Captain Marcy explained to the chiefs that he had been chosen to survey the country and to select a site for their reservation. Iesh informed Marcy that although he realized that the "Great Father had the abundant power to send" his people wherever he chose, the Caddos preferred to live on the Brazos at a point below Fort Belknap in order to receive protection from the Northern Comanches. Although his tribe had been driven from its home many times by the whites, Iesh said he preferred to live near them since "they generally allowed him to eat a portion of what he raised, but that the Comanches took everything." The other headmen concurred with this opinion.[5]

There was only one parcel of land below Fort Belknap on the Brazos that had yet to be claimed by onrushing whites, so Marcy and Neighbors traveled there, accompanied by the Wichita and Caddo chiefs. Situated about fifteen miles below Fort Belknap near the old Caddo and Wichita villages, the tract consisted of 8 leagues, or 37,152 acres. Within the tract was a "large body of valley land of the most preeminent fertility upon either side" of the Brazos. The uplands were "covered with luxuriant gramma grasses," which provided the tribes with good pastureland. There were several streams of fresh spring water, which afforded "an abundance of water at all seasons." The tribes gladly accepted this rich land as their reservation, which came to be known as the Brazos or Lower Reserve. Marcy and Neighbors chose another parcel of land higher up on the Clear Fork of the Brazos for the Penateka Comanches. This reservation was called the Comanche or Upper Reserve.[6]

At the same time, the federal government began negotiations for the purpose of securing a permanent home for the Taovayas and Kichais who remained in the Indian Territory. In treaties signed in the 1820s and 1830s, the Choctaws and Chickasaws had gained legal possession of the land on which these tribes resided. On June 22, 1855, following lengthy discussions in Washington, a treaty was concluded in which the Choctaws and Chickasaws agreed to lease to the United States the territory between the Canadian and Red Rivers and the 98th and 100th meridian for the settlement of the Wichitas and whatever tribes the federal government might desire. Thus, just as the Wacos and Tawakonis were receiving a home on the Brazos Reserve in Texas, the Kichais and Taovayas gained the right to settle in the so-called Leased District of the Indian Territory.[7]

The reservation experiment began in Texas in late October, 1854, when the three Caddo tribes began settling on the Brazos Reserve "without assistance or encouragement." They set up houses for the winter, and small parties of hunters ranged between Fort Belknap and Comanche Peak in search of game. Over the winter Agent Hill began distributing rations—consisting of flour and beef—to the tribes. In November Waco and Tawakoni warriors returned stolen horses to Hill at the Comanche Reserve and "evince[d] anxious desire" to settle on the Brazos Reserve since they were starving in the Indian Territory. Hill furnished them with the remaining rations but convinced them to wait until spring to move south of the Red since he had no more food.[8]

Finally, on March 1, 1855, Agent Hill gathered the Caddos and the two Wichita tribes together and, after consulting with the headmen, distributed the land. The Kadohadachos, along with the small group of Delawares they were associated with, chose land near the east line of the reserve near Caddo Spring, on the north bank of the Brazos. The Nadacos and the Hainais settled on the same side of the Brazos, about one and a half miles west of the Kadohadacho village, at the mouth of Anadarko Creek. As a result of Iesh's leadership over the two tribes, the term Nadaco began to be used for both tribes, and the designation of Hainai was dropped for the time being. The Waco and Tawakoni village was located five miles west of the Nadacos, one mile north of the Brazos, near Salt Creek.[9]

The federal government also assigned the Tonkawas, a non–Caddoan-speaking tribe, to the Brazos Reserve. This decision ultimately proved to be a mistake, for the Tonkawas were neither linguistic kinsmen of the Caddos and Wichitas nor fellow agriculturalists. Instead,

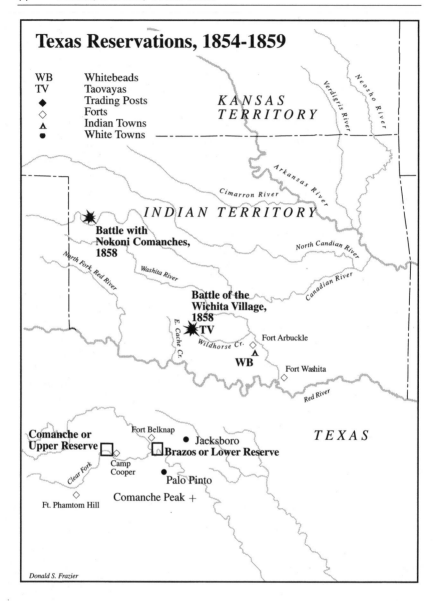

Texas Reservations, 1854-1859

WB   Whitebeads
TV   Taovayas
◆   Trading Posts
◇   Forts
▲   Indian Towns
●   White Towns

KANSAS TERRITORY

Verdigris River
Neosho River

Arkansas River
Cimarron River

INDIAN TERRITORY

Battle with
Nokoni Comanches,
1858

North Candian River

North Fork Red River
Washita River

Canadian River

Battle of the
Wichita Village,
1858
TV

E. Cache Cr.
Wildhorse Cr.
◇ Fort Arbuckle

WB
▲

◇ Fort Washita

Red River

Fort Belknap
◇

Comanche or
Upper Reserve ☐ ◇

● Jacksboro

☐ Brazos or Lower Reserve

TEXAS

Camp
Cooper

Clear Fork

● Palo Pinto

◇
Ft. Phamtom Hill

Comanche Peak +

Donald S. Frazier

they scratched out a meager existence in southwestern Texas hunting
small animals—the Comanches had shut them out of the buffalo country—and gathering plants and roots. The poverty of the Tonkawas had
caused them to provide assistance to the Republic of Texas in the wars
against the Penateka Comanches, Wichitas, and Caddos, thus earning

the everlasting distrust of their future co-settlers on the Texas reserves. Agent Hill assigned land five miles west of the Waco and Tawakoni villages to the two hundred and fifty remaining Tonkawas, who were en route to the Brazos Reserve from Fort Inge on the Nueces.[10]

Agent Hill decided to construct the agency buildings of the Brazos Reserve about one and a half miles north of the Waco and Tawakoni village, six hundred yards south of the north line of the reserve. Upon completion, the agency buildings consisted of a double log house for the agent's dwelling, a single log house for his office, a single log house for the commissary store, a double log house for the laborer's dwelling, one schoolhouse, a blacksmith shop, a house for the interpreter, a privy, and a spring house. Laborers' houses were also built at the villages of the Kadohadachos and the Wichitas.[11]

The Indians immediately began setting up permanent villages and planting crops in the adjacent fields. By all accounts, their efforts met with great success, ostensibly proving the feasibility of the reservation system. By 1856 the various tribes were described as having "neat cottages," made of both grass and logs. During the following year the Kadohadachos built seven log houses and the Nadacos ten, while the Wacos and Tawakonis raised sixteen between them. The leading members of each tribe were housed in these nontraditional abodes, some of which were quite impressive. The log house of the Nadaco caddi, Iesh, was estimated to be worth $150. In 1859 it was noted that both the Kadohadachos and the Nadacos had raised seventy-three traditional grass houses, the Wacos and Tawakonis another forty-nine. The Indian agents attributed the general good health of the reserve tribes "to the cleanliness of themselves and their lodges."[12]

The Caddos and Wichitas—including, for the very first time, the Waco and Tawakoni men—went to work in the fields immediately upon their arrival in March, 1855. With the assistance of two white farmers and two laborers, the tribes (along with the late-arriving Tonkawas) were able to plow and plant corn on 295 acres of land. However, the late period of planting, coupled with dry weather, caused the yield to be fairly small, only a little over a thousand bushels. In addition to the corn, the Indians raised a "good supply" of melons, pumpkins, and beans.[13]

Following the harvest in 1855, each tribe was provided with a five-yoke team of oxen as well as plows, a wagon, and "all the necessary farming utensils." Three hundred head of cattle, along with a few chickens and hogs, were also distributed among the tribes in an effort to wean them away from the chase. With the new equipment, the tribes made great progress in preparing their fields for planting in 1856. The Kadohadachos were able to cultivate 150 acres of land, the Nadacos only 10 less. The Wacos and Tawakonis together planted 150 acres, the Tonkawas 100. All of the tribes built fences around the crops to protect them from the cattle and pigs. Despite all their efforts, the tribes' crop yield again was not high. Grasshoppers destroyed the first crop in the spring, and summer dryness caused the second crop to produce only half of what was expected. The new Indian agent on the Brazos Reserve, Shapley P. Ross, realized that raising corn was difficult, if not impossible, this far west and began making preparations to raise wheat the following year.[14]

Finally, in 1857 the Brazos Reserve Indians had a successful agricultural year. The Kadohadachos and the Nadacos were very industrious, keeping their wagons and oxen "constantly at work, hauling in their crops and fencing their farms." The labor of the two tribes was rewarded, for they raised two thousand bushels of corn apiece, and together, in their first attempt, raised six hundred bushels of wheat. In addition, there was "a very large crop of peas and beans, an abundance of pumpkins and squashes [and] . . . a large crop of melons." Working "admirably," the Wacos and Tawakonis raised eighteen hundred bushels of corn apiece; however, their wheat crop was destroyed by a spring frost. The Brazos tribes also had success in stock raising, and some of the Caddo women were actually learning to milk the cows and make their own butter. According to Agent Ross, the crops of the Brazos Reserve Indians were better than those of the average white settler in the area. The agent gave the Kadohadachos and Nadacos permission to make small hunting parties in the winter, as a reward for their diligence, which had proved them "perfectly reliable." This was done, "more [as] a matter of recreation than profit," for the Caddos had raised enough food in 1857 to make a winter hunt unnecessary.[15]

The year 1857 proved to be the agricultural high point for the Indians of the Brazos Reserve. Their efforts were greatly hampered the following two years by troubles with both the Northern Comanches and the white settlers. Much of their stock was stolen by the raiding Comanches, and white hostility forced the tribes to remain on the reservation, unable to collect the cattle that had roamed out on the open range. In addition, the increased tensions caused the tribes to pay much less attention to their crops.[16]

Despite the setbacks, the Brazos Indians were still able to keep a good stock of domestic animals. By 1859 the tribes of the reserve had collected 597 hogs. Even after many of their horses and cattle had been run off by the Comanches and the whites, the Nadacos still owned 127 head of cattle, 4 yoke of oxen, and 346 horses; the Kadohadachos had fewer animals, with 93 head of cattle, 259 horses, and 4 yoke of oxen. The Wichita tribes were less successful than the Caddos at stock raising, for the Wacos had only 109 horses and 32 head of cattle, while the Tawakonis owned 116 horses, 48 mules, and 23 head of cattle. Except for the oxen, the animals were held individually rather than communally. The tribal members had always owned their own horses, and this form of ownership was extended to the rest of the stock they acquired. Following tradition, the leading members of the tribe owned more animals than the rest. For example, out of a total of 600 hogs on the reservation, Iesh and his sisters owned 120.[17]

The success the Caddos and Wichitas experienced on the Brazos Reserve is best demonstrated by their ability finally to stabilize their population after centuries of decline. The Caddo census of March 31, 1855—taken soon after the opening of the reserve—numbered 364, a loss of 110 people since the previous enumeration in 1851. The Wichita population had dropped from 255 to 202 in the same period. Much of this loss can be attributed to the defection of many tribal members north of the Red River, but Agent Hill also claimed that many Indian children had died during that period for "want of proper food, and increase of exposure."[18]

The first census taken after the opening of the Brazos Reserve counted 31 Nadaco families totaling 204 people, and 23 Kadohadacho families totaling 160. Once settled on the Brazos Reserve, the Caddo population grew continually, from 364 in 1855 to 445 two years later, and to 462 in 1859. The Nadaco totals peaked in 1857 (before a few defected) at 232, an increase of 28 people, while the Kadohadachos gained 84 members to reach 244 in 1859.[19]

Statistics for the Wacos and Tawakonis demonstrate the same increase. In March, 1855, there were 85 Wacos grouped in 15 families, and

115 Tawakonis grouped in an undetermined number of families. Both tribes' populations peaked in December, 1857; the Waco population nearly doubled to 161 members, while the Tawakonis gained 98 members to reach a total of 213.[20]

Most of the increase can be attributed to the return of the refugees from the Indian Territory; the agents noted a continual stream of these new arrivals from the north. Overall, 181 refugee Wichitas and 105 refugee Caddos joined the Brazos Reserve during its four-year existence. However, the conditions on the reserve in and of themselves were sufficient for a natural increase in population. In the words of Agent Neighbors, "by being well clothed, having houses to live in, and relieved from the continued anxieties of attending a roving life, their health has greatly improved, and [the Indians on the Brazos Reserve] now, for the first time in several years, begin to raise healthy children." In fact, there were 22 Caddo children born between 1855 and 1859, but there were only 7 deaths. The Waco and Tawakoni numbers are less dramatic—6 births and 3 deaths.[21]

In addition to the material success the Caddos and Wichitas experienced on the Brazos Reserve, the tribes also accepted changes in the areas of education and religion. As the various tribes gathered on the two reservations in 1855, Major Neighbors noted that among the population there were 344 children under twelve years of age. The agent claimed that all of the tribes of the Brazos Reserve were "anxious to have a school for their children."[22]

On August 31, 1855, Rev. John W. Phillips of San Antonio, presiding elder of the Methodist Episcopal Church South, wrote to Neighbors and inquired whether the Indians on the Brazos Reserve would accept a missionary and a school. Neighbors replied that the Indians had agreed to receive both in the treaty of 1846, and he heartily endorsed the proposal both to Reverend Phillips and to Commissioner of Indian Affairs Charles E. Mix.[23]

Government officials took no action on the proposal in 1856, although Agent Ross alerted them that a number of children were "growing up in ignorance and superstition, which might be averted by a suitable appropriation for educational purposes." Ross claimed that the majority of the Indians on the Brazos Reserve understood "that schools would prepare the rising generation for the more useful walks and occupations of life."[24]

In light of such endorsements, five thousand dollars was appropriated by Congress in 1857 for the establishment of a school on the Brazos Reserve. Despite being suggested by officials of the Methodist church, the school was not tied in any way to that body. Agent Ross reported in September, 1857, that the Indians "all express a desire to have their children educated, and it is gratifying to them to know" that the schoolhouse was nearly completed.[25]

Although the building was ready in the fall of 1857, the school was not opened until the following summer. In the meantime, a Methodist missionary, Rev. Pleasant Tackitt, visited the reservation and preached to a gathering of the Indians. According to Tackitt, following his sermon several chiefs held a council and told him they "were pleased with the talk, and will return to hear more of it." Tackitt preached a few more times to the Indians in 1858, but he gained no actual followers. However, it was the first time since the Spaniards' attempt to convert the Caddos in the previous century that they had heard the Christian gospel; it was the very first time for the Wacos and Tawakonis.[26]

On June 1, 1858, the school on the Brazos Reserve was finally opened by Zachariah Ellis Coombes, an optimistic twenty-five-year-old teacher. Sixty students enrolled in the school, most of them boys. Coombes reported that average attendance, however, was only about thirty students a day. Although the children knew no English and were hard to control, "being accustomed to no restraint or coercion," a good many of the students had learned the alphabet by September, 1858.[27]

Most of the children were Kadohadachos and Tawakonis, for those two tribes "manifest[ed] considerable interest in getting their children to school." Coombes prepared a "report card" on October 19, which listed fifteen "scholars." There were nine Kadohadacho students, two Nadacos, three Tawakonis, and one white child. All of the Nadaco and Tawakoni children who attended were boys, but only five of the Kadohadachos were males. Reflecting the Caddos' history of close relations with Euro-Americans, nine of the eleven children had white names, such as Bob Taylor and Tom Smith; all three Tawakoni students, however, had traditional names. Among the comments that Coombes made was that Sam Houston, a twelve-year-old Kadohadacho boy, had "learned his letters [and was] very kind." Fourteen-year-old Kadohadacho Jim Shot Gun had "progressed well at first, but is very headstrong." Shantano, a Nadaco boy of thirteen, "progressed slowly at first [but] advances now rapidly." A twelve-year-old Tawakoni named Nahquah was progressing slowly because he was "fond of talk and trade."[28]

Following six months of school, Coombes felt that the students needed a rest, and the children were given a month's vacation. Coombes reported that by the end of the first session in November, 1858, one student was studying *Ray's Arithmetic,* sixteen were studying reading and writing, seventeen were studying spelling, and twenty others were learning the alphabet.[29]

Unfortunately, the progress made during the first school session was not matched by the second, which opened on January 10, 1859. As a result of the murders of seven Caddos by hostile whites in late 1858, the whole reserve was thrown into an uproar, and it was difficult for Coombes to get the children to attend. On February 28 he reported that the number of scholars at the school had dropped from sixty to forty-six, because of the parents' fear for their children's safety. Despite the trouble, Coombes remained optimistic and believed that it "would be very difficult in any school of red or white people to find as much good will and as great harmony as in this school."[30]

Cause for optimism about the school, however, quickly dwindled. By the end of March Coombes felt that neither the pupils nor the parents had a desire to continue the school. Average attendance during April, 1859, dropped to only twelve students per day. By June the school was closed as the Reserve Indians were forced off their lands by the Texans. It would be many years before the Caddos and Wichitas would again receive educational instruction.[31]

The Caddos and Wichitas, therefore, had done their part in proving the feasibility of the reservation system. The tribesmen had eagerly set up houses and farms, gladly accepted whatever innovations the whites proposed, sent their children to school, and were even willing to hear the Christian gospel. They were able to support themselves and seemed well on the way to adapting to the changes that had occurred around them. In order to complete fully the transformation to the reservation way of life, however, the tribes would need more time. Unfortunately, patience with any Indians, friendly or hostile, was not a virtue many white Texans had to spare.

Although the tribes of the Brazos Reserve made great strides within the reservation system, uncontrollable external forces hampered the overall success of the reserve. The unsettled Comanches to the north-west emerged as the primary enemy, attacking both the Indians on the Brazos Reserve and the frontier white settlements. Despite the Caddos' and Wichitas' many demonstrations of friendship, the Comanches' unceasing attacks upon the hapless Texans caused them to become increasingly suspicious of the Reserve Indians as well and eventually to oppose their existence. Although the Reserve Indians might have been able to withstand the attacks of the Comanches, the additional hostility of the Texans placed them in a untenable situation.

Northern Comanche hostilities actually grew out of a treaty they, as well as the Kiowas and Kiowa-Apaches, signed with the United States in 1853. In the so-called Treaty of Fort Atkinson the federal government agreed to present the tribes with eighteen thousand dollars' worth of trade goods annually in return for free right of travel on the Santa Fe Trail and the right to establish military posts in Indian country. Assured of receiving goods from the United States at Fort Atkinson in Kansas, the Northern Comanches began to raid into Texas with impunity. Headed by Buffalo Hump and Sanaco, warriors from the Penateka Comanche bands, which had refused to settle down with Ketumse's group on the Comanche Reserve, occasionally joined in on these raids. These actions only caused the Texans to suspect all Comanches, including those on the reserve.[32]

Northern Comanche raiding began almost as soon as the Indians on the two reserves had settled down. On September 14, 1855, Agent Ross received word that a white settler named Skidmore had been killed by two Comanches ten miles above Fort Belknap. Ross sent runners to the various tribes on the Brazos Reserve asking for their assistance, and the next morning sixty-six warriors were mounted and ready to pursue the raiders. The party stayed on the trail of the Comanches for two days before they concluded that it would be impossible to overtake them.[33]

The following week, however, a Comanche raiding party stole forty head of horses from the Reserve Indians as well as an undetermined number from the white settlements. A combined Kadohadacho-Delaware force pursued the Comanches across the Red River, skirmished with them, and recovered the horses. On this expedition they learned that the Comanches had "declared war upon all people south of Red River, white and red."[34]

In the spring of 1856 Comanche raids upon the Brazos Reserve and the surrounding white settlements increased dramatically. In response, the future hero of the Confederacy, Col. Robert E. Lee—who had recently helped open Camp Cooper near the Comanche Reserve—mounted a punitive expedition in June, 1856. Fifteen Brazos Reserve Indians, mainly Delawares and Caddos, accompanied Colonel Lee's Second Cavalry as scouts. Jim Shaw, the Delaware chief, led the Indian troops.[35]

After following Indian trails for a few days on the upper reaches of the Colorado and Brazos Rivers, Lee split his force in two; Lee remained in command of the Second Squadron, while another future Confederate general, Maj. Earl Van Dorn, led the First Squadron and the Indian auxiliaries. On July 2 Van Dorn's force surprised a party of four Comanches, killing two and capturing a woman. Twelve stolen horses and saddles were recovered. Upon questioning, the woman reported that she had accompanied twelve men on a raiding expedition through Mexico and Texas. The party had split up and was returning to their village when Van Dorn found them. Although she was a Northern Comanche unattached to the Upper Reserve, she was taken there by the Indian scouts because she claimed to have relatives living among the Penatekas.[36]

The return of the woman and the news that the Caddos had joined Colonel Lee's expedition against the Comanches caused about seventy-five Penatekas from the Comanche Reserve to march on Iesh's village on July 23. Led by Ketumse and Buffalo Hump (who had temporarily decided to settle down), the Penateka Comanches advanced to within one hundred yards of the Nadaco camp before being met by Iesh, who told them that his men were ready for battle if they wanted to fight.[37]

Faced with this bold stance, the Penatekas replied that they wanted only to talk. Agent Ross was summoned, and a council was held between the headmen of both tribes. Ketumse protested the Caddo scouts' assistance to the white troops and inquired if Iesh intended to continue allowing his tribe to fight the Comanches. Agent Ross answered for the caddi, insisting that the Caddo tribe had every right to take measures to detain and kill any thieving Indians. Ross then persuaded the Penatekas to return peacefully to their own reservation. However, both the agent and the angry Penatekas were certain that the Caddos had not been "dissuaded from stopping [the Comanche's] stealing."[38]

Depredations upon the Brazos Reserve and the white settlements continued throughout the fall and winter of 1856. Fourteen horses were stolen from the Nadacos in October by the Comanches, but a party of eight Nadacos and four Kadohadachos was able to recover them. The following month two white teamsters were killed about forty miles from Fort Belknap. A party of fifteen Brazos Reserve Indians, led by Jim Shaw, took to the trail in pursuit but were unable to overtake the killers, who were thought to be Comanches.[39]

As the depredations increased in intensity in 1857 so did the white hostility to the Reserve Indians, although they were "always rendering assistance to citizens in pursuing thieves." The country around the reservations was rapidly filling with white settlers, many from the "older states who are not accustomed to Indians." In early 1857 Young County (in which the Brazos Reserve lay) was organized. Agent Ross claimed that when the reservations were opened in 1854 only 12 families lived in the area embraced by the county. Three years later he estimated that about 150 families resided in Young County. The other surrounding counties were experiencing a similar growth. The new emigrants to the area, exasperated by Indian attacks, were inclined to lay the blame for hostilities at the feet of the Reserve Indians, particularly the Penateka Comanches, who lived in their midst.[40]

"Reckless and designing men" helped encourage the prejudices of the white citizenry against the Reserve Indians. Chief among these unprincipled few was John R. Baylor, who had been dismissed for negligence by Neighbors from his position as agent for the Comanche Reserve in 1857. The vengeful Baylor began to do all that he could (scrupulous or not) to secure the removal of the Texas Indian agent. In 1858 he stated in a confidential letter that he was collecting "all the evidence I can against the Indians and Neighbors," for he wanted his friend, Allison Nelson, to take Neighbors's position and promised to do "all in my power to aid him." Over the next two years Baylor, Nelson, and others spread many libelous and dangerous rumors among the white settlers designed to raise their ire toward the two reserves and the Indian agents who presided over them.[41]

The attacks of the Comanches, however, continued to be aimed at the Brazos Reserve tribes as well as the whites. In February, 1857, a Kadohadacho scout named Jack Hunter was killed by raiding Comanches. Iesh assembled the tribe for the purpose of enlisting men for a campaign against their foe, but Agent Ross convinced them to postpone their attack until after the spring planting. The Caddos were given the opportunity to fight the Comanches the following month after white settlers reported fifteen horses had been stolen. Unfortunately, the band of Reserve Indians who pursued the raiders was unable to find them. During the summer of 1857, though, various hunting parties of Indians from the Brazos Reserve were successful in recapturing stolen horses and mules from the Comanches.[42]

Indian attacks upon the white settlers on the Brazos and Colorado Rivers reached a new intensity beginning in November, 1857. Within two months the Indians had killed seven whites, stolen about six hundred horses, and damaged an estimated sixty thousand dollars' worth of property. Investigations by Nadaco warriors, led by second chief Jim Pock Mark, discovered the guilty parties to be the Comanches, Kiowas, and Kickapoos, all of whom resided north of the Red River.[43]

Many white settlers, however, placed the blame on the Indians of the Comanche Reserve. On December 15, 1857, the citizens of two Texas counties presented separate petitions to the Secretary of the Interior calling for the removal of Major Neighbors as Indian agent. In the petitions, the citizens charged the Comanche Reserve Indians with stealing the horses of whites, while Agent Neighbors "persists in the face of proof" to do nothing to stop them. The whites claimed to be "satisfied that the very Indians we are taxed to feed and clothe are the ones who inflict the greatest injuries upon us."[44]

Capt. W. G. Evans of the Second Cavalry at Camp Cooper was ordered to investigate the charges, and he reported that he was "fully convinced that robberies in the neighborhood were committed by the Northern Comanches" but did not rule out the possibility that they may "have many facilities afforded them by their relations" on the Comanche Reserve. According to Captain Evans, every citizen in the area believed the Indians of the Comanche Reserve were involved in the depredations.[45]

In a letter addressed to Commissioner Mix, Major Neighbors denied any involvement on the part of the Reserve Indians in these attacks. Fearing for the safety of the Indians on both reservations, Neighbors implored Mix to initiate measures to prevent the Northern Comanche raids, such as increasing military protection. Unless the attacks were stopped, he felt it would "be impossible to prevent the people of Texas from making an indiscriminate war on the Indians" in which the reservations would also be destroyed.[46]

In response to the increased white hostility, the tribes of the Brazos Reserve took matters into their own hands in an attempt to prove their friendliness. On January 14, 1858, a party of Waco warriors took up the trail of the raiders and returned thirty days later with two captured Comanches, sixty-seven stolen horses, and seven stolen mules, all of which they turned over to Agent Ross. A council was then held by the headmen of the Brazos Reserve, along with Agent Ross. The two Comanche prisoners were questioned, and they assured their inquisitors that the raids had been committed by the Northern Comanches, Kiowas, and Kickapoos. It was agreed by the council to execute the two prisoners, and on February 15 they were shot by a firing squad of Indians chosen from the several tribes. The council then assured Agent Ross that "they would use every means in their power to maintain the friendship of the whites, [and that they] were willing and ready whenever called upon to cooperate with the government forces in putting a stop to all stealing and marauding on this frontier."[47]

The Brazos Reserve tribes were soon given the opportunity to show that their pledge to Agent Ross was not empty. The citizens of Texas had elected a new governor, Hardin R. Runnels, on a platform that included a promise to provide the frontier settlements with adequate protection from attacking Indians. Governor Runnels implemented that policy on January 28, 1858, when he appointed John S. (Rip) Ford as senior captain of the Texas Rangers and authorized him to enlist another one hundred men to take action against the hostile Indian forces. By late February, Ford had established Camp Runnels on the Clear Fork of the Brazos, near the two Indian reserves, in preparation for a campaign against the Northern Comanches.[48]

Captain Ford enlisted the help of Agents Neighbors and Ross in the recruitment of the Indians of the Brazos Reserve to be used as scouts and auxiliaries. Ross encouraged as many Indians as could be spared from farming to join Ford "in order to satisfy the minds of the citizens" that they were on the side of the Texans. The recruitment was successful, for on April 22 when the 102 Rangers finally broke camp, they were joined by 109 auxiliaries from the Brazos Reserve. The Caddo contingent, led by Jim Pock Mark, was the most numerous, providing 29

Nadaco and 20 Kadohadacho warriors. In addition there were 35 Tonkawas, 16 Tawakonis, and 9 Wacos.[49]

The target of the campaign was the Kotsoteka tribe of Comanches, whom Ford had learned were camped in the Indian Territory along the Canadian River. On April 29 the expedition crossed the Red River, and eleven days later the Indian scouts began reporting signs which showed a large Comanche encampment nearby. At dawn on May 12, Ford's force, with the Indian allies leading the way, set out for the Comanche camp. Before they could reach their destination, however, the Reserve Indians came upon five Comanche lodges, which they attacked, killing four men and taking two prisoners. Two Comanches escaped to warn the main village of Kotsotekas which was three miles away.[50]

Once again the Indian auxiliaries led the way, in a ruse designed to make the Comanches think that it was only an Indian attack. In response, Kotsoteka chief Iron Jacket rode out of the village to meet his Indian foes but was immediately killed by the well-armed troops of the Brazos Reserve. Ford then launched his Rangers upon the village, the inhabitants of which scattered, and the rout was on. After a few hours of slaughter and destruction, Ford's troops counted seventy-six dead Comanches, eighteen women and children captured, and three hundred Comanche horses taken, most of which were turned over to the Reserve Indians. Only one Waco had been killed as well as two Texas Rangers. Ford learned from the prisoners that Buffalo Hump's band of Penatekas was camped only twelve miles away, so he ordered his force to return quickly to Texas.[51]

Rip Ford's fight with the Comanches on the Canadian River was an overwhelming success, thanks in no small part to the role played by the Indians of the Brazos Reserve. Ford acknowledged the effort of the Indian troops in his report to the governor, claiming that "in justice to our Indian allies I beg leave to say they behaved most excellently on the field of battle. They deserve well of Texas and are entitled to the gratitude of the frontier people." Upon hearing the news of Ford's success, Governor Runnels addressed a message to the men of the expedition which stated that the "deeds of gallantry and valor, performed by each and all of you who were engaged in the fight, gallant Rangers and brave Indian allies . . . will be held in grateful remembrance by the people of Texas."[52]

A great celebration was held at the Brazos Reserve upon the return of the victorious warriors, for the situation at the reservation had been tense since the Indian troops had left. Two white families had been murdered eighteen miles north of the reserve only a few days after the Indians had joined Ford's command. This incident only increased the suspicions of the surrounding white settlers concerning the reserve, and in an attempt to prevent a confrontation, the agent had not permitted the remaining Indians to leave the boundaries of the reserve to collect their stock. However, the news of the returning warriors' participation in Ford's successful campaign quieted (temporarily, at least) the fears of the white citizenry. Agent Ross optimistically noted that a "great change of feeling has taken place in the minds of our frontier citizens in favor of the [Reserve] Indians . . . and . . . they have obtained both credit and position that will allay any prejudice existing against the Reserve."[53]

Soon after the return of the Indian troops to the Brazos Reserve, Major Neighbors traveled to Washington to inform the government of the tense atmosphere which surrounded the reserves in Texas. As a result, Thomas T. Hawkins, a special agent, was sent there to investigate Neighbors's administration of Indian affairs. Though he stayed at both reserves for five weeks, and in that time invited complainants to appear before him and testify, very few did so. In fact, no one came to present evidence against Neighbors. In his report Hawkins commended the agents very highly and stated that the Reserve Indians had made "great moral and physical advancement."[54]

Hawkins was not alone in these conclusions. Many settlers living near the reservations did not believe the Indians were guilty and readily endorsed the administration of Neighbors. Captains Ford and E. N. Burleson of the Texas Rangers, both of whom had been directed by the governor to watch the reserve Comanches closely, had found no evidence of guilt. Captain Ford particularly praised Agent Ross, calling him an "able, efficient and energetic agent, whose successful manner of conducting the affairs of the Agency can be seen by anyone who will examine the houses, the fields, and the Indians."[55]

In the fall of 1858 the Indians of the Brazos Reserve were once again given the opportunity to demonstrate their worth to the white settlers of Texas. Captain Ford's successful campaign against the Comanches had quieted them during the spring and early summer, but by August they had resumed their raiding. The Comanches aimed many of their forays at the stock of the Brazos Reserve Indians, for they expressed "a determination to revenge themselves . . . for damage done them by the expedition of Captain Ford."[56]

This time the army of the United States responded, and Maj. Earl Van Dorn was ordered to lead the Second Cavalry into the Comanche country to search for warring bands. Van Dorn, like Ford, sought the assistance of the Indians of the Brazos Reserve. Once again they responded to the call, and while preparations for the campaign were still under way, Agent Ross's son, Lawrence Sullivan (Sul) Ross, led a force of 125 Reserve Indians to Otter Creek, north of the Red River. Here they established a base named Camp Radziminski and were joined by Van Dorn's force in late September, 1858.[57]

Waco and Tawakoni spies soon learned that an encampment of six hundred Comanches, mainly Buffalo Hump's Penatekas, was located near the Taovaya village on Rush Creek, about ninety miles northeast of Camp Radziminski. As his force made its way to Rush Creek, Major Van Dorn was unaware that Buffalo Hump was in the process of making peace with the United States authorities in the Indian Territory. Following Ford's attack on the Kotsoteka village in May, the Penatekas under Buffalo Hump had begun stealing horses from the Taovayas in the mistaken belief that they had given assistance to the Texas Rangers. The Taovayas finally convinced the Penatekas that they had not been with Captain Ford and invited Buffalo Hump to come to their village for a council on August 22 with Lt. J. E. Powell from Fort Arbuckle. New Taovaya chief Isadowa related the misunderstanding to Lieutenant Powell, who then gave the Penatekas permission to settle on Rush Creek, provided Buffalo Hump promised to travel to Fort Arbuckle in the near future to finalize a peace agreement.[58]

Tragically, Buffalo Hump was making preparations for his peace mission to Fort Arbuckle on the morning of October 1 when Van Dorn and the Indian allies reached the Comanche village. Van Dorn ordered an attack, and in the resulting ninety-minute fight, the Comanches were once again routed. Their losses were heavy since their retreat was hampered by the Reserve Indians who had stampeded their horses. Van Dorn labeled the so-called Battle of the Wichita Village a "complete and decisive" victory. The bodies of fifty-six Comanches were counted in the vicinity, and many more were presumed to have been killed.

More than three hundred horses were captured, and the entire camp of 120 lodges burned. Only five members of Van Dorn's command were killed and twelve were wounded, including the major himself. The Indians of the Brazos Reserve lost no men, and only a few were wounded. Coombes reported that the Reserve Indians returned from the expedition on October 11 "all safe and bringing in a few ponies as the fruit of their victory." The teacher looked forward to seeing the tribe perform an "exulting victory dance."[59]

The Taovayas, however, were not so lucky. Fearing the surviving Comanches would accuse them of a double cross, they abandoned their village on Rush Creek (and its one hundred acres of corn) and took refuge with the Whitebead Caddos near Fort Arbuckle on the Washita. They were soon joined by the Kichais and the newly appointed Wichita agent, Samuel Blain. Agent Blain had arranged for the refugee Wichitas to be cared for over the winter, but 754 blankets purchased for their warmth failed to arrive after the steamboat that was carrying them sank. In the spring of 1859 the Taovayas and Kichais were uncertain if they should plant crops, for the Indian agents could not decide whether the Wichitas should be allowed to remain with the Whitebead Caddos.[60]

Ultimately, the federal government's hand was forced by a crisis concerning the Indians of the Brazos Reserve. The crisis was precipitated in the latter portion of November, 1858, when Tom, a Choctaw who had married into the Nadaco tribe, received permission from Agent Ross to take a group—consisting of twenty-seven Nadaco and Kadohadacho men, women, and children—below the agency boundary. The young men in the party, one the nephew of Iesh, had just returned from Major Van Dorn's campaign, and they wanted to graze their horses in the luxuriant grass that grew on the banks of the Brazos River downstream from the reserve. The men were eager to get their horses ready for another expedition against the Comanches which Van Dorn had scheduled for the spring of 1859.[61]

Choctaw Tom's party was encamped above Golconda, the Palo Pinto county seat, and spent much of early December "conducting themselves in a peaceful and quiet manner," visited occasionally by friendly white settlers who lived nearby. A few white citizens, however, did not approve of the Indian presence in their midst and went to Choctaw Tom's camp and "firmly but kindly" told them to return to the reservation.

The whites told the Caddos that they would not permit them to hunt near their settlements and that if they did not leave, the whites "would raise men and kill them."[62]

Choctaw Tom and his group agreed to return to the Brazos Reserve, but before they left they were invited by a group of friendly whites to camp farther downstream to hunt for a few bears that had recently been sighted. On this invitation, the Caddo party moved the camp farther down the Brazos to the mouth of Keechie Creek. On December 19 Choctaw Tom bought an ox-wagon and a yoke of oxen from a white citizen living nearby and began his return to the Brazos Reserve, having left instructions for the rest of the party to follow in a few days.[63]

However, before the group could break camp they were attacked while they slept by a group of white men in the early morning hours of December 27. Four Caddo men and three women were killed. Three men, two women, and three children were severely wounded. One Nadaco man was able to rise from his bed and kill one of the attackers before being shot to death himself.[64]

A few of the survivors raced back to the reserve and informed Iesh and Tinah of the massacre. The young men of the Caddos immediately took to arms in order to "go back and execute summary vengeance on the murderers." As he had done before, Iesh stepped in and persuaded them to wait and attempt to seek justice through the whites' channels. Since Agent Ross was absent at the time, the following morning the two headmen went to the agency farmer, J. J. Sturm, with the grim news. Sturm, with four white men and thirty Kadohadacho and Nadaco warriors, started immediately for Choctaw Tom's camp and arrived there shortly before sundown on December 28.[65]

Sturm characterized what he viewed as being "a more horrible sight I never expect to see." Lying on their beds were the riddled bodies of "the best and most inoffensive Indians on the reserve . . . their eyes closed and their bodies stretched at full length, their countenances indicating that they passed from calm sleep to the sleep that knows no waking." The relief party covered the bodies with brush and stones and attended to the wounded. Sturm and the Indians found a place near the camp where the murderers had evidently awaited their chance to surprise the sleeping Caddos.[66]

The relief party camped that night about five miles from Golconda and were met the next morning by a Palo Pinto County citizens' committee which had been sent to explain the circumstances. They informed Sturm that on the evening of December 26 a party of twenty white men from Erath County, led by Peter Garland, had encamped near Golconda. They continued that in the middle of that night Garland's party had broken camp only to return to Golconda in the morning with the news that they had attacked Choctaw Tom's camp. Garland and his men happily claimed that through this attack "they had opened the ball and the people there should dance to the music."[67]

Believing that Garland's men had precipitated an Indian war, the settlers in Palo Pinto County began to abandon their homes. The citizens' committee explained to Sturm and the Caddo headmen that they did not approve of the attack on the Indian camp and that they wished to "live in peace and amity." The Caddo chiefs immediately assured Sturm that they would not "retaliate on the innocent" and asked that a messenger be sent to inform the people to return to their homes.[68]

Despite the assurances of both parties, tensions on the frontier remained high. Upon the return of the Caddo party to the agency with the details of the slaughter, a few members of the reserve tribes, including Choctaw Tom and his family, decided to abandon the reserve and cross the Red River. Fearing further attacks, the Indians that remained on the reserve left their villages and assembled around the agency buildings "for their better protection." Although they were ready to defend themselves in case of attack, they showed no "disposition to seek the usual mode of revenge practised by wilder tribes."[69]

Capt. T. N. Palmer of the Second Cavalry was ordered to take a detachment of troops from Fort Belknap to the Brazos Agency to prevent a collision between the whites and the Reserve Indians. Captain Palmer arrived on January 5, 1859, and found the Indians "much alarmed" because they had heard a rumor that the citizens of Palo Pinto and Erath counties were assembling to attack and break up their reserve.[70]

The rumor proved to be partly true. On January 4 Peter Garland and his band had published a signed letter, addressed to the "people of Texas," in which they took full responsibility for the attack on Choctaw Tom's camp. They claimed they had had the "wool pulled over" their eyes long enough by the Indians of the Brazos Reserve and thus offered no apology for what they had done. They further asserted they were "sustained by hundreds" of their fellow citizens. Two days later two hundred citizens of Coryell, Bosque, Comanche, Erath, and Palo Pinto counties began assembling at Stephenville. The whites chose an executive committee of twenty-four men, five of whom had been involved in the attack on the Caddo camp. They also formed a military organization they called the "frontier guards" and organized companies headed by those who had attacked Choctaw Tom. Capt. Allison Nelson, the man Baylor had been pushing to replace Agent Neighbors, was unanimously chosen commander-in-chief.[71]

The executive committee then selected three commissioners to travel to the Brazos Reserve to evaluate the situation and attempt to reach a peaceful agreement. The commission arrived on January 8 and met with Captain Palmer and Farmer Sturm, who was acting in place of the still-absent Agent Ross. Three days later the headmen of the various tribes met with the commissioners, who quickly became "satisfied that there was no danger to be apprehended" from the Indians of the Brazos Reserve. On January 12 they returned to Palo Pinto County and made their report to the assemblage, after which it was agreed that everyone should return to his home. Further violence had been temporarily averted.[72]

The authorities in Texas responded to the attack on the Caddos in a manner which seemed to indicate that Garland's vigilantes would be prosecuted. On January 10 Governor Runnels issued a proclamation that denounced the attack upon the Caddo camp and "warned all persons against joining any hostile expeditions" aimed at the Reserve Indians. The governor directed that the offenders should be arrested and brought to trial; he additionally requested that "all good and law abiding citizens give all necessary and lawful aid" to the authorities.[73]

On January 14 District Judge N. W. Battle of Waco ordered the arrest of the men of Garland's party, but the civil officers of the area refused to carry out those orders out of fear for their lives. Three days later Judge Battle ordered Captain Ford of the Texas Rangers to arrest Garland. Major Neighbors, anticipating a trial, hired E. J. Gurley, a Waco lawyer, to act as counsel for the Caddos in order to ensure they would be "properly represented before the legal tribunals" of Texas.[74]

Neighbors finally arrived at the Brazos Agency on January 22, eight days after the return of Ross. The Indians were still gathered around the agency buildings, and Neighbors held a council with the headmen there. He read them the governor's proclamation and explained to them the measures taken by state authorities to have the murderers apprehended and brought to trial. The chiefs of the tribes agreed to remain peaceful and to "abide by the decision of the civil authorities" of Texas. Following the reassurances of Neighbors, the Indians agreed to return to their villages and farms, which had suffered from neglect after being left unattended for nearly a month.[75]

The Texas authorities soon demonstrated, however, that they were not serious about apprehending Garland and his men. Captain Ford, despite being a friend of the Caddos, informed Gurley that he could not legally arrest the murderers since he could only act as an assistant to a civil officer. He stated that he would need an order from the governor to implement Judge Battle's command. Neighbors then protested the lack of action to Governor Runnels. The governor advised Judge Battle to issue new writs of arrest to a civil officer and promised that Captain Ford would assist in their execution. Despite these promises, by mid-February Garland and his men remained free.[76]

The Indians of the Brazos Reserve received another blow to their cause in February when the U.S. Army decided that nearby Fort Belknap would be abandoned in the near future. The troops stationed at the fort had provided the Reserve Indians with at least some protection from the raiding Comanches and hostile whites, and their removal would leave the Indians totally exposed. Agent Neighbors, realizing it would be "impossible to maintain the reserve without a military force," suggested to the commissioner of Indian affairs on February 22 that the Indians be removed north of the Red River and that they "abandon the reserves to the lawless bands of white barbarians" who abounded nearby.[77]

In the meantime, the Indians of the Brazos Reserve returned to their farms and began planting their crops and repairing their fences. Unfortunately, in their absence much of the Indians' livestock had run off the limits of the reserve. This stock was in danger of being permanently lost because the Indians refused to leave the reserve for fear of being killed by the whites of the surrounding counties. In addition, raiding Comanches and unscrupulous white men had stolen many reserve horses while the tribes had taken refuge around the agency buildings.[78]

On February 23 another eighty horses were stolen from the Caddos by marauding Comanches, who also raided a few white ranches. Agent Ross sent a message to Captain Ford, who was encamped nearby with a group of Rangers. Despite his earlier refusal to arrest the Garland party,

Ford agreed to assist the Caddos in a retaliatory expedition against the Comanches. On the morning of February 24, forty Kadohadacho and Nadaco warriors joined Ford's rangers for this ill-timed campaign.[79]

The citizens of Erath, Jack, and Palo Pinto counties, learning that the Caddo warriors had left the reserve with Captain Ford, began raising a force to attack the unprotected Brazos Reserve and to prevent any attempt to arrest Garland's party. Agent Ross received the news from various sources on March 2 and immediately requested a company of troops from Maj. George Thomas—the future Rock of Chickamauga—commander of the Second Cavalry at Camp Cooper.[80]

On March 5 Ross held a council with the headmen of the reserve tribes and informed them that the citizens were planning to attack the agency. Although twenty of the Kadohadacho and Nadaco warriors had returned from their fruitless pursuit of the Comanches, the Indians of the reserve nevertheless left their villages and took up a defensive position around the agency buildings. Iesh was very angry with the lack of protection given his tribe by the government, and in protest he refused to accept presents distributed by Ross on March 11. Fearing the worst, both the Nadacos and the Kadohadachos began to talk of leaving the reserve for the Indian Territory as soon as the danger passed.[81]

By March 20 about one hundred whites, under the command of Neighbors's enemy, John R. Baylor, had gathered at Rock Creek, about twelve miles from the Brazos Agency, where they awaited Captain Nelson's reinforcements, who were gathering at nearby Jameson's Peak. On March 23, however, Capt. John King arrived at the agency with an artillery piece and troops from Camp Cooper. This strong show of force caused the citizens to lose their nerve, and only thirty-five whites—not enough to assist Baylor—showed up at Jameson's Peak. On March 26 Baylor and Nelson resolved to "suspend operations" for six weeks to allow the government "peaceably" to remove the Indians from the state. Even though the danger of an attack had passed for the moment, both the Kadohadachos and the Nadacos refused to return to their villages long after the other tribes had abandoned the agency buildings.[82]

It was becoming obvious to all parties that the situation in Texas was untenable for the Reserve Indians. Finally, on March 30, 1859, Commissioner Mix informed Major Neighbors that the two reserves in Texas "must be discontinued . . . the Indians removed where they can be protected from lawless violence, and effective measures adopted for their domestication and improvement." Mix believed that the Reserve Indians should be moved, along with the Wichitas and Caddos living near Fort Arbuckle, to the Leased District. Mix ordered Elias Rector, Indian Territory superintendent, to proceed with Wichita Agent Blain, to the Leased District and choose sites for an agency, a military post, and a suitable location for the Indians to settle. Since all this would necessarily take some time, Mix did not believe that the Reserve Indians could be removed until the fall or winter, and he hoped they would be "permitted to remain in peace and quiet, where they are, till then."[83]

Unfortunately, this was not to be. Neighbors notified Governor Runnels immediately after receiving the commissioner's notification for removal and then had the news published in all the leading newspapers on the frontier. This action, however, only led Baylor and his group to undertake "more energetic endeavors to bring about hostilities" between the whites and the Indians. Rather than indict Garland and his men for murder, the grand jury of Palo Pinto County charged Iesh with stealing a mule. The grand jury also characterized the Brazos Reserve as an "intolerable nuisance" and concluded their report by claiming that "it is now the prevailing sentiment that we must abandon our homes and take up arms against the Reserve Indians."[84]

On April 25 Captain Baylor and his cronies held a meeting in Golconda and made speeches using "very threatening language against the agents and Indians." One hundred twenty-eight men signed a petition which demanded the immediate resignation of Neighbors and his assistants. Baylor and about fifty armed men subsequently left Golconda with the "avowed intention of taking scalps of reserve Indians." Upon being informed of Baylor's activities, Agent Ross notified the Indians and sent for reinforcements from Camp Cooper. The frightened tribesmen once more assembled around the agency buildings.[85]

It was at this inopportune moment that about sixty or seventy warriors from the Brazos Reserve once again decided to join Major Van Dorn in an expedition against the hostile Comanches. As usual, the opportunity to exact revenge on their foes, to recover stolen horses, and to gain other booty proved too much for the Reserve Indians to resist. In addition, the Reserve Indians continued to hope that their friendly actions might cause the surrounding whites to cease their hostilities.[86]

The expedition—the third and final one the Reserve Indians would participate in against the Comanches—rode out from Camp Radziminski on April 30 and traveled north in search of their enemies. On May 10 they entered Kansas Territory, and two days later Van Dorn's command attacked a Penateka Comanche village on Crooked Creek, a tributary of the Cimarron River. The village contained about a hundred people led by the ill-fated Buffalo Hump. Major Van Dorn's force successfully routed the Comanches—killing forty-nine warriors and capturing thirty-six. One hundred horses were recovered from the Comanches, and all of their camp supplies were either taken or destroyed. Four of the Reserve Indians were killed, and several were wounded. Major Van Dorn's casualties were two dead and fifteen wounded.[87]

Although the Reserve Indians had aided Van Dorn, their absence only served to embolden their white enemies. On May 7 a Kadohadacho man named Fox, along with six other warriors, was returning from Fort Arbuckle in the Indian Territory with messages to Major Neighbors from Agent Blain. Just as they reached the boundary of the Brazos Reserve, they were fired upon by fifteen white men. The shots killed three of their horses, but all of the Kadohadacho party except for Fox made it safely back to the agency to report the attack.[88]

Lt. William E. Burnet had arrived from Camp Cooper, and he led one hundred Indian warriors, two soldiers, and Farmer Sturm in search of Fox. They went to the site of the attack, found the dead horses, and concluded that Fox had been taken prisoner. They followed the trail for a mile and a half until they came upon a postal station. The employee there told Lieutenant Burnet that fifteen men, calling themselves the Jacksboro Rangers, had arrived at the station about three hours before with Fox and a pair of saddlebags containing the mail from Fort Arbuckle. They "cursed and abused" Fox and told him he had no business with the papers and no right to be there. They then read the letters and continued on the road to Jacksboro with the captured Kadohadacho warrior.[89]

Lieutenant Burnet and the party followed the trail for twelve miles until they found Fox's body lying about twenty steps from the road; he had been shot through the chest and scalped. The Indians, including Fox's brother and cousin, gathered around the body "and each looked at him, but no one spoke a word." They wrapped him in a blanket, carried him to a ravine, and covered him with branches.[90]

The party followed the trail into Jacksboro and camped for the evening. It rained heavily that night, and the next morning the trail was impossible to follow. Lieutenant Burnet decided to abandon the chase, and the group returned to the agency. Burnet characterized the Indians as being "very much exasperated" and vowing to "have revenge for these things some time or other."[91]

For the time being, however, the Indians were forced to remain gathered around the agency buildings awaiting the next move of the hostile whites. Baylor—eager to bring his two-year vendetta to a successful climax—quickly began gathering more men at Jacksboro, and by May 20 he had led five hundred armed men to a position about eight miles below the Brazos Reserve. They began stealing cattle from the Indians and those whites in the area who had refused to join the band. In an attempt to starve out the inhabitants they intercepted a wagon train loaded with flour headed for the reserve.[92]

In response, Capt. Joseph B. Plummer arrived from Camp Cooper with the First Infantry to begin directing the defense of the agency. The troops erected a picket work, arranged with flanking bastions and traverses, large enough to protect the gathering of Indians and soldiers. A six-pound cannon was brought over from Camp Cooper and placed within the works. By May 22 the agency was ready for Baylor's attack.[93]

The following morning Indian scouts reported that a party of between 250 and 300 men were a mile and a half from the agency and were moving forward. The soldiers of Captain Plummer's command took up their position and at the same time the Indians mounted their horses for a cavalry attack. Baylor and his men halted half a mile from the troops and waited. Captain Plummer sent Capt. Charles C. Gilbert with fifty men to ask Baylor why he had "come upon the reservation with an armed body of men." Baylor answered that he had "come to assail certain Indians" of the reserve, but he did not wish to fight the troops. Nevertheless, Baylor warned Gilbert that if the troops did fire at his men, he would attack them as well.[94]

Captain Gilbert returned to the agency and informed his commander of Baylor's message. Captain Plummer in turn sent Lieutenant Burnet to direct Baylor to leave the reserve, as he intended to carry out his orders to protect the Indians from "the attacks of armed bands of citizens." Baylor defiantly answered that this message did not alter his determination and that he was intent on destroying the Indians on both reserves even "if it cost the life of every man in his command." Lieutenant Burnet returned to the agency buildings, and the troops and the Indians prepared themselves for Baylor's attack.[95]

It never came. Instead, Baylor's party apprehended an old Indian couple in their nineties and retreated. While still in sight of the Reserve Indians, they killed and scalped the man and the woman; this brutality infuriated the warriors, and about sixty or seventy mounted Indians attacked the retreating whites. A running fight ensued for six or seven miles before the whites finally took shelter at the ranch of William Marlin. Baylor's party occupied the house, outhouses, and livestock pens in anticipation of the fast-approaching warriors. Throughout the rest of the day, the Indians "annoyed" Baylor and his men but were unable to draw them out to fight. Jim Pock Mark rode up to the house and called for Baylor to "come out and give him single combat," an invitation the once-boastful Baylor "respectfully declined." The Indians returned to the agency at nightfall. During the battle, five Indians were wounded, and one, Caddo John, was killed. Two of Baylor's men were killed, and six were wounded.[96]

The troops and Indians at the agency remained on their guard, as they fully expected another attack from Baylor and his men who had returned to their encampment eight miles away. Baylor did send numerous scouting parties throughout the area to intimidate the Indians, who remained gathered at the agency for several days. The agency's close quarters and unclean conditions caused the outbreak of a disease, "something like the Cholera." In five or six days about forty Indians died, and many more were very sick; the disease then spread to the soldiers but did not cause any deaths.[97]

Although it was quickly becoming necessary to break up the camp and send the tribes back to their villages, Baylor's army nevertheless remained in the way. Luckily, Major Van Dorn had just returned to Camp Cooper from his campaign against the Comanches, and Lieutenant Burnet wrote him and requested that he send back the Indian auxiliaries and any other troops he could spare. Immediately, Van Dorn sent these Indians and three companies of soldiers to the Brazos Agency and also sent two companies to protect the Comanche Reserve. Upon hearing the news of Van Dorn's advance, Baylor's men broke camp and fled back to their homes. This retreat allowed the Reserve Indians finally to return to their villages, and the spread of the sickness abated.[98]

Although the Reserve Indians had survived Baylor's "attack," they did suffer serious losses during his "campaign." The tribes lost a large portion of their stock to marauders in addition to the crops they had planted in the spring, and forty Indians had succumbed to disease. With danger ever present, the Indians refused to take up cultivation again. Neighbors considered the reserve "virtually broken up." He held a council with the headmen of the various tribes and reported that "although they think themselves badly treated," they "expressed full confidence that the general government will do them justice" and hoped they would be allowed to move immediately north of the Red River.[99]

The newly appointed commissioner of Indian affairs, A. B. Greenwood, recognizing the gravity of the situation in Texas, authorized Major Neighbors on June 11 "to take measures forthwith for the removal" of the Reserve Indians to the Leased District. Neighbors was instructed to "proceed at once" in order to gather the Indians and their movables and "make everything ready to start them as soon as" the U.S. troops arrived to provide a military escort. The reservation experiment in Texas was over.[100]

Chapter Four

The Civil War Era, 1859-67

This great war has driven us from our own country and from our homes, and we cannot raise corn and provisions for our women and children, and a great many of our people have been sick this year with the smallpox and a good many of them have died, and left widows and orphan children, and a good many of our people are sick now. From this cause many of our hunters could not go out to hunt the Buffalos for food, and to buy clothing for their families, as they could when in their own country. We have always been told by our white Father that they would help us when we needed help, and we need it now very much and we hope you will tell our Agent to give us bread for our women and children and clothing for them before the next snow falls. We hope our white fathers will not forget their red children when they are suffering.

—Chiefs and Headmen of the Taovaya, Kadohadacho,
Waco, Kichai, Tawakoni, Nadaco, and Hainai tribes
to President Abraham Lincoln,
October 14, 1864

The Wichitas and Caddos now hoped that the reservation experiment could be successfully carried out in the Indian Territory where they would be protected from intruders. But the Civil War, which broke out only twenty months after the successful removal of the tribes to the Leased District, shattered that dream. Both tribes were forced to abandon their new home in 1862 and take refuge in Union-controlled Kansas. The Wichitas and Caddos probably suffered more in the five years they spent in Kansas than at any other period in their troubled pasts. They were unable to raise crops successfully or hunt buffalo and were dependent upon the meager rations the weak Union forces could supply. Hunger, combined with exposure and disease, caused both tribes to experience great population losses.

Nonetheless, the period between the Wichita and Caddo settlement in the Leased District and their return in 1867 was very important. For the first time in their long histories, all the tribes of each confederacy—the Kadohadachos, Hainais, and Whitebeads of the Caddo and the Taovayas, Wacos, Tawakonis, and Kichais of the Wichita—were settled together in close proximity to one another. Therefore, the foundations were laid for the future unification of each tribe. In addition, the miserable years the Caddos and Wichitas spent together in Kansas worked to tighten the bonds between them, thus ensuring that their fates would be intertwined for many years to come.

Tensions remained high near the Brazos Reserve in the late spring of 1859 despite the retreat of Baylor's forces. In response, on June 6 Governor Runnels appointed a five-man peace commission to travel to the reserve and do everything in its power to "prevent all future violence" between the frontier whites and the reserve tribes. Governor Runnels empowered the commission to call, if necessary, for a force of one hundred men "for the purpose of preserving the peace." The governor informed Captain Nelson of the appointment of the peace commission and requested that the captain use his "best exertions to delay hostilities on the part of the people" until the arrival of the commissioners.[1]

The five commissioners left Waco on June 10 and upon reaching Parker County—just east of Palo Pinto—they found that "extensive and formidable preparations" for another attack on the reserves had been undertaken in all of the surrounding counties. Further demonstrations of the citizens caused the commissioners to raise a troop to be commanded by John Henry Brown. The troop was ordered to "act as a police force, to keep the Indians inside the reserve" until they could be removed to the Indian Territory. The commissioners believed that this was the only way to prevent the citizens from attacking the tribes.[2]

The frontier whites, however, were enraged by the actions of the commissioners. Baylor chaired a meeting of the citizens of Parker County which branded the raising of Brown's force a "gross insult" to the settlers of the frontier. The citizens' council went on to recommend that the county organize a militia for the "purpose of the immediate removal of the Indians and the utter destruction of all reservations on our fron-

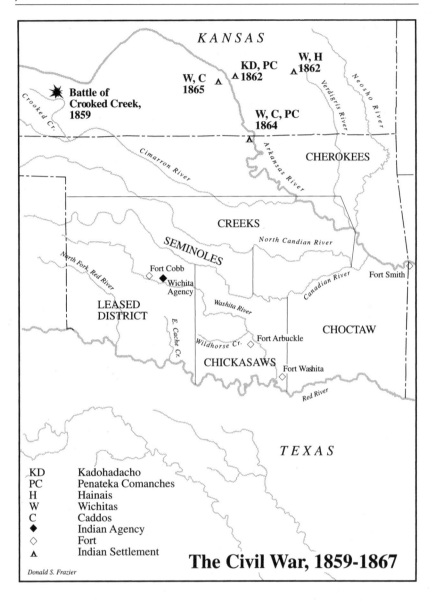

KANSAS

W, H
▲1862

KD, PC
▲1862

W, C ▲
1865

✴ **Battle of
Crooked Creek,
1859**

Crooked Cr.

W, C, PC
1864
▲

Cimarron River

Arkansas River

CHEROKEES

Verdigris River

Neosho River

CREEKS

SEMINOLES

North Canadian River

North Fork, Red River

Fort Cobb
◇ ◆ Wichita
Agency

LEASED
DISTRICT

Washita River

E. Cache Cr.

Wildhorse Cr.

Fort Arbuckle
◇

Canadian River

Fort Smith
◇

CHOCTAW

CHICKASAWS Fort Washita
◇

Red River

TEXAS

KD   Kadohadacho
PC   Penateka Comanches
H   Hainais
W   Wichitas
C   Caddos
◆   Indian Agency
◇   Fort
▲   Indian Settlement

The Civil War, 1859-1867

Donald S. Frazier

tier." The citizens appointed a committee to correspond with other counties to request that they raise a militia as well. The continued hostile stance of the frontier whites forced the Indians of the Brazos Reserve to remain confined within its boundaries, unable to collect their stock which had wandered off during Baylor's previous campaign.[3]

In the meantime, the Indians of the Texas reserves, as well as the Wichitas and Caddos in the Indian Territory, began to make preparations for their removal to the Leased District. On June 18 Taovaya chief Isadowa, Whitebead Caddo headman George Washington, and a few Kichais and Delawares traveled to the Leased District to pick out village sites with a party headed by Superintendent Elias Rector and Wichita Agent Blain. In the hope of continuing their traditional agricultural methods, the Indians selected fertile river bottoms as the locations for their settlements. The Caddos and Delawares chose a plain, about two and a half miles wide, located near the mouth of Sugar Creek, on the north bank of the Washita River. The Taovayas and Kichais chose a "similar small valley," twenty miles to the north in the Canadian River Valley. Superintendent Rector, however, was disappointed with the agricultural possibilities of the land and believed that it would only be suitable for grazing.[4]

On their return to Fort Arbuckle, Rector's party was met by Major Neighbors and the headmen from each of the six tribes from the two Texas reserves. A council was held on July 1 in which the two agents informed the Texas Indians of the sites selected for their new homes. They apologized to the assembled chiefs for having to relocate them but promised that the federal government would pay for all losses incurred by the removal. The agents explained that after the removal the Indians would occupy the territory, between the Red and Canadian Rivers and the 98th and 100th meridian, not belonging to any state and would remain there "as long as the waters should run, protected from all harm by the United States." The headmen of the reserves "declared themselves entirely satisfied" with the sites—all of them very well known to the Indians—and proclaimed that they were ready to relocate immediately.[5]

Neighbors and the headmen returned to the Brazos Reserve and began preparations in earnest for the Indians' departure to their new homes. The tribes of both reserves gathered whatever possessions that could be easily transported to the Leased District. Neighbors appraised all of the Indians' immovable property—such as their houses—so the government could repay them for their losses. Because they could not survive the long trip, nearly six hundred hogs belonging to the Reserve Indians were sold to the surrounding white settlers.[6]

The preparations carried out entirely within the boundaries of the agency went smoothly, but the matter of collecting the tribes' lost stock caused further conflict with the neighboring whites. At least seven hundred head of cattle and horses had been lost from the two reserves since March. The majority of the stock had strayed from the reserve, but a considerable number had been stolen by the whites; these horses and cattle were being sold openly in public auction at Jacksboro. Since Rector had forecasted that grazing would be very important in the Leased District, it was imperative that the Indians recover their scattered stock.[7]

Gathering the stock, however, proved to be very dangerous. Captain Brown, commander of the one hundred Texas state troops who were guarding the reserves, had orders to consider as hostile any Indian found off the reserve unaccompanied by an "agent, or some responsible white man." Neighbors took "every precaution" and assigned all available white employees of the agency to accompany the members in their stock-gathering expeditions. Unfortunately, the agency employees—who had their hands full with the work of closing up the reserves—did not have much time to spare, and the amount of cattle actually collected was limited.[8]

Despite the precautions taken by Neighbors, violence did occur. On July 22 a Tawakoni warrior was killed fifteen miles off the Brazos Reserve by a white rancher named Patrick Murphy. Two days later a more serious engagement took place near the Comanche Reserve between a detachment of Captain Brown's troops and a party of Reserve Penatekas. Two whites and one Indian were wounded in the skirmish. To avoid future incidents of this nature, the Reserve Indians abandoned any further attempts to collect their stock. Neighbors arranged for friendly white settlers to gather whatever strays were left after the Indians' departure.[9]

Neighbors pressed on with the final preparations for the trip. He purchased provisions for the march north and made arrangements for cattle to be slaughtered en route. Neighbors also hired eighty ox-drawn wagons to carry the Indians' goods. Despite the obvious intent of the reserve tribes to move north of the Red River peacefully, Baylor and the other hostile whites threatened to attack the Indians on their march. Because Captain Brown's regiment had shown that it could not be trusted to protect the Indians, Major Thomas, commanding at Camp Cooper, was ordered to provide federal troops to accompany Major Neighbors. Arrangements were made for Thomas and two companies of the Second Cavalry and one company of the First Infantry to meet Neighbors, Ross, and the Indians of the Brazos Reserve at Salt Creek, three miles north of the Brazos Agency, on July 31. Comanche Agent Matthew Leeper, accompanied by one company of the First Infantry, was to lead the 370 Penatekas from the Upper Reserve the same day and meet Neighbors at the Red River.[10]

During the rain-swept day of July 31 the Brazos Reserve tribes gathered at the camp on Salt Creek to begin their own "trail of tears," leaving, once and for all, their traditional homeland south of the Red River. Agent Ross distributed firewood, coffee, sugar, tobacco, and flour to the Indians for the trek. The size of the gathering was huge; in addition to the 1,049 Indians—462 Caddos, 344 Wichitas, and 243 Tonkawas—there were at least 1,000 horses and 500 head of cattle to be driven. As a result, the great caravan traveling north would necessarily be slow-moving.[11]

The following morning, Agent Neighbors, the Indians of the Brazos Reserve, and the U.S. troops commanded by Major Thomas began their march northward. The trip, undertaken through very dry country during the hottest month of the year, proved to be a difficult one. Finding sufficient water—for both the humans and the animals—was the primary goal each day. Although the party was able to encamp near adequate water each night, it usually was "not very pleasant to drink" because the water was gathered in stagnant "holes and ponds." The animals, particularly the oxen that pulled the wagons, suffered the most. A great many beasts died, including one of the four yoke of oxen owned by the Nadacos.[12]

After a journey of ten miles, the caravan spent the first night at the ranch of Judge Peter Harmonson on Salt Creek. On the following day, the party was forced to travel twenty-one miles before finding suitable water at the West Fork of the Trinity River. On August 3 a trek of twenty-two miles took the weary travelers to the Little Wichita River, where they rested the following day. The expedition then began three days of travel in which they covered thirty-six miles, reaching the Red River on August 7. Here, two miles below the mouth of the Big Wichita, they were joined by Agent Leeper and the Penatekas of the Comanche Reserve.[13]

Because of the threats of attack by the Texans en route, the date of their departure had been kept a secret. Captain Brown did not learn of the withdrawal of the Reserve Indians until August 2. He and his command immediately took up the trail in order to monitor their progress. The next day Brown's troops were met by Patrick Murphy, who charged that the Reserve Indians had stolen five horses from him as they were leaving. In an attempt to investigate Murphy's charges, Brown hurriedly continued his quest to overtake the slow-moving caravan before it crossed into Indian Territory.[14]

In the meantime, the Indians of the two reserves spent the entire day of August 8 in the slow but safe crossing of the Red. Camp was made that night three miles north of the river on Whiskey Creek. Neighbors felt that by fording the Red River he had "crossed all the Indians out of the heathen land of Texas and [was] now out of the land of the philistines."[15]

The "philistines," in the form of messengers from Captain Brown, nevertheless, arrived at the camp that night. They charged the Reserve Indians with the theft of Murphy's horses and expressed dismay that they had not been allowed to examine the Indians' livestock for stolen property before the Indians left the reserves. Major Thomas answered that the citizens had been given every opportunity to search the Indians' herd for stolen cattle and that since then none of the Indians had left the line of march or caused any mischief. This bold stance induced Brown's messengers to cross back into Texas without causing any further difficulties.[16]

After resting for a day, the caravan traveled twelve miles to Beaver Creek on August 10. Before leaving that morning, Neighbors sent an express of four Kadohadacho warriors to locate Agent Blain—who had left Fort Arbuckle for the Leased District on July 26 with the Taovayas, Kichais, and Whitebead Caddos—and inform him of the approach of the Reserve Indians. The caravan traveled twenty-one miles over the next two days before reaching a different branch of Beaver Creek, where they encamped on the evening of August 12. Here an abundance of good water and grass prompted the expedition to stop and rest the animals on August 13. An express from Camp Cooper arrived the same day ordering Major Thomas to return at once with his two cavalry companies; the remaining two companies of infantry were ordered to join them as soon as the party reached the Washita.[17]

Before Major Thomas could depart, however, the Kadohadacho messengers arrived and explained that they had been attacked by nine

Kiowas on their return from Agent Blain's camp. The Kiowas had made off with all of their horses, and one of the Kadohadacho warriors was severely wounded. The Indians also reported that a group of Comanches had attacked Blain on the Washita. The news of hostile Indians lurking in the area caused Major Thomas to decide to remain with the reserve tribes.[18]

In order to forestall an attack by the Kiowas or Comanches, Major Thomas and the two companies of cavalry led the column on August 14. By traveling twenty miles over the next two days, the caravan finally arrived at waters which flowed into the Washita. On the sixteenth, Major Thomas and the cavalry departed for Texas, leaving the caravan in the hands of Captain Plummer and the infantry for the final day of travel. After seventeen grueling miles, the party arrived safely at its destination, the Washita River, and camp was made opposite the mouth of Sugar Creek. On the following day the camp was moved four miles upstream where there was spring-fed water and good grazing land. All the remaining rations, one week's worth, were distributed to the Indians on the eighteenth, and they settled down to await the arrival of Agent Blain and his party.[19]

The removal of the reserve tribes to the Indian Territory, although in itself a sad event, must be considered a great accomplishment. In the face of tremendous obstacles—withering heat and the opposition of both the Texans and hostile Indians—the huge caravan had traveled over 150 miles in seventeen days. Only six deaths were recorded on the trip, and the tribes' property and livestock were transported without damage. In addition, one baby was born.[20]

Both the Reserve Indians and Major Neighbors were very happy with the success of the trip and with their new home. While waiting for Agent Blain, the headmen of the various tribes accompanied Neighbors on a tour of the countryside. They inspected the village sites that had been chosen and found them "to their entire satisfaction." Neighbors, unlike Superintendent Rector, was very pleased with what he saw and claimed that the area was "truly a splendid country." He believed the land to be "eminently suitable for farming, and convenient to an abundance of good water and timber for building and fencing." In addition, Neighbors optimistically proclaimed that the new reserve would be "capable of sustaining a very dense population."[21]

Agent Blain, the Taovayas, Kichais, and Whitebead Caddos arrived at Neighbors's camp on August 19. The next day Captain Plummer returned to Camp Cooper with his infantry troop. On September 1 Neighbors officially transferred jurisdiction over the Indians to Agent Blain and headed for home. The Texas Indians were greatly saddened by the departure of their old friend, and every warrior shook hands with the major before he left. Some of the older men clung to Neighbors, refusing to let him go; the Tonkawa chief, Placido, "cried like a child." When Neighbors—accompanied by Agents Ross and Leeper—finally did ride away, the Indians "threw themselves upon the ground, yelling, in the wildest grief." Neighbors stated he was so moved that it required all of his "fortitude to leave them."[22]

But the major's troubles did not end when he gave up jurisdiction of the Texas Indians. On the return to Texas, Neighbors and his party were attacked by hostile Indians, and Leeper was severely wounded. After crossing the Red River, they were halted at the town of Belknap because of high waters on the Brazos. On the morning of September 14 Neighbors was walking in the streets of the town when he was approached by the vengeful Patrick Murphy. Angrily, Murphy spoke to Neighbors, but before the major could answer he was shot in the back and killed by Edward Cornett, Murphy's brother-in-law. Driving the Reserve Indians out of Texas apparently had not quenched the bloodthirstiness of the angry white settlers. Soon after the murder of Neighbors, a citizens' meeting in Belknap convened to discuss the fates of Leeper and Ross, but ultimately the two were left unpunished.[23]

The man who had most tirelessly devoted himself for thirteen years to the cause of the Indians of Texas was rewarded with death. The close ties Major Neighbors had developed with the Indians caused him to be the enemy of frontier whites. Commissioner Greenwood felt that Neighbors had incurred the "vengeful animosity" of many Texans by "his zealous and uncompromising efforts to protect the Indians and their property from wrong." Neither Neighbors nor his agents nor the Reserve Indians had been able to overcome the intense prejudice of the frontier whites of Texas. The reservation experiment in Texas, through no fault of the Indians, had proved to be a disaster. Unfortunately, even within the supposed safe enclave of the Indian Territory, the tribes would still not be free from the problems caused by the whites.[24]

Nonetheless, the various tribes were eager to begin settlement of what had been promised to be their permanent homes. Upon receiving jurisdiction of the Indians, Agent Blain decided to construct the agency—named the Wichita Agency—upon the site of Neighbors's camp. However, the Indians were still grouped around the camp. They had refused to depart for their newly chosen homes until they were guaranteed military protection, because the hostile Comanches and Kiowas were "still hovering" around the agency and were threatening the new arrivals. Fortunately, the tribes did not have long to wait for military protection; on October 1, 1859, Maj. William H. Emory established a post called Fort Cobb on the west side of Pond Creek, three miles west of the Wichita Agency. The post was occupied by two companies of the First Cavalry and one company of the First Infantry.[25]

With the troops in place, the Indians now felt it was safe to take up residence at their villages, all located from three to ten miles from the agency. Because of their fear of the hostile Kiowas and Comanches, the Wichita tribes settled in the Washita Valley near Fort Cobb rather than near the Canadian River as planned. The Wichitas formed two separate villages; Isadowa's Taovayas settled in one, while the Kichais joined Acaquash's Wacos and Ocherash's Tawakonis in the other. The Caddo tribes moved to their chosen site near the mouth of Sugar Creek and began constructing shelters for the winter. The chiefs of the three bands—Iesh of the Nadacos, Tinah of the Kadohadachos, and George Washington of the Whitebeads—had log cabins built for them. The other tribal members lived in "picket houses" covered with grass. By January, 1860, the Caddos were "comfortably situated" and had "gone foremost" among the tribes of the agency in building houses. By September, 1860, they had constructed eighty-two picket houses, while all the other tribes, except for the few Shawnees and Delawares who lived in their midst, continued to live in grass houses or tepees. The Wichitas refused to build picket houses because they felt their two villages near Fort Cobb were only temporary.[26]

None of the tribes of the Wichita Agency were able to raise crops the first winter and were thus wholly dependent upon the rations provided by the federal government. However, like Major Neighbors, Superintendent Rector believed that the object of the Wichita agent was to "teach these Indians to become tillers of the soil and raisers of stock, and to supplement themselves without expense to the government, and this within the briefest period practicable." In view of this policy, Agent Blain held a meeting with the headmen of the various tribes in early

January, 1860, and "advised them to prepare for farming" because he did not believe that the government would continue to issue rations after the current year ended.[27]

The chiefs understood Blain's message and over the next few months "gave substantial evidence of their willingness to labor for their own support." The tribes immediately began fashioning oak rails for fences and soon thereafter had built many "horse lots and cowpens." Agent Blain had a blacksmith's shop and woodwork shop constructed, and the Indians kept the employees busy throughout the winter by having them repair their wagons and plows for the spring planting. The agent procured seed corn and seed sweet potatoes so that the tribes could plant their fields in April.[28]

The Wichitas and Caddos, as usual, were very industrious and planted their crops in the traditional method—dividing them into many "different fields or patches"—with some having "tolerably good fences." The Kadohadachos cultivated a total of 84½ acres, the Nadacos planted 76½ acres, and the Whitebeads had 14 acres in crops. The Taovayas cultivated an additional 141 acres, while the combined effort of the Wacos, Tawakonis, and Kichais yielded 73 acres. As a counterpoint, the Tonkawas planted only 23½ acres, and the Penateka Comanches none. Unfortunately, all the tribes' corn crop failed from exposure to excessive heat and drought. As a result, the federal government was forced to renew the contract to provide rations to the tribes of the Wichita Agency for the following year.[29]

Drought was not the only problem the agency Indians had to contend with. Their old enemies—the hostile Indians and the Texans—continued to hound them north of the Red River. In early 1860, however, the Kiowas and Comanches diverted their raids from the Wichita Agency to the frontier of Texas. In February a band of hostiles swept into Erath and Bosque counties, killed seven men, and kidnapped four women; in addition, they made off with four hundred horses.[30]

Predictably, the Texans blamed the settled Indians of the Wichita Agency. Two citizens of Bosque County addressed letters to President James Buchanan in which they blamed the Kadohadachos in particular. They demanded further protection by the U.S. troops and warned "if the government doesn't do something . . . the people here will risk the fight." In response to the charges, Sam Houston—serving as governor of Texas once again—wrote Agent Blain on March 20 to inquire whether any of the Indians of the Wichita Agency were involved in the attacks.[31]

Blain called together the headmen of the various tribes and read them Houston's letter. The chiefs responded bitterly to the governor's suspicions by stating in a letter to Houston that they had always fought "for the security . . . of our homes and yours." The chiefs believed that the success of the various campaigns against the Comanches was largely attributable to the efforts of the tribes of the Brazos Reserve. The chiefs added that despite their assistance, "suddenly in the midst of these successes against your real enemies, [we] were compelled to leave the homes which [we] were fighting for, without a cause and without a hearing."[32]

The chiefs insisted that since moving north of the Red River they had continued to help the white citizens; for instance, they often informed the Texans of "trails of wild bands of Indians, who were making their way through this country to Texas." In addition, they actually attacked several parties of marauding Indians who passed by the agency on their way south of the Red River. However, the chiefs disappointedly concluded to Governor Houston that "we are still to be made the scape goat [sic] upon whom is to be thrown all the crimes committed on your frontier, whether the same be the work of the white or red man."[33]

Soon afterward, the tribes of the Wichita Agency had occasion once again to prove their friendliness to the Texans. In early May a hunting party of agency Indians skirmished with a band of Kiowas and Comanches about thirty miles west of Fort Cobb; they killed five enemy warriors and brought one Comanche prisoner back to the agency and "held a war dance over him." On May 8 a band of agency Indians found another fresh trail of seven Kiowas nearby. Blain led a war party in pursuit the following day and, after a long chase of thirty to forty miles, finally overtook the Kiowa band and killed six of them. The only friendly casualty was that of Toweash, the old Hainai caddi, who was wounded and had his "fine war horse killed." Blain informed Governor Houston of the successes and asked him to "please keep these facts before the people."[34]

In the late summer of 1860, some Caddo, Wichita, and Tonkawa warriors actually joined a regiment of Texas Rangers in a campaign against the hostile tribes. They attacked a camp of Kiowas and Comanches near the head of the Canadian River. A number of Comanches were killed, including women and children. One of the Caddo warriors killed a prominent Kiowa named Bird-Appearing, which only heightened the bad feelings between the two tribes.[35]

Despite these friendly demonstrations to the Texans, the frontier whites continued to doubt the merit of the Wichita Agency tribes. The civil authorities of Palo Pinto County insisted that Iesh finally be brought to trial for the charges of stealing a mule, and Commissioner Greenwood agreed to their demands. However, both Superintendent Rector and Matthew Leeper—who had replaced Blain as Wichita Agent in August, 1860—refused to hand the caddi over to the Texans. Rector informed the commissioner that Iesh "has the reputation of being the best and most influential Indian in the Leased District, he stands high both with white men and Indians." Rector was sure "his people will never surrender him . . . without resistance" and that if the caddi was turned over to the Texans, all the Indians would leave the agency, and the reservation would be destroyed. Commissioner Greenwood did not press the issue, and Iesh was allowed to remain with his people.[36]

Troubles with the hostile tribes as well as with the Texans continued throughout the fall and winter. In October Agent Leeper reported that there were large numbers of "wild Indians . . . in or near the borders" of the Wichita Agency; members of these tribes threatened that they intended to "overwhelm the reserve this winter." This news alarmed the agency Indians, and they became very apprehensive about splitting rails for their farms with the Comanches and Kiowas nearby.[37]

Attacks upon the Kadohadachos began in earnest in December. On the twenty-second Crow Bonnet, brother of Bird-Appearing, led a Kiowa raiding party onto the reserve. The Kiowas killed and scalped a Kadohadacho man named Dutch John on Sugar Creek, eight miles from the agency. They then skirmished with a nearby party of twenty Kadohadacho warriors. A few days later five Kadohadacho women were attacked and fired upon on their way from the agency to their village, but they escaped unharmed.[38]

Indian depredations committed in January, 1861, in Jack County caused the Texans to suspect the Reserve Indians yet again. Agent Leeper, however, claimed that the only Indians that had recently left the reserve was a group of women who went to the Red River to collect pecans and a few small parties of men grazing their horses just beyond the agency boundaries. Leeper complained that the Reserve Indians were placed "between two fires; denounced from Texas and attacked by wild Indians as well."³⁹

A third fire was added in the spring of 1861 with the outbreak of the Civil War. Just as before, the Caddos and Wichitas found themselves again caught in the midst of another Euro-American struggle, this time between the Confederate and Union armies. On March 18 the newly promoted Lieutenant Colonel Emory was ordered to abandon Fort Cobb and report to Fort Washita, downstream from the Wichita Agency, where all Union troops in the Indian Territory were being concentrated. Emory was ordered to notify the Indians of his withdrawal so that they "may have a chance to move temporarily to the vicinity" of Fort Washita.⁴⁰

The Reserve tribes, however, were in the midst of planting their crops for the year and did not wish to be forced to move from their new homes once again. Upon the "earnest appeal" of Agent Leeper, who believed that "disastrous results would follow" the removal of the troops, Emory authorized two companies of cavalry to remain at Fort Cobb to protect the Indians from the Kiowas and Comanches.⁴¹

By the time Colonel Emory reached Fort Washita with his command, however, the Confederate forces from Texas were already on the way north and were threatening the Indian Territory's southernmost military posts. In view of the superior number of enemy troops in the vicinity of Fort Washita, the colonel abandoned the fort to the Confederates on April 16 and started back to the aid of forts Arbuckle and Cobb. En route to Fort Arbuckle, however, Colonel Emory received new orders directing all Union troops in the Indian Territory to retreat north into Kansas. On May 3 Emory relieved the troops at Fort Arbuckle and sent orders ahead to Fort Cobb commanding the two remaining companies to leave the post and meet him on the road to Fort Leavenworth, Kansas. They abandoned Fort Cobb on May 9, and the post was occupied the following day by Texas troops under the command of Col. William C. Young.⁴²

The Wichita Agency tribes now found themselves at the mercy of their old enemies from Texas. They agreed to enter into a temporary peace treaty with Colonel Young "on the condition that the Confederacy issue them supplies and protect them as had been done by the United States government." However, many of the Reserve Indians—

fearful of the Texans' motives—abandoned their homes and fields and took refuge elsewhere in the Indian Territory.[43]

The Confederates immediately took steps to solidify their position in the Indian Territory. Gen. Albert Pike, appointed by President Jefferson Davis as Confederate commissioner to the tribes of the Indian Territory, wrote Leeper on May 26 and asked him to stay on as Wichita agent for the new government. He instructed Leeper to gather the agency Indians—many now off the reserve—and inform them that the Confederacy would "comply with arrangements made by the United States." Pike also told Leeper to warn the Texans not to do any harm to the tribes of the Wichita Reserve. Furthermore, Pike instructed Charles B. Johnson, contracted by the Union to feed the Reserve Indians, to continue to do so as under the conditions of his previous contract.[44]

General Pike—who had first met the Taovayas in 1832 and had accompanied Superintendent Rector to the Leased District in 1859—returned to the Indian Territory to make treaties with the numerous tribes that had settled there. In his treaties with the Choctaws and Chickasaws, Commissioner Pike included a provision authorizing the Confederate government to use the Leased District as a reservation home for the Texas Indians. On August 6, 1861, the headmen of the Reserve tribes—many of whom had only recently returned to their villages—met General Pike, accompanied by Confederate soldiers and sixty Creek and Seminole warriors, at the Wichita Agency.[45]

On the afternoon of his arrival, the general hurriedly assembled a council of the Wichita, Caddo, Tonkawa, Penateka Comanche, and Delaware and Shawnee headmen. He distributed two thousand dollars' worth of presents to the tribes and promised to give them more when the council closed. During the next few days Pike set forth the terms of the proposed Confederate agreement, which was finally signed by the headmen of all the Wichita Agency tribes on August 12. Basically, the treaty was a restatement of the treaties with the United States. The tribes agreed to "place themselves under the laws and protection of the Confederate States of America in peace and war forever." The Indians retained the right to stay in the Leased District, where the Confederate government would supply them with agricultural implements, stock, and seed. The tribes were promised rations "for such time as may be necessary to enable them to feed themselves." The treaty also asserted that all hostilities between Texas and the reserve tribes were ended and "to be forgotten and forgiven on both sides."[46]

The Wichita Agency tribes really had no option but to sign the treaty. The Union troops were gone, and the Confederates obviously were in possession of the Indian Territory. The tribes retained the same agent, while the new government made the same pledges as the United States and backed its claims with presents. By aligning themselves with the Confederacy, the Wichitas and Caddos were doing just what they had previously done when they had transferred their loyalties from France to Spain and then to the United States. When the Confederate Congress ratified the treaty in December, 1861, the Wichitas and Caddos yet again had a new "father."[47]

The tribes' relationship with the Confederacy, however, proved to be short-lived. It quickly broke down for various reasons, and the Wichitas and Caddos were left to meet the hazards of the Civil War— except for minor assistance from the Union—on their own. In the first place, neither tribe trusted the rebel government to protect them from the Texans as the federal government at least had attempted to do. Second, the Confederates were unable to provide the Indians of the Wichita Agency with sufficient military protection from the Kiowas and Comanches. The Texan troops under Colonel Young soon abandoned the area. To serve as their replacements the Confederacy enlisted about thirty agency Indians into the army to guard the reserve. Among these troops—who were supplied with weapons and ammunition—were George Washington and members of his band.[48]

These events did not inspire confidence among the Indians of the Wichita Agency. Small groups abandoned the agency during the winter of 1861 to join other refugee tribes who had gathered at the Neosho River in southeastern Kansas, still held by the Union. Among these refugees were twenty Caddos, five Taovayas, and eighty-three Kichais. E. H. Carruth was appointed U.S. agent to these tribes, and in April, 1862, he sent a request to the Wichita Agency asking the Indians to cooperate with a Union expedition which planned to drive the Confederates out of the Indian Territory. The arrival of Confederate troops to occupy Fort Cobb in May, however, did not allow the tribes to respond to Carruth. Because these troops were from Texas, they only served to frighten the Reserve Indians even more. The Texans collected and guarded supplies during the summer but eventually abandoned the fort in August.[49]

That summer the Wichita Agency tribes suffered a serious blow with the death of one of their leading spokesmen, Iesh. The esteemed Nadaco caddi had led the Caddos through the troubled times which had followed the Texas Revolution, and whatever small successes the tribe had enjoyed since then were largely a result of his firm guidance. The present confusing state of affairs demanded quality leadership, but no one, neither Kadohadacho chief Tinah nor any of the Wichita headmen, proved up to the task.[50]

Following the departure of the Texan troops in August, tension arose around the Wichita Agency. Once again the Indians' corn crop failed from excessive drought, and though rations continued to be delivered, the tribes were said to be "suffering." In September Buffalo Hump, who had only recently settled his band of Penatekas on the reserve, quarreled with Agent Leeper and threatened his life, causing the agent to take his family to safety in Texas. During Leeper's absence, rumors abounded that a Texas army was on its way to attack the reserve. Without Iesh present to quiet them, about half of the Caddo people, along with many members of the Wichita tribes, panicked and fled from the reserve.[51]

Some of the refugees joined a group of Indians—Shawnees, Delawares, Osages, Seminoles, and Cherokees—who had been armed by the Union forces and were on their way to destroy the Wichita Agency. On the evening of October 23, the same day Agent Leeper returned from Texas, the group attacked the agency, burned it to the ground, and killed four white employees. Agent Leeper was at first reported killed, but a friendly Comanche had provided him with a horse upon which he fled to safety in Texas.[52]

During the burning of the agency, the Indians heard a rumor claiming that the Tonkawas had killed a Kadohadacho boy. The Caddoan-speaking tribes of the reserve had never been close to the Tonkawas, despite having lived on the same reservation for six years. The Tonkawas spoke a different language, were not as agriculturally advanced, and had always been on friendly terms with the Texans. In addition, they were the only tribe at the Wichita Agency which had remained unshakably loyal to the Confederacy; none of the Tonkawas had fled to Kansas.[53]

The morning after Fort Cobb was destroyed, an infuriated mob of Kadohadacho warriors—along with some agency Indians—pursued the Tonkawas who had already fled toward Fort Arbuckle. The attackers overtook the Tonkawas, and in a running fight that lasted nearly all day, they killed almost half of the fleeing tribe. Only about 140 Tonkawas, "in a most miserable and destitute condition," were able to gain the refuge of Fort Arbuckle.[54]

The destruction of the Wichita Agency and the attack upon the Tonkawas caused the remaining Wichitas and Caddos—except for George Washington's band of Whitebeads—and the rest of the Reserve tribes to abandon the Indian Territory, despite the orders of the Confederates that they remain. Deprived of the unity provided by Iesh's leadership, the Caddo tribes splintered. By December the Hainais and the Nadacos—with the death of Iesh these two tribes collectively became known as the Hainais—arrived in Woodson County, Kansas, and settled, along with the four Wichita tribes, near the Verdigris and Fall Rivers. At nearby Belmont, Agent Carruth had established a temporary agency and supply depot for the refugees. The Kadohadachos, however, chose to remain aloof from the whites and wintered with the Penateka Comanches on the Arkansas River far to the west of the temporary agency.[55]

In May, 1863, Agent Carruth began making arrangements to hold a council for all the Indians belonging to the Wichita Agency. He sent a contingent of Taovayas (including Isadowa), Hainais, Wacos, and Tawakonis to the Arkansas to request that the Kadohadacho and Penateka Comanche headmen attend the council. On June 8 Tinah and the new Penateka chief, Toshaway, arrived at the council grounds on Fall River and received presents from the agent. Carruth invited the two tribes to move to Woodson County with the other agency Indians so that they could receive clothes and rations from the government. Both the Kadohadachos and the Penateka Comanches refused, insisting that they receive their supplies at the mouth of the Little Arkansas River (present site of Wichita, Kansas). They told Carruth that "we do not want to live near the whites, because of troubles between them and us in regard to ponies, timber fields, [and] green corn." The Wichita agent was forced to agree with their sentiments and acceded to their wishes. For the rest of the year the Kadohadachos continued to live apart from their brethren.[56]

All of the Wichita Agency Indians supplemented the slight Union rations by entering the booming, uncontrolled cattle trade that had developed in Kansas. With the Civil War raging, there was a great demand for beef, and many whites in Kansas were offering high prices for cattle. At first the Reserve Indians were content to return to the environs of the Wichita Agency and round up their own cattle to sell. Increasingly, however, the whites offered the Reserve tribes "liberal sums of money" to go south into the abandoned Creek and Cherokee lands and drive in that cattle as well. Although some of the headmen tried to prevent this cattle rustling, a "good many" tribal members went ahead and participated in it.[57]

Milo Gookins, who was appointed Wichita agent following the death of Carruth, noted that most of the Indians of his agency "seem to have plenty of money, the proceeds mostly, I suppose, from the cattle trade." Unfortunately, the moneyed Indians attracted many opportunists, and the Wichitas and Caddos were plagued by swarms of whites who sold them whiskey, stole their horses, and "cheat[ed] and robb[ed] them of everything they have worth stealing." By late 1863, when intensely cold weather swept through Kansas, many of the Reserve Indians were left with "an insufficient supply of clothing, blankets, and shelter." The shipment of these articles did not arrive until January 12, 1864; by then, many had already died from exposure, and others were severely weakened. At this point, a smallpox epidemic swept through the area and killed many of the infirm.[58]

Once the weather warmed in April, the Wichitas and Caddos abandoned Woodson County for the healthier region to the west. They settled along with the Kadohadachos—the Penatekas having returned to the Indian Territory where they joined the Whitebead Caddos on the Washita River near Fort Arbuckle—in modern Cowley County, Kansas, at the confluence of the Walnut and Arkansas Rivers. They told Southern Superintendent W. G. Coffin that they preferred to "subsist on buffalo and antelope" rather than on government rations. Before they left, however, Coffin gave the tribes a "liberal amount" of flour and ammunition, and from April to October the Wichitas and Caddos were not supplied by the government at all.[59]

At first, all went well in their new villages except for the problem of the "vicious . . . vagabonds of whites" who followed the tribes hoping to rob and cheat them. The headmen complained to Agent Gookins about these "bad white men" who created "much trouble and difficulty." Superintendent Coffin gave Gookins full authority to "expel and drive out of the country" every white person found in the area without a legitimate reason to be there. In case they refused his orders, Gookins was to call on the nearest military post for assistance.[60]

In October Agent Gookins was able to resume the provisioning—albeit slight—of the Reserve tribes located in Cowley County. On October 14 Gookins held a council with seventy headmen of the Caddo and Wichita tribes. Since the Kadohadacho caddi, Tinah, had yet to return from a hunt, Nadaco Jim Pock Mark, "an intelligent man, spoke at considerable length" for the Caddos and the Wichitas. He stated that since they had left the Wichita Agency for Kansas, the tribes had not had an agent to advise them "and often did not know what to do." He complained of the "bad white men" who hounded them and stole their horses, and he asked Gookins to keep them away from the Indian camps, "and then there would be no trouble."[61]

Gookins reported that all of the headmen "express a strong wish, and seemed to expect, that the government would do something for them." As a result, the headmen of the tribes addressed a memorial to President Lincoln "our great Father . . . and say to him that we are his friends, and friends to the Government, and to all white men who do right by us." They complained that they had been driven off their lands and had suffered greatly because they had been unable to raise crops or kill enough game, did not have adequate clothing or shelter, and had been decimated by disease. The headmen concluded that "we have always been told by our white Father that [the whites] would help us when we needed help, and we need it now very much and we hope you will tell our Agent to give us bread for our women and children and clothing for them before the next snow falls. We hope our white fathers will not forget their red children when they are suffering." Three Caddos and seven Wichitas placed their marks on the document.[62]

Unfortunately, the federal government did not answer the Caddo and Wichita plea. After receiving Gookins' report of the council, Superintendent Coffin informed the agent that he did not have enough supplies to go around, and therefore he had to support the "more destitute" Indians who lived in the Cherokee nation. Coffin felt these Indians were more needy because of their proximity to "robbers, thieves, and rebels," while the Indians of the Wichita Agency were safe out on the frontier.[63]

The Wichitas and Caddos, however, felt they were not far enough away from the whites and, accompanied by a large group of Shawnees and Delawares, moved their villages farther west to winter at the mouth of the Little Arkansas River. Unfortunately the tribes' suffering only increased at their new homes. Realizing something needed to be done to help the ailing Indians, Agent Gookins obtained a "very limited and very inadequate supply" of food for them. This consisted of a daily ration of 1¾ ounces of flour and "just enough sugar and coffee for them to quarrel over, but not enough to do them any good." Gookins also arranged for the tribes to receive a shipment of clothing, but winter was nearly over when it finally arrived on February 14, 1865.[64]

The Indians attempted to supplement the government rations in various ways. They continued their involvement in the cattle trade, but Gookins reported that by April, 1865, they had completely run out of stock and had no money left. By hunting buffalo and other game the Indians were also able "partially to supply themselves with provisions and to keep up considerable traffic in robes, skins, furs, and tallow." Game, however, was becoming increasingly scarce because of constant white encroachment; in fact, by fall of 1865 the buffalo range was a full one hundred miles west of the Wichita and Caddo camps.[65]

Agent Gookins also took great pains to get the Indians to raise their own crops for the first time since they had abandoned the Indian Territory. On February 16, 1865, he wrote Superintendent Coffin to ask for agricultural supplies. Receiving no reply, he traveled to Fort Leavenworth in March, only to find Coffin absent. Taking matters into his own hands, Gookins purchased nine hundred dollars' worth of seed and farming implements for the tribes and returned to the Little Arkansas. In April the Reserve tribes "went to work earnestly, fencing and preparing their grounds, and planting their fields and patches." The prospects for an abundant yield were good until July, when extremely high water flooded most of their fields.[66]

By the end of the year, Gookins was forced to admit that the Indians under his care were "very poor." He warned that their numbers were "decreasing at a rapid rate" from the "extreme destitution to which they have been exposed." A census taken in September, 1866, provides a rough estimate of the severity of the population decline. Together, the four Wichita tribes numbered 800 members, down from about 1,100 in 1859, nearly a 30 percent decline. Waco chief Acaquash, as well as Tawakoni chief Ocherash, were among the dead. Nearly one-fourth of the Kadohadachos and Hainais had died since the beginning of the Civil War; the Caddo population—excepting the 200 or so White-beads—fell from 476 to 362. Gookins reported that very often the head-men asked "when and where the Government will provide a permanent home for them." Because the Civil War had ended, both the Wichita Agent and the new southern superintendent, Elijah Sells, recommended that the Reserve Indians be moved back to the Indian Territory "where lands may be set apart for their permanent occupation."[67]

The federal government, however, took no action on these propos-als during the following year. Once again Gookins encouraged the In-dians to raise their own crops, and in April, 1866, they began planting corn, pumpkins, and other "garden vegetables." Their work was ham-pered by their having had no plows and only an "inadequate supply" of hoes. Gookins also found that he had to prod the weary Indians be-cause all of them were "indolent and improvident," except for the Caddos.[68]

Although the tribes were busy in their fields, troubles occurred with the whites, whose numbers increased daily. Gookins reported that whiskey was prevalent in the camps, and he was powerless to stop the "unprincipled white men" from carrying on this trade. Gookins did, however, arrest and prosecute one trader in May, causing the others to be more cautious. Soon afterward, though, other whites stole several horses from the Kadohadachos. In retaliation, a band of Kadohadacho warriors randomly stole horses from the first white man whom they encountered. Because of the growing tensions between the whites and Indians, Gookins insisted to his superiors that the tribes be returned to the Indian Territory "at the very earliest practicable period."[69]

By June the tribes had successfully planted their crops which ap-peared "to be doing very well." The continued small amount of rations, however, caused many members to leave their crops and head west to hunt buffalo. This trek proved to be disastrous for the tribes of the Wichita Agency. While out on the plains the Reserve Indians were met by bands of Cheyennes and Arapahos. They refused to allow them to hunt and robbed them of what little they did have. The Reserve Indians returned empty-handed to the Little Arkansas only to find that, yet again, a good portion of their crop had been destroyed by flooding.[70]

Henry Shanklin, Agent Gookins's replacement, arrived at the camps soon after the hunting parties had returned from the plains. He found the Indians starving and in "utter destitution." Shanklin urgently sent a dispatch to Superintendent Sells stating that unless the Indians "receive immediate relief, starvation—actual starvation" would be the result. The Wichita agent complained that he was "besieged daily by old and young, entreating, begging, urging me to give them something to eat." He attempted to convince the warriors to return to the plains to hunt, but they refused out of fear of the hostile Indians. Superintendent Sells, in his annual report, stated that the Indians of the Wichita Agency were "probably the most destitute" of all the tribes in his care and warned that "unless some relief is furnished, they must suffer the horrors of both hunger and cold, as they are greatly in need of subsistence and clothing."[71]

This time the government responded. On August 3 rations finally arrived and were distributed to the Reserve Indians. Upon learning that the refugee Caddos were being fed, George Washington's Whitebeads abandoned the Indian Territory and joined their brethren in Kansas. Three hundred Penateka Comanches followed them north soon thereafter. In September the government arranged for the Indians to receive daily rations, consisting of one pound of beef and either ¾ pound of flour or 1½ pints of corn per person. Two months later Shanklin purchased two hundred dollars' worth of cooking utensils for the tribes. Unlike as in previous years, blankets, clothing, and socks arrived before the really cold weather had set in, and these goods were distributed to the Indians in early December.[72]

Meanwhile, plans were finally begun to move the refugee tribes back to the Leased District. On December 21, 1866, the southern superintendent informed the commissioner of Indian affairs that he would relocate the tribes in the following spring. Because the Indians had "but few ponies, and these generally in bad condition," he felt they would require one hundred two-horse team wagons to carry the Indians and their goods. On March 30, 1867, Agent Shanklin received instructions to move the tribes back to the old Wichita Agency on the Washita River and was forwarded ten thousand dollars to implement the move. J. J. Chollar was hired as special agent to "superintend and control the removal," and he began to collect the necessary wagons and supplies for the trip.[73]

It was quickly becoming imperative to move the refugee Indians from the area around the mouth of the Little Arkansas. The land they occupied had been a part of the Osage Reserve. The Osages—traditional enemies of the Wichitas and Caddos—had recently sold this land to the United States, and, as a result, about eighty to one hundred white families had settled near the refugee Indian villages by June. The Osages, whom Shanklin characterized as being "miserable thieves," were stealing stock from the white settlers and blaming the refugee tribes for the thefts. In addition, the Osages attempted to exact rent (in horses) from the Wichita Agency Indians, who refused to pay. Thus, the Osages stole the refugees' horses, and in turn, the Reserve Indians retaliated by taking the Osage ponies. Shanklin feared if the refugee Indians were not "removed at the earliest day," this "bitter feud . . . may terminate disastrously."[74]

Luckily, Special Agent Chollar arrived at the refugee camps in mid-June with eighty wagons. Unfortunately, though, the return trip to the Washita River did not go as smoothly as the Indians' removal from Texas. There were no whites present who had the leadership abilities of Major Neighbors, and the Indians themselves were divided. Bad luck also hampered their efforts. At first, heavy rains and high water in the rivers held up the removal process. Shanklin procured a small boat, and an attempt was made to cross the swollen Arkansas River on June 24. One of the Indians was drowned, and the Wichita agent decided to suspend further attempts "until such times as the streams could be crossed with safety."[75]

Unhappy with this delay, newly appointed Southern Superintendent James Wortham took charge of the removal process a few days later. Unfortunately, his accession did not improve matters. Cholera broke out in the Taovaya village, killing eighteen tribal members in five days. The sickness quickly spread to the nearby Waco, Tawakoni, and Kichai village, and even more Wichitas died. Despite the epidemic, the Wichitas refused to abandon their villages on the grounds that they needed to mourn their dead. They also refused to abandon their fields, feeling that the Great Spirit would be offended if they did not harvest the corn they had planted in the spring. The Indian agents were helpless in dissuading the Wichitas from this belief, and the tribes remained in their villages.[76]

In the meantime, most of the Caddos and Penateka Comanches, along with a few Shawnees and Delawares, decided to head to the Leased District on their own before the cholera could reach them. On July 1 rations to be consumed en route were distributed to the refugees. Tinah, as leader of the entire Caddo tribe, signed a receipt for rations to feed 531 Caddos, and most of them began the trip south. One hundred Caddos, along with nearly four hundred Shawnees and Delawares, remained behind, however, waiting to depart with Chollar and the wagons. On August 3 this group had just crossed to the south bank of the Arkansas River when cholera struck, and thirty-four Indians died on the way to the Wichita Agency, a destination that was finally reached a few weeks later.[77]

The Wichitas did not begin their own troublesome trek to the Leased District until October 1. Along with Agent Shanklin, they crossed to the south side of the Arkansas, where they were supposed to meet the hired wagons, but only ten wagons showed up equipped "with poor mules and oxen that gave out." Although Shanklin was able to hire a few more wagons from local farmers, many of the Wichitas were forced to walk, causing one observer to lament that "it was a pitiful sight to see the women and children, old men and old women trudging along on foot, most of them barefooted and nearly naked." A prairie fire only added to the Wichitas' misery on October 24 as high winds fanned the flames and burned to death eighty-five of their hobbled horses. Fortunately, the rest of the trip was uneventful, and the Wichitas arrived at the Washita River in mid-November.[78]

Twenty-one years after the Wichitas and Caddos had acknowledged their dependence upon the United States, the two tribes were finally able to settle upon lands they believed they could permanently call home. The tribes' reservation experience, which would last another thirty-four years, was now truly ready to begin.

Chapter Five

Reestablishment of the Wichita Agency, 1868-78

The Indian [is] like the white man. The Great Spirit had made them both, only He had made the white man wiser than the Indian. . . . He had put him on a broader road and told him to take care of the Indian and show him the way . . . so far they had not found the road. They were worse off than when they started, but . . . to day they hoped to find the road. Long time ago their father took the white man by the hand, and now they wished to do the same. This land they saw all around them, for many miles, belonged to their fathers. . . The bones of [my] people lie where the post [Wichita Agency] is being built. [I hope my] people [will] never be made to leave this country.

—Address of Waco chief Buffalo Good,
April 7, 1869

As the Wichitas and Caddos made their way back to the Wichita Agency in the fall of 1867, they hoped to resume the reservation experiment that had been proven viable at the Brazos Reserve before outside aggressors caused its dissolution. Following the hardships and wandering caused by the Civil War, both tribes desired to settle on land they could securely call their own, firmly protected by the U.S. government. They were more than willing to incorporate customs into their culture, such as stock raising and English education, which they felt would be beneficial to their survival. This practice would be nothing new for the Caddos and Wichitas; in fact, the people of both tribes had been absorbing "white" ways into their lives ever since the European intrusion three centuries before.

In the wake of the Civil War, the Indian policy of the federal government seemed to agree with the desires of the Caddos and Wichitas and promised to bring ultimate success to the reservation experiment. The prewar program of "civilizing" the Indians was now reinvigorated by a new crusading zeal, deeply influenced by Christian humanitarianism. This ambitious plan, which came to be called the Peace Policy, was developed in the waning days of President Andrew Johnson's administration and fully implemented by his successor, Ulysses S. Grant. It called for treaties of peace to be negotiated with all tribes in which they would be granted land on reservations, where, in the hope that one day the Indian could enter society as the white man's equal, he would be taught the "arts of civilization."

Although there was not much new in this part of the Peace Policy, its innovative administration promised to separate it from the failed prewar program. Instead of having army officers or dishonest and incompetent civilians implement the Peace Policy, President Grant turned the administration of the reservations over to various religious organizations, which would then nominate the agents and other agency employees. It was hoped that these men of higher morals would not only be more dedicated to the Indians' needs but also provide them with a living example of the profits of civilization and Christianity.[1] Although the Wichitas and Caddos had always been blessed with good agents, the promise of a group of devoted men, fully supported by the federal government, working in concert with the Indians to achieve shared goals, seemed to guarantee success.

However, even as the Wichitas and Caddos were returning to the Wichita Agency, a treaty was being negotiated on Medicine Lodge Creek in southwestern Kansas that would drastically change the nature of their reservation and undermine the gains the Peace Policy promised them. On October 21, 1867, the United States entered into an agreement with the Comanches and Kiowas (and later, unilaterally included a small number of Apaches) which set aside all the land south of the Washita River in the Leased District to these tribes for a reservation.[2] Land the Wichitas and Caddos considered their own—as promised in the Fort Arbuckle Agreement of July 1, 1859—was being given to the enemy tribes that they had assisted the United States in fighting for more than a decade. Not only were the Kiowas and Comanches far larger and more powerful than the Wichitas and Caddos, they were not—despite signing the treaty—wholly ready to give up their warlike, nomadic ways in favor of a settled life on the reservation. To make matters worse, in

1869 President Grant issued an executive order which assigned approximately five million acres of land north of the Washita to the buffalo-hunting Cheyenne and Arapaho tribes.[3] Thus, within two years of their resettlement at the Wichita Agency, the Caddos and Wichitas had no land they could firmly call their own and once again were threatened on all sides by former enemies.

Unfortunately for the Caddos and Wichitas, the Peace Policy ultimately would be applied more vigorously to the nomadic, warlike tribes, which guaranteed its failure, than to the settled, agricultural tribes, which could assure its success. Because visible gains appeared limited, the federal government eventually abandoned the plan altogether in favor of yet another program which would ultimately cause the Indians even greater harm than the flawed Peace Policy.

The winter of 1867–68 was a harsh one for all of the tribes that had returned to the Wichita Agency in the fall; these tribes were reported to be in "greatly destitute condition, dependent on the government for support." The tribes, however, hoped to alleviate their suffering by finally being able to settle down and raise a crop for the first time in nearly a decade. Unfortunately, this settlement would not occur in 1868. As a result of a "gross misstatement" made to them by Comanche Agent Col. J. H. Leavenworth in Agent Shanklin's absence, all the Indians were mistakenly directed to settle on the south side of the Washita River on the new Kiowa-Comanche Reservation instead of at their old homes on the north bank. Among these misguided Indians—who also had the misfortune of planting crops on their former enemies' land— were the 600 Kadohadachos and Hainais under Tinah, Black Beaver's 100 Delawares, and the 650 Shawnees led by John White. However, the 4 Wichita tribes—Isadowa's 280 Taovayas, Kewakasitz's 123 Kichais, Buffalo Good's 135 Wacos, and Dave's 157 Tawakonis—despite also having settled on the south side of the Washita, planted crops in their old fields on the north bank, near the mouth of Sugar Creek. Three hundred Penateka Comanches, led by Toshaway and Esahabbe, settled nearby but did not raise a crop.[4]

The seriousness of Agent Leavenworth's error did not become evident until he compounded it in February, 1868, by establishing the Kiowa-Comanche Agency just downstream from the Wichita Agency tribes instead of at Cache Creek in the southeastern part of the Leased District as previously planned. Thus, great numbers of Kiowas and Co-manches—together their population totalled nearly five thousand—arrived to trade and pick up rations just as the Wichita Agency tribes were carrying out their spring planting. Not only did they intimidate the Wichita Agency Indians, but also they knocked down fences and allowed their horses to graze in the newly planted fields. Since federal troops had not yet reoccupied the region, in May a Comanche war party helped itself to all the supplies stored at the Wichita Agency be-fore heading for Texas. Upon the Comanches' return, they burned one of the few agency buildings and threatened to kill the post doctor.[5]

This aggressive behavior caused the Wichita Agency tribes to give up their fields and concentrate on protecting their livestock from the thieves. The Shawnees, realizing that "it would be impossible to raise a crop or two in peace," left the Leased District altogether and settled on land vacated by the Seminoles on the Canadian River. The Delawares moved south to the Little Washita, while the two Penateka bands, along with eighty Kadohadachos, moved down the Washita toward the Chickasaw line. By the end of the year, only the Wichitas and the rest of the Caddos remained near the agency. Obviously, the tribes' situa-tion had not improved in their first year back in the Leased District; once again they were reported to be in "a very destitute condition, and are really suffering." Agent Shanklin, before permanently abandoning his post in November, 1868, because of illness, claimed that it was a "mystery as to how they will subsist this winter."[6]

Following this dire warning, the federal government took steps to stabilize the chaotic situation in the Leased District. First, Col. A. G. Boone, newly appointed Kiowa-Comanche agent, helped the Wichita Agency tribes survive the winter by distributing thirty-six hundred dol-lars' worth of goods in December. The following month, Gen. William B. Hazen, military commander of the southern district of the Great Plains, directed interpreter Philip McCusker to take temporary charge of the Wichita Agency. At the same time, Hazen made McCusker's job a bit easier by establishing the Kiowa-Comanche Agency (as well as his own headquarters, eventually called Fort Sill) thirty miles to the south on Cache Creek, near the old Taovaya village.[7]

Thus freed from the annoyances caused by the Kiowas and Coman-ches, most of the Wichita Agency tribes reestablished their villages in the Leased District in the spring of 1869. The four Wichita tribes set up

*Philip McCusker, scout and interpreter, and Buffalo Good, Wichita (Waco) chief,
1870s. Courtesy Fort Sill Museum*

their trademark grass houses in the midst of their fields along Sugar
Creek on the north bank of the Washita. The Kadohadachos, because
of the death in the winter of Tinah, their leader since Iesh's death in
1862, broke into three separate camps, even though a new caddi,
Guadeloupe, had been acknowledged by all. The largest Kadohadacho
village was located on the north side of the Washita, ten miles above
the Wichitas, while a smaller Kadohadacho group settled alongside the
Delawares on the south side of the river. A third group of Kadohadachos,
George Washington's Whitebeads, lived on the south bank of the Canadian River near the Chickasaw Reservation. The Hainais lived fifteen
miles below the Wichitas on the north side of Washita. For the time
being, the Penatekas settled with their kinsmen near Fort Sill.[8]

With the assistance of McCusker, who served as interpreter and also distributed stock, plows, and seeds, the tribes resumed their agricultural pursuits in 1869 to good results. The ever-industrious Caddos and Delawares planted nearly 700 acres of corn, which yielded almost 9,000 bushels. They were also successful husbandmen; by the end of the year they had nearly 2,000 horses, 600 head of cattle, and 750 pigs. As was their custom, the men of the Wichita tribes—including the Waco and Tawakoni men who had farmed on the Brazos Reserve—refused to engage in agriculture. Instead they preferred to tend to their 2,200 horses and hunt for buffalo, the robes of which they sold to the agency trader, William Shirley. The Wichita women, however, planted 230 acres of corn, which provided the four tribes with a harvest of nearly 2,500 bushels. For the first time, then, the Wichita Agency tribes were able to supplement their meager daily rations with their own crops and were not plagued by hunger.[9]

In 1869 the Wichitas, Caddos, and Delawares met with two delegations sent from the East, providing them at least a glimmer of hope for the future. In April, Vincent Colyer, heading a government inspection tour of the Indian Territory, visited the Wichita Agency along with General Hazen and held a talk with the chiefs. He told them that "now the good white men had united together to take care of the good Indians" and that President Grant wished to establish schools among them. Waco chief Buffalo Good responded warmly and told Colyer that his tribe "had been a long time looking for a school-house and a teacher, and were glad to now hear that they were to have them." Four months later, in a council held with a delegation from the Society of Friends, Wichita and Caddo chiefs stated once again "that they were very desirous of having schools established among them."[10]

The Quakers came to the Wichita Agency because President Grant, as a part of the Peace Policy, had assigned the central superintendency to the Orthodox Friends, who appointed Enoch Hoag as its head. An Iowa Quaker farmer, Lawrie Tatum, was chosen as agent for the Kiowa-Comanche Reservation, including the Wichita Agency tribes, and he assumed his position at the agency near Fort Sill on July 1, 1869. Tatum soon realized that he had his hands full with the Kiowas and Comanches; thus, in April, 1870, Jonathan Richards, a Quaker employed as a clerk in the office of Superintendent Hoag, was appointed to the position of agent for the Wichita Agency tribes.[11]

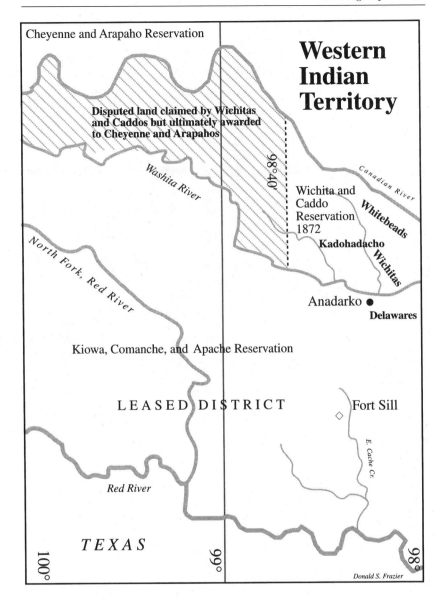

Western
Indian
Territory

Cheyenne and Arapaho Reservation

Disputed land claimed by Wichitas
and Caddos but ultimately awarded
to Cheyenne and Arapahos

Washita River

98°40'

Canadian River

Wichita and
Caddo
Reservation
1872

Whitebeads

Kadohadacho

Wichitas

North Fork, Red River

Anadarko ●

Delawares

Kiowa, Comanche, and Apache Reservation

LEASED DISTRICT

Fort Sill ◇

E. Cache Cr.

Red River

TEXAS

100°

99°

98°

Donald S. Frazier

Agent Richards proved to be everything the government hoped for when it implemented the Peace Policy. He was honest, sober, industrious, and truly dedicated to providing assistance to the Wichita Agency tribes. Although he may have overestimated the Indians' desires to fully accept Christianity and become "white men," he never underestimated

Guadeloupe, 1872. After becoming the Kadohadacho caddi in 1869, he became the first chief of the entire Caddo tribe in 1874. Courtesy Smithsonian Institution, National Anthropological Archives

their wishes to improve their condition, nor did he lose his optimism in trying times. While his personality did not inspire the Wichitas and Caddos to love him as they had Major Neighbors, they did come to appreciate Agent Richards as a true friend.

The Wichita, Caddo, and Delaware chiefs met with Richards, Agent Tatum, and Lt. S. P. Jocelyn in council a few days after the new agent's arrival at the Wichita Agency in May, 1870. The headmen "expressed themselves emphatically in favor of having a separate agency" from the Kiowas and Comanches who "continued in their nomadic and depredating habits." They told the delegation that, even though they believed they owned all the country between the Red and Canadian Rivers, they would accept only a portion of that area if they could assuredly tell their children "this is your home, and it is to be the home of your children." A few days later they outlined the boundaries of the proposed reservation to Agent Richards: bounded on the east by the 98th meridian, the north by the Canadian River, the west by a line north and south through the mouth of Pond Creek (near Fort Cobb), and on the south by a line drawn from the mouth of Pond Creek to the point where the Washita River struck the 98th meridian. General Hazen and Superintendent Hoag jointly recommended this land be permanently set aside for the Wichita Agency tribes on June 15, 1870.[12]

In the meantime, while waiting for Congress to take action on the recommendation, Agent Richards earnestly began to make permanent improvements at the Wichita Agency. Because there were no agency buildings, Richards was forced to rent Trader Shirley's storehouse and dwelling for his family and the agency employees who began arriving in the fall. By February, 1871, work was completed on a twenty-by-twenty-eight-foot two-story house for use as the agent's dwelling. A fenced corral and stables were built nearby as were a carpenter shop, corn crib, and pig pens, "mostly of a temporary character." However, with the arrival of a sawmill—with an attached grain mill—in the fall of 1871, work of a more permanent nature was begun. By the summer of 1872 two frame buildings had been completed to house the agency employees, along with a sixteen-by-forty-foot warehouse, a "grain and buggy house," and an icehouse. An agency farm of 180 acres was brought under cultivation, around which was planted nearly one hundred peach, apple, and cherry trees. Within two years of his arrival then, Agent Richards had established the basic outline of the Wichita Agency, about a mile north of the Washita River, from scratch.[13]

Agent Richards also quickly won the favor of the Wichita Agency Indians by being responsive to their concerns about their rations. The daily rations were issued weekly and consisted of ½ pound of flour, 1½ pounds of beef, ¾ pound of bacon, along with 4 pounds of coffee, 8 pounds of sugar, and 1 pound of salt per every 100 rations. Immediately upon Richards's arrival, the Indians complained of the "inconveniences and disadvantages they are subjected to" by having to travel the thirty miles to Fort Sill every week to pick up their rations. Not only was it too far for many of the aged and infirm, but also their women were subjected to the taunts and offers of the white employees and soldiers stationed there. Agent Richards relayed their complaints to Superintendent Hoag, and by the beginning of 1871 rations were issued from the Wichita Agency commissary. The following year, the Wichita Agency tribes pointed out to Richards the poor quality of the issue flour, which he once again was able to rectify through Hoag. The agent was not as successful, however, in getting his superior to approve of the monthly issuance of rations for bands such as George Washington's which lived thirty miles from the Agency. Despite the failure in this case, Richards's efforts on their behalf did not go unappreciated by the Indians.[14]

Inspired by the new agent, some of the Wichita Agency Indians began working just as hard on their own settlements. By the fall of 1871, with the assistance of the agency employees, nearly all of the Indians' fields were fenced in. As usual, the Caddos and Delawares took the lead in agricultural improvements; Richards characterized them as appearing "anxious about their farming," displaying "a commendable spirit in joining in the work." Even prior to the spring planting in 1871, Kadohadacho caddi Guadeloupe asked Agent Richards for wagons, harness plows, axes and "other things necessary for advancing their labors." Although these items did not arrive in 1871, the Kadohadachos, Hainais, and Delawares together raised nearly 8,000 bushels of corn. The following year, Agent Richards assigned a farmer with a span of mules to assist the tribes, and the yield was increased to 14,550 bushels of corn, in addition to 450 bushels of oats raised by the Delawares. All three tribes continued their stock-raising efforts to great success; by 1873 they had accumulated some 2,600 horses, 1,350 head of cattle, and 1,650 hogs.[15]

Two individual farmers, Kadohadacho George Washington and Delaware Black Beaver, stood out from the rest of their fellow tribesmen. By 1873 George Washington and his Whitebead band, which numbered 127 (about one-fifth of the total Caddo population), owned three-fifths of the Caddo horses, nine-tenths of the cattle, and just under half of the swine. In addition, Washington's Canadian River band had accumulated 12 of the 16 plows the Caddos owned, and half of the tribe's 26 wagons. Black Beaver and his extended Delaware family fenced in over 200 acres of land—50 acres more than the rest of the tribe put together—on the south bank of the Washita nearly half a mile downstream from the agency. With these two leading the way, the Caddos and Delawares began the process of establishing individual family farms.[16]

The Caddos and Delawares also made great strides in improving their housing, especially after the sawmill arrived in late 1871. With the help of the agency employees, the Indians began building log houses the following spring for the chiefs of each tribe. By 1873 almost all of the six hundred or so Caddos and Delawares lived in sixty-three log houses. In addition, Agent Richards had two frame houses, measuring

Showetat, or George Washington, 1872. Leader of the "progressive" Whitebead band of Caddos from the 1840s to the 1880s. Courtesy Smithsonian Institution, National Anthropological Archives

eighteen-by-twenty-six feet, equipped with stone fireplaces and chimneys, built for the two Penateka Comanche chiefs, Toshaway and Esahabbe, upon their tribe's return to the Wichita Agency in 1872. Other buildings constructed in 1873 included a blacksmith and wheelwright shop.[17]

The close relations of the Caddos and Delawares eventually caused them to meet in council and unite under one chief. In 1874, probably at the insistence of Agent Richards, the Hainais and the Delawares officially accepted Kadohadacho caddi Guadeloupe as their political leader. Richards felt that the "necessity of separate bands, with a chief for each, appeared undesirable," and that they could better protect themselves if they were united. Although the Delawares reestablished their independence in 1879, from this point on, the Kadohadachos and Hainais would be recognized together as one single tribe, the Caddos.[18]

As the Caddos and Delawares became settled at the Wichita Agency, they also began to send their children to school for the first time in a generation. Josiah Butler, a Quaker from Ohio, opened the first Indian school in the area at Fort Sill on February 20, 1871. Although the school—housed in a formidable building measuring thirty-by-sixty feet—was erected mainly for the Kiowas and Comanches, the only students that attended during the first term (which lasted until July, 1871) were twenty-four Penatekas and Caddos, who were brought personally to the school by George Washington. A temporary school, housed in a "small room over the commissary," was also opened in the spring of 1871 at the Wichita Agency. Only about six pupils attended this school, which closed as soon as the hot weather set in.[19]

It was not until Quaker teachers Alfred Standing and Thomas Battey converted the Wichita Agency commissary into a boarding school in the fall that a full-scale effort was made to provide an education for the Indian children. Eleven Caddo and Delaware children attended the opening session of the school—which would eventually be called the Riverside Indian School—on November 15, 1871. Battey and Standing attempted to recruit more students throughout the term (which lasted until June 14, 1872) but succeeded in getting only an additional twenty-seven to attend. Most were Caddo and Delaware boys, since the Wichita tribes refused to send their children to the school. The teachers emphasized math, geography, and the reading and writing of English, in addition to a "series of New Testament lessons, then Genesis." Although Riverside had the full support of Caddo and Delaware leaders—including Guadeloupe and Black Beaver, both of whom visited the school and stressed the importance of education to the students—the Quaker teachers had a hard time keeping the pupils in school; they often ran away or were taken back home by their parents. The boys that remained were subjected to taunts by Caddo and Delaware young men who called them women for "studying with white folks" and claimed they were not men "and never will be."[20]

Despite the ridicule, attendance grew by six students to forty-four during the second school term, which lasted from September, 1872, to June, 1873. A few of these new students were Taovaya and Kichai children, who were treated with "tender affection" by their Caddo and Delaware classmates. On March 28, 1873, the students were transferred to a brand-new twenty-by-sixty-foot two-story building which contained schoolrooms, a dining room, kitchen, and sleeping quarters for the students. In addition to this boarding school, a day school was opened on January 14, 1873, mainly for the Wichita tribes who were still uneasy about having their children spend the night away from home. However, by the time school reopened following the summer break in September, 1873, the Wichitas had changed their minds and began sending their children to the boarding school, thus alleviating the need for the day school. Although seventy students attended the boarding school during the 1873–74 term, only forty regularly went to class, since the Wichita children's "wild nature carries them back to their camps." Despite the Wichitas' vacillation toward the school, Agent Richards was optimistic about its future, and plans were laid to create more housing space in 1874.[21]

While the Caddos and Delawares began establishing their settlements in earnest, the four Wichita tribes, forced off their land so many times before, hesitated to make permanent improvements. They continued to live in their traditional grass houses and lagged behind the Caddos and Delawares agriculturally, for the men still refused to engage in farm work. In 1871 the Wichita women planted 148 acres of corn, melons, and beans in various small patches and raised nearly 2,500 bushels of corn. The following year a few Kichai men began working in the fields only to lose interest and "abandoned it after a few day's trial." By 1873 the Wichita women still only had 150 acres in cultivation. The Wichita men continued to prefer to look after their horse herd which, unfortunately, had declined by about half—mainly because of theft from Texans—from 2,870 head in 1872 to only 1,484 the next year. Even the 345 Penateka Comanches had nearly 100 more horses than the 671 Wichitas by the end of 1873.[22]

The Wichita reluctance to establish long-lasting settlements was the result of the federal government's lack of action concerning the confirmation of their reservation. In February, 1871, nine months after the Wichita Agency tribes had detailed the boundaries of their proposed reservation, Richards reported that the Indians were "very anxious about the land . . . being secured to them." No action had been taken by August, 1871, forcing Richards, in his annual report, to "call the attention of the Department [of Interior] to the necessity of prompt action in urging upon Congress the importance of extending to these deserving Indians" a reservation with defined boundaries. Despite the pleas of the agent, nothing was done for the Wichita Agency tribes for another full year.[23]

What caused the federal government finally to take note of the Wichita Agency Indians' plight was, fittingly, the breakdown of the Peace Policy at the Kiowa-Comanche Reservation. Unhappy with the small rations and inadequate annuity gifts, and unwilling to settle down on the reservation, Kiowa and Comanche warriors resumed their raiding into Texas in 1870. The following May a Kiowa war party ambushed a supply train near Fort Richardson, Texas, and killed seven whites. Upon their return to the reservation, three Kiowa chiefs were seized by the military and held for trial, an action fully supported by Agent Tatum. Despite this show of force, the Kiowas and Comanches continued their depredations during the winter of 1871–72, causing Toshaway and Esahabbe's Penateka bands to take refuge at the Wichita Agency. The dangerous situation also caused the Department of Interior to send a delegation, headed by retired army captain Henry E. Alvord, to the Leased District to investigate the situation at the Kiowa-Comanche Reservation as well as to meet with the Wichita Agency tribes and the Cheyennes and Arapahos.[24]

Captain Alvord reached Fort Sill on August 25, 1872, and over the next three weeks visited the three agencies and held councils with all of the tribes of the area, except the absent Cheyennes. He then invited the tribes to send a delegation of chiefs to Washington so they could meet the Great Father and the commissioner of Indian affairs. Without consulting Agent Richards, Captain Alvord hastily chose nine headmen from the Wichita Agency—including Kadohadacho caddi Guadeloupe and George Washington, Taovaya chief Isadowa, Tawakoni chief Dave, and Kichai chief Kewakasitz—to accompany him on the trip east. In all, forty headmen from all three agencies left in wagons with Captain Alvord on September 20, finally reaching Washington by rail on October 2. President Grant quickly received them at the White House, but it was a full two weeks before the Wichitas and Caddos were finally able to meet with Commissioner of Indian Affairs Francis A. Walker.[25]

Tired from their travels and the extended stay in Washington, the Wichita Agency headmen were surprised by Commissioner Walker on October 19 when he informed them that "he had brought them to Washington to tell them where the boundaries of their reservation would be fixed." In his October 10 report to Walker, Captain Alvord had stated that the boundaries of the Wichita Reservation had not yet been established and that it was "very important that [the Wichitas and Caddos] should be satisfied in this respect." He claimed that all of the bands were represented in this delegation and were "prepared to discuss and settle the reservation question at the present visit." Alvord also recommended that the land between the Washita and Canadian Rivers and the 98th meridian and 98° 30' be set as the boundaries, which Commissioner Walker reiterated to the headmen at the meeting.[26]

The Wichita and Caddo delegation responded to this shocking news by informing the commissioner (through Interpreter McCusker, Trader Shirley, Farmer Sturm, and Black Beaver) that they had only been chosen by Alvord to travel to Washington and did not have the authority of their tribes to make such a decision pertaining to land. In any case, they protested, claiming that their country stretched much farther to the west, all the way past the Antelope Hills to the 100th meridian, as stated in the Fort Arbuckle Agreement of July 1, 1859, instead of at Pond Creek, which they had informed Agent Richards they would accept in 1870. Walker did extend the boundary westward ten minutes—or just a few miles west of Fort Cobb—and told the Indians the issue was settled and they should sign an agreement to that effect. The Caddo and Wichita headmen objected but finally signed the document under protest, all the while insisting they had not relinquished rights to any land they might possess. Upon their return to the Wichita Agency a few weeks later, the headmen "were abused by their people for having signed such a paper," and the tribesmen wholly disavowed the agreement.[27]

Despite the Indians' repudiation at the Wichita Agency, the Wichita Agreement of October 19, 1872, as presented to the Senate three months later, included a clause in which the Wichitas and "other affiliated bands" relinquished all "right, title, interest, or claim of any nature whatsoever in and to any lands in Texas, Louisiana, Indian Territory, or elsewhere within the limits of the United States," in addition to accepting the boundaries of the reservation set by Commissioner Walker. Although the agreement was never ratified by the United States Senate, Congress would eventually take action based upon the fiction that it was an actual ratified agreement.[28]

In the meantime, however, the Wichita Agency tribes believed that the federal government had yet to guarantee them a reservation of any size. Their insecurities were only heightened by the unsettled situation which surrounded the agency over the next few years. White despera-does from Texas continued their predatory incursions across the Red River in 1873–74, further depleting the horse herds of all of the Wichita Agency tribes. In one of the worst instances of horse theft, Texan thieves stole sixty horses from the Indians on February 9, 1874. Agent Richards and a group of agency Indians followed the trail to the Red River and informed the Texas authorities, but they were "unable or unwilling to interfere with" the thieves, despite their identities being well known. Taovaya headman Utstutskins protested to Richards, demanding the government compensate them for their losses. Despite gaining the sup-port of Cyrus Beede, chief clerk in Superintendent Hoag's office, on the issue, no compensation of stolen property was forthcoming.[29]

Another cause for unrest at the Wichita Agency was the murder of Taovaya chief Isadowa by a group of Osage Indians in May, 1873. Isadowa and a group of Taovayas had obtained a pass from Agent Richards and traveled off the reservation to hunt buffalo. The Taovaya chief was sepa-rated from his fellows during the chase and met up with a group of Osages, who "killed him without any known provocation." Upon learn-ing of the murder, the Taovayas flew to arms and enlisted the services of the other agency tribes (as well as the Kiowas, Comanches, Cheyennes, and Arapahos) in seeking retribution from their traditional foe. Before they could mount an offensive, however, Agent Richards called a council and persuaded the Taovayas to agree to a negotiated settlement with the Osages. Soon thereafter, the Osage chiefs sent a letter of apology to the Taovayas in which they placed blame on a "band of lawless men of the tribe." Ultimately, the matter was settled at a Taovaya-Osage council in which the Osages made retribution in the form of money, horses, and goods. Taovaya warriors then met and chose Tsodiako to be their new chief.[30]

Although the Taovaya-Osage dispute was settled without further bloodshed, the main cause of the Wichita Agency tribes' insecurities— the unsettled situation on the Kiowa-Comanche Reservation—led to death and destruction in the summer of 1874. Captain Alvord's visit to the Leased District and the resulting trip to Washington had done noth-ing to ease the tensions among the Indians, their agents, and the mili-tary. Kiowa and Comanche warriors continued to raid into Texas, while the agency officials tried to bully the Indians by threatening to withhold their rations and annuities. Finally, in July, 1874, a war party of three hundred Comanches and Cheyennes, along with a few Kiowas and Arapahos, attacked a group of white buffalo hunters at Adobe Walls in the Texas Panhandle, thus initiating the so-called Buffalo War. Army officials, having lost patience with the Peace Policy, responded by deciding to terminate the Indians' fighting capabilities forever. Plans were drawn up by Gen. Philip Sheridan ordering five separate military expeditions to converge on the hostile Indian camps in the Panhandle and force them to surrender their arms and return to the reservation, no matter how long it took or how many Indian men, women, or children were killed. To avoid being considered hostile by the troops, all Indians had to be enrolled at their agencies by August 3.[31]

Although all of the Wichita Agency tribes were enrolled by the deadline, the Wichitas and Caddos were alert for trouble since most of the Comanches and many Kiowas were still off their reservation after August 3. Several days later Chief Red Food's band of renegade Nokoni Comanches, having missed the deadline, sought refuge at the Wichita Agency and established their sixty lodges near the commissary among the tepees of the Penatekas. They were later joined by a large group of Kiowas headed by Lone Wolf. Agent Richards just happened to be absent at this crucial moment, and the agency had been left in the hands of a clerk named J. Connell. When Red Food began demanding rations, Acting Agent Connell realized he was in over his head and dispatched a messenger to Fort Sill to inform the commander, Lt. Col. John W. (Black Jack) Davidson, of his predicament. At ten o'clock on the evening of August 21 Lt. Colonel Davidson led four companies of the African-American Tenth Cavalry out of Fort Sill; fourteen hours later they reached the Wichita Agency at high noon on the following day.[32]

August 22 was issue day, and the area was full of activity since all the Wichita Agency tribes had arrived to collect their weekly rations. Caddo and Wichita warriors met Lt. Colonel Davidson and escorted him to the Nokoni camp. Urged by Penateka headmen Toshaway and Esahabbe, Red Food agreed to have his men turn over their guns. However, when Davidson's adjutant insisted that the Comanches also give up their bows and arrows, they refused. Red Food gave a war whoop, and the battle was begun. Following an initial skirmish, the Nokonis headed for the bluffs behind the agency buildings, and when Lt. Colonel Davidson's soldiers turned to face them, they were fired upon from the rear by Lone Wolf's Kiowas who had hidden behind the commissary. The Kiowa fire was returned by about twenty of Guadeloupe's Kadohadachos, which turned the fight into a disorganized melee among the black soldiers, Wichita Agency tribes, and the Kiowas and Comanches. The fighting lasted throughout the rest of the day and well into the following morning before Waco chief Buffalo Good finally convinced the invaders that there had been enough killing and that they should leave.[33]

When the smoke finally cleared following the Battle of the Wichita Agency, it was found that one Kadohadacho woman had been killed and two Penateka women had been wounded. In addition, six agency employees had been killed and three soldiers wounded. The Kiowas and Comanches also had burned the commissary and looted and ransacked Trader Shirley's store. They also damaged Black Beaver's farm as well as destroyed many of the agency Indians' fields. Unfortunately for the Wichita Agency tribes, it would be almost a full year before the federal troops—assisted by Caddo and Wichita scouts—would bring in the last remaining hostile Comanche band; Quanah Parker's Quahadas finally surrendered on June 2, 1875, thus ending the Indian wars on the southern plains once and for all.[34]

In the meantime, many of the Wichita Agency Indians abandoned their crops—most of which had been destroyed by drought or the Kiowas and Comanches—and sought refuge elsewhere. About a hundred Caddos—mainly Hainais—and Delawares joined with the Shawnees, north of the Canadian River, not to return until 1877. However, almost two hundred Wichitas—mainly Taovayas and Wacos—left the Wichita Agency for good. Despite Agent Richards's claim that they joined with the Kiowas, it seems more likely they attached themselves to their linguistic cousins, the Pawnees, who were in the process of moving from Nebraska to land set aside for them in the Indian Territory. In addition, some two hundred Penateka Comanches abandoned Toshaway and Esahabbe and joined their kinsmen on the Kiowa-Comanche Reservation.[35]

Those tribespeople who did remain at the Wichita Agency suffered greatly. Because of insufficient appropriations from Congress, all rations except for beef had been exhausted by early winter. The Wichita Agency Indians were unable to supplement their meager rations because their crops had been destroyed, and they could not leave the reservation to hunt buffalo because the military operations were still being carried out. By the spring of 1875, most of the members were starving; Delaware chief Black Beaver claimed that it was the "first time he had ever been in want of food." Finally, on March 11, the agency received one hundred sacks of flour, which were issued to the desperate Indians in less than twenty minutes.[36]

Despite the great disruption to the Wichita Agency's progress caused by the battle with the Kiowas and Comanches, over the next four years the Indians were able to overcome the setback. As the planting season for 1875 approached, Agent Richards visited each tribe separately and informed them that "all would be done for them that could be done" to procure seeds and to provide them with plows and other tools lost over the past year. With these assurances the Wichita Agency Indians "seemed to take courage, and as spring opened they commenced their farming with spirit and energy beyond that of any previous year." These activities included the Wichita tribes (only the women) and the Penateka Comanches as well as the Caddos and Delawares, who not only replanted their old fields but also brought new land under cultivation. For the first time since returning to the Wichita Agency in 1868, the Indians enjoyed good weather, and together all four tribes raised a bumper crop of 45,000 bushels of corn (in addition to abundant crops of melons, peas, and beans), which tripled the agency's previous high.[37]

The bounteous production of 1875 was repeated and even surpassed by the Indians of the Wichita Agency over the next three years; by 1878 the amount of acres cultivated had increased from 1,500 to 1,900, upon which 50,000 bushels of corn were raised. The various tribes also continued to experiment with new crops to great success; in 1878 they raised 400 bushels of wheat and 3,000 bushels of oats and barley in addition to their traditional harvest of melons, peas, and beans. Stock raising continued to be important, particularly to the Caddos and Delawares, who by 1876 owned 1,552 horses and mules (a decrease by 750 from theft since 1873), 1,176 head of cattle (a decrease of 200), and 1,810 swine (an increase of 160). The four Wichita tribes concentrated on their horse and mule herd (which had declined from 1,484 in 1873 to 1,180 three years later) to the neglect of other domestic animals; they owned only 26 cows, 16 pigs, and 10 goats in 1876. The following year a small detail of soldiers from Fort Sill was stationed at the Wichita Agency to provide protection from Texas horse thieves. For the most part they were successful, and the tribes' stock increased over the next couple of years.[38]

Although the Wichitas did not raise as much cattle and swine as the Caddos and Delawares, they made up for it by hunting buffalo. With the end of hostilities on the southern plains in 1875, Wichita men, along with Penateka warriors, resumed their winter hunt and returned to the agency with 2,300 dollars' worth of buffalo robes. The Wichitas and Penatekas hunted with a military escort the next two years and were able to increase their yield by collecting 20,000 dollars' worth of buffalo robes in 1876 and 30,000 dollars' worth in 1877. Unfortunately, the Indians and whites overhunted the buffalo, and the herd dwindled to near extinction over the next few years. In 1878 the Wichitas and Penatekas only sold 11,500 dollars' worth of buffalo robes. By 1882 they had completely given up the buffalo hunt they had engaged in nearly every winter since long before the European intrusion.[39]

With their successes in agriculture and hunting, the Wichitas and the Penatekas joined the Caddos and Delawares in the building of permanent log houses. By 1878 nearly three-fourths of the Wichitas and Penatekas had forsaken their traditional lodges for log cabins, while almost the entire Caddo and Delaware population lived in the new style of home.[40]

The Riverside school continued to attract students, including Wichita children, after the Battle of the Wichita Agency. Thirty-six Wichitas (26 boys, 10 girls) attended the school during the 1875–76 term, along with 50 Caddos and Delawares (33 boys, 17 girls) and 7 Penateka Comanches (all boys), thus necessitating the construction of an extension to the boarding-school buildings. By the 1877–78 term attendance had risen to 111 children, with the average daily attendance holding steady at 88. Unfortunately, on the evening of March 29, 1878, the school caught fire and "in one hour and a half, the finest school building in the Indian Territory lay in ashes." Black Beaver's grandson, who was sick in bed with pneumonia, was the only child to die in the blaze. Despite this great setback, the school was reorganized at the agent's house, and 44 students attended every day.[41]

Thus, within four years of the catastrophic Battle of the Wichita Agency, the tribes were actually able to improve and surpass their previous accomplishments and showed great hopes for continuing their progress in the future. All these improvements had been carried out despite the loss of two of the most important men at the Wichita Agency,

Agent Richards and the Caddo caddi Guadeloupe. Richards had re-signed his post in February, 1876, after five years of exemplary service. He was replaced by fellow Quaker Andrew Williams, who continued to uphold Richards's tradition of steadfast loyalty to the tribes during his two-year term. However, Guadeloupe died thirteen months after Richards's resignation without a clear-cut successor as Caddo caddi. On March 20, 1877, the Caddos elected Winasaw (Big Man) as their chief, a man characterized by Agent Williams as being a "progressive and industrious Indian." Although he was a fine leader, Big Man was not a hereditary caddi, and, therefore, power within the Caddo tribe would become more diffused over the next few decades, despite the actual unification of the Kadohadachos and Hainais in 1874.[42]

Despite the great strides (or possibly because of them) made by the Wichita Agency tribes in the first decade after their return to the Leased District, the Indian Office decided in 1878 to consolidate the Wichita Agency with the Kiowa-Comanche Agency and establish the new head-quarters on the south bank of the Washita River. This move had been under consideration since Captain Alvord's visit in 1872, basically as a means of saving money. The consolidation had been opposed, how-ever, by the military officers at Fort Sill, mainly because they would have to divert a number of troops to protect the new agency on the Washita. Finally, in the spring of 1878 the Indian Office won out over the War Department's protests, and it was announced that the consoli-dation of the two reservations would take place later in the year.[43]

Needless to say, the Wichita Agency tribes were outraged and alarmed by the decision, which they feared would result in the destruc-tion of a decade's worth of hard work, because of the federal government's fiscal concerns. Representatives of the Caddos, Wichitas, Delawares, and Penatekas met with Agent Williams in council on June 21 and "entered their earnest protest against consolidation." They claimed that "most of us have taken the white man's road, have houses and little fields and are raising cattle and hogs and chickens." The Kiowas and Comanches, however, were "entirely uncivilized" and "could not but be detrimental to them" because they would kill the Wichita Agency Indians' cattle and steal their horses. The Wichita Agency headmen felt that the Kiowas and Comanches "hate us more than they do the white man, because we are Indians and fought against Indians, and fear that if we had to meet them, or they had to come to draw rations, somebody would be killed." The Wichita Agency tribes were supported in their protest by Lieutenant Colonel Davidson, whom the headmen had met with in July. They informed Davidson that they did not want their children to attend school with the "wild tribes" and that they were sure that the Kiowas and Comanches would "depredate in some degree upon their farms and gardens."[44]

As usual, the tribes' protests fell upon deaf ears, and the consolidation of the two agencies took place on September 1, 1878, when ex-army officer P. B. Hunt assumed control over the new Kiowa, Comanche, and Wichita Agency. Hunt's appointment as agent signaled the end of the idealistic Peace Policy, which was now considered to have been a failed experiment. The Wichitas and Caddos had done everything they could to prove its viability and had worked closely with their Quaker agents in rebuilding the Wichita Agency. The federal government, however, rewarded their efforts by abandoning the Peace Policy and callously uniting the Wichitas and Caddos with those tribes that had threatened their very existence for the past three decades, the Kiowas and Comanches.

Chapter Six

Life on the Wichita Reservation, 1879-1901

The Indians of the Wichita Reservation are a class different entirely from those on the Comanche and Kiowa reservations. They are the remnants of once powerful tribes, and have been beaten and driven from pillar to post for a hundred years or more, until now they are actually afraid to call their lives and property their own. Still they are a comparatively indus-trious people, and I believe if their rights of land property could be settled that they would be a self-supporting people. They have a large number of cattle and hogs, and have grown almost enough this season to support themselves till the crops of another season come.

—Report of Captain Frank D. Baldwin,
Kiowa, Comanche, and Wichita Agent, August 29, 1896

Soon after Agent Hunt consolidated the Kiowa, Comanche, and Wichita Agency in the fall of 1878, most of the Caddos (and the associated Dela-wares) who lived near the Washita River abandoned their lands out of fear that the Kiowas and Comanches would relocate nearby and steal their livestock. They moved to the northern part of the reservation and began reestablishing their farms over the winter. This move led to a misunderstanding between the two tribes and an angry Agent Hunt, for he had hoped that the Kiowas and Comanches might, from the good example set by "their more civilized brethren" north of the Washita, learn to be self-sufficient farmers. In response to the abandonment of their lands on the Washita, Hunt charged that the Caddos were "retro-grading" and "not progressing as they should, doubtless from the belief they have that they will always be fed and there is no use for them to make an effort." Therefore, the agent notified them that their entire ration, including beef, would be suspended on July 1, 1881, and they would be left to "depend upon their own resources."[1]

Although the Caddos eventually regained their right to receive rations, they, along with the Wichitas, did greatly "depend upon their own resources" for survival over the remaining twenty-three years of the reservation's existence. For, although the federal government's presence on the reservation expanded greatly in the final years of the nineteenth century, the Wichitas and Caddos north of the Washita were neglected by the bureaucrats in favor of the Kiowas and Comanches (as well as the much fewer Apaches) who lived to the south. Not only did the latter tribes outnumber the former by a margin of three to one, they had only recently been forced to relinquish warfare and buffalo hunting and, therefore, were seen to need more attention from the agents and support personnel, who were determined to teach them the "arts of civilization." The high turnover of agents—there were ten in the sixteen-year period which followed Hunt's seven-year stint—only reinforced the predilection to focus on the Kiowas and Comanches, since the agents never had enough time to pay much attention to the needs of the less troublesome Wichitas and Caddos.

Ironically, the two tribes actually benefited from the relative neglect of the federal government's agents. Just enough attention was paid to the tribes to provide them with basic needs—rations, protection from the hostile tribes, agricultural assistance, and education—without the agents appearing overbearing. Therefore, the Wichitas and Caddos were free to develop a life within the confines of the reservation experience that borrowed from the Euro-American culture while retaining many of the traditions they had developed over the previous centuries of interaction with whites. Admittedly, the United States in this period exerted more pressure on the Wichitas and Caddos to adopt the white man's ways than at any other point in their history. However, the government's haphazard methods, combined with the Indians' strength and determination, allowed the tribes to adapt while maintaining a degree of control over their own lives.

Hunt's first order of business upon assuming his position as Kiowa, Comanche, and Wichita agent was to relocate the agency headquarters from Fort Sill to the south bank of the Washita River, opposite from the somewhat decrepit Wichita Agency that Jonathan Richards had constructed nearly a decade before. In the fall of 1878, building began on the new agency site, called Anadarko, after the Nadaco tribe of Caddos. Anadarko, which by the end of the year contained only the agent's office, house, and warehouse, would be transformed into an actual village as the federal bureaucracy constantly grew on the reservation (and elsewhere in the West) over the course of the next two decades. By 1888 a commissary, steam saw and corn mill, a blacksmith and carpenter shop, and a dispensary had been added to the agency buildings. To these were added, by 1892, a harness shop and houses for the families of the agency employees, whose numbers had doubled by 1901 from the original twenty-four in 1878. Various schools and churches founded in this period only added to the population of Anadarko, which, with the arrival of the telegraph and railroad, had become the most important nonmilitary center in the western portion of the Indian Territory by the end of the century.[2]

Obviously, the position of agent had certainly changed since the 1840s when Robert Neighbors had handled the affairs of all the Texas Indians by himself. The Kiowa, Comanche, and Wichita agent increasingly was saddled with the management of the agency bureaucracy in the last two decades of the nineteenth century and rarely dealt directly in any meaningful way with the Indians of the reservation. The agents themselves, along with the support personnel they appointed, tended to be spoilsmen with little experience in Indian affairs, anyway. Hunt, who served as agent from 1878 to 1885, was a Republican Kentuckian who had been employed in the Bureau of Internal Revenue. With the election of Democrat Grover Cleveland as president in 1884, the new administration appointed J. Lee Hall to replace Hunt. Hall admitted that he had entered the Indian Service to become rich, and he was ultimately relieved of duty in October, 1887, for misappropriation of funds. He was replaced by Special Agent E. E. White, who had participated in his investigation. After eleven months on the job White was replaced by William D. Myers, a lumberyard manager from Missouri. Thirteen months later Myers lost his job to new Republican President Benjamin Harrison's appointee, a Baltimore grocer named Charles E. Adams. Adams lasted two years only to be replaced by fellow Maryland Republican George D. Day, who filled the post until Grover Cleveland and the Democrats won back the White House in 1892.[3]

Caddo village, 1880s. Note the transition from purely traditional housing to shelters that are a combination of Caddo and Euro-American styles. Courtesy Smithsonian Institution, National Anthropological Archives

In that same year Congress enacted a law authorizing the president the option to appoint army officers as agents. President Cleveland responded by appointing Capt. Hugh G. Brown to the position of Kiowa, Comanche, and Wichita agent. Although the shift from civilians to military officers produced somewhat more capable agents than before, their longevity in the position did not immediately increase. Captain Brown only lasted six months, and his replacement, Lt. Maury Nichols, held the position for only ten months. Maj. Frank D. Baldwin's assumption of the position of agent in November, 1894, ended a decade of constant turnover, for he remained at his post for four years. Baldwin's civilian replacement, an Oklahoma newspaperman named William T. Walker, held the position of agent for only a year until he surrendered the agency to Lt. Col. James F. Randlett on July 1, 1899. Agent Randlett would oversee the dissolution of the reservation two years later.[4]

The rapid turnover of agents, who were almost wholly unfamiliar with the complicated situation at the Kiowa, Comanche, and Wichita Agency, led to the relative neglect of the Caddos and Wichitas in the late nineteenth century. The goal of the federal government continued to be the transformation of the Indians into self-sufficient farmers and husbandmen who could easily be assimilated into white society; to any newly arrived agent at Anadarko, a quick survey of the situation clearly demonstrated that the Caddos and Wichitas were much farther "advanced" along this path than the Kiowas and Comanches, who greatly outnumbered them. Consequently, what little attention the agents could afford to pay to the Indians while managing the reservation was focused on the "backward" tribes that lived south of the Washita River. The best result the agents could hope for in regard to the Caddos and Wichitas was that they would continue on the road towards civilization and not cause too much trouble. Likewise, the two tribes north of the Washita felt the same about the agent; as long as he continued to give them a minimum of support and did not interfere too strongly in their affairs, they would not inconvenience him.

Upon the consolidation of the agency, however, Caddo and Wichita headmen immediately met with Agent Hunt to demand that he guard them from the Kiowas and Comanches, whom they feared would move from Fort Sill to the south bank of the Washita. Hunt's assurances of protection eased the Wichitas' fears, and they remained at their settlements along the lower reaches of Sugar Creek. The Caddos, though, were not convinced, and, as noted, they relocated their farms northward to be as far away from the Kiowas and Comanches as possible. Ultimately, the Caddos' apprehension proved to be unfounded as neither of the two "wild" tribes—except for a few Penatekas—moved north to the Washita, and friction among the tribes of the reservation was kept at a minimum. The danger of a Kiowa or Comanche attack, which had been ever present over the past three decades, was finally removed, and the Wichitas and Caddos were at last secure on the reservation.[5]

This security afforded the Wichitas and Caddos the opportunity to make improvements on land they believed to be theirs. Although the tribes received encouragement from Agent Hunt, the Wichitas and Caddos did almost all the work themselves. The Wichitas, realizing that they would no longer be able to supplement their income through buffalo hunting, revolutionized their farming methods; for the very first time the men joined the women in the fields. The Wichitas also began the practice of farming individual plots of land—something the Caddos had traditionally done—instead of communal gardens. By 1885 all but nine Wichita families had established their own private farms. The

Taovayas and Wacos concentrated their farms on the lower reaches of Sugar Creek, from two to five miles north of Anadarko. One group of Tawakonis, led by Tawakoni Jim, established farms a few miles above their kinsmen on Sugar Creek, while Niastor's band of Tawakonis settled with the Kichais on Keechi Hollow, a tributary of Sugar Creek, about fifteen miles from Anadarko.[6]

Most of the Wichita farms, on which the tribespeople grew corn and raised livestock, were relatively small, ranging from five to fifteen acres in size. Their livestock usually included less than ten horses and ten head of cattle per settlement. By 1885 most of the log houses the Wichitas had constructed in the previous decade had fallen down; thus, the average Wichita family lived in a traditional grass house. The Wichita headmen, however, took advantage of their elite status to build up much larger, more comfortable establishments. For example, Tawakoni Jim's ranch contained fifty acres, upon which he had two hundred head of cattle as well as fifty hogs, a peach and apple orchard, and a "good dwelling and outhouse." Waco chief Left Hand lived in a log house and owned fifteen head of cattle, forty horses, and hogs. Taovaya chief Tsodiako lived on twenty acres, and Taovaya headman Achittermax owned 150 head of cattle. Many Wichita leaders also raised poultry on their farms.[7]

Whereas only a small group of Wichita elite was able to establish large farms with many animals, most Caddos and Delawares success-fully built homesteads that equalled or surpassed those of the Wichita leaders. Of the twenty-five Caddo and Delaware farms located on Sugar Creek from twelve to fifteen miles above its mouth, only five were less than ten acres in size, while eight were larger than fifteen acres. All of the Caddos were housed in log dwellings, although the Delawares pre-ferred homes constructed of bark. Many Caddos and Delawares had placed fruit trees on their farms, and almost all of them had horses, cattle, hogs, and poultry. The eleven Caddo families that settled near George Washington's ranch near the Canadian River were even more successful. Each ranch was at least ten acres in size, and three con-tained twenty acres and one fifty. All the Canadian River Caddos had constructed log houses, and many had "good outhouses" and fences, within which they kept great numbers of stock. The few Caddos and Delawares—most were women who were married to either whites or Muskhogeans—who settled along Spring Creek, east of the agency, had

Tawakoni Jim, early 1870s. Chief of the Tawakonis throughout the reservation period, he gradually became the most important of the Wichita leaders as well. Courtesy Wilbur S. Nye Collection

the largest farms of all; none contained less than twenty acres, while four had between fifty-five and eighty acres. Another small group of Caddos and Delawares established fairly large farms on the Washita River, near old Fort Cobb; all lived in "good houses" and owned large numbers of horses and cattle.[8]

The Caddo elite, like the Wichita headmen, accumulated more property than their fellow members; the difference was that the elite group was much larger among the Caddos. By 1885 Winasaw, who had been elected Caddo chief in 1877, and George Washington, leader of the Whitebeads, were dead. Instead of only two men emerging to replace them, many Caddo leaders came to the fore. This diffusion of power was reinforced by the agent's decision to divide the Caddos into groups led by "beef chiefs," whose job it was to supervise the division of rations. The Caddos on Sugar Creek were led by five men—George Parton, Kahnoustu, White Bread, Inkanish, and John Wilson—all of whom owned large farms with much livestock. White Bread alone had two hundred horses, Kahnoustu had fifty hogs, and John Wilson owned fifty head of cattle, forty hogs, and twenty horses. The Canadian River Caddos were led by large property owners such as Caddo Jake, Nouche, Coffee, and Johnson. Being rich, however, did not always translate to political power. There were many Caddos (like Bill Pardier, who had an eighty-acre farm on Spring Creek) who never assumed the position of chief. Hereditary ties were still needed to become an important political figure; both White Bread and Caddo Jake—the two unofficial Caddo leaders by the turn of the century—were descendants of caddis from the past.[9]

While the traditionally hierarchical Caddos opened up their political system on the reservation, ironically, the more democratic Wichitas tightened theirs. Not only did the Wichita elite accumulate more property than the average tribesman, they monopolized political power as well. The richest Wichita, Jim of the Tawakonis, was considered to be the chief of the Wichitas at the turn of the century. In part, this economic success was the result of his longevity; he was one of the few Wichita chiefs who was in office during the entire reservation period. The Taovaya chief, Tsodiako, died around 1892 and was succeeded by two men, Kecatesquocuddyow and Kewitsiddy. Chief Left Hand, of the Wacos, died in the late 1880s only to be replaced by a succession of short-lived chiefs. Only Kauwiddyhuntis, the Kichai chief, joined Tawakoni Jim in leading his tribe through the turn of the century. Unlike the Caddos, however, the Wichitas did not divide into beef bands—it is unclear whether they refused or the agents did not make the attempt—and political power, as well as economic advantages, remained in the hands of only a few men.[10]

Although the Wichitas and Caddos were able to establish individual homesteads soon after the consolidation of the reservation, they still needed to find a way to raise money for the items they needed—such as plows and harnesses—to work their farms. In the past the Wichitas and

Caddos had been able to supplement what they raised in their gardens through the chase; they would keep the meat and sell the hides (mainly buffalo for the Wichitas, deer for the Caddos) to the official traders. The beef ration helped a bit to make up for the absence of hunting but did not bring in any money. Agent Hunt, though, provided them a source of outside income, beginning in July, 1879, by hiring men from all the tribes on the reservation to work as freighters, carrying supplies from the nearest railhead—either at Caldwell, Kansas, about 150 miles away, or Arkansas City, Kansas, 175 miles away—back to the agency. The few Indians who owned wagons, such as George Washington, used their own, while Agent Hunt allowed the others to purchase wagons on credit, paying for them with what they earned hauling goods. All of the eighty or so Indians who ended up carrying freight provided their own animals to pull the wagons. Freighting proved to be a "perfect success" for the first few years, and the Indians earned about ten thousand dollars per year, or between one hundred and two hundred dollars per freighter. In 1885, however, bad weather made the streams on the road impassable, and much of the year's supplies sat at the railhead in Kansas. Over the next few years the railroads began to approach the reservation—first reaching Henrietta, Texas, eighty-five miles away, and then Paul's Valley, Oklahoma, only seventy miles down the Washita River from Anadarko—and the freighter's haul became much easier. Since the volume of delivered goods increased, the Indians' income remained about the same despite the shorter distance they now traveled.[11]

A few Caddos and Wichitas also earned extra money by working in the sawmill or joining the Indian police, whose main job consisted of keeping Texas cattle rustlers off the southern part of the reservation where the Kiowas and Comanches grazed their herds. In the 1890s all the tribes of the reservation earned "grass money" by leasing the unoccupied portions of their lands to white cattle raisers. These leases tended to be bargains for the cattlemen; for example, in 1898 twelve grazing leases, amounting to 220,000 acres, were granted for the Wichita portion of the reservation. In return for leasing nearly one-third of their lands to the cattlemen, the Wichitas, Caddos, and Delawares received about fourteen thousand dollars, or fourteen dollars for every man, woman, and child. Although no one on the reservation got rich from the outside income, the extra money did allow the tribes north of the

Washita to purchase items such as farm tools, seed, stock, and lumber for their houses to make the necessary improvements on their farms. By 1895 nearly every Wichita and Caddo family lived on a well-fenced farm in a wooden house, for the Wichitas had finally abandoned their traditional grass abodes during the previous decade.[12]

Despite the great efforts the Wichitas and Caddos made on their farms—generally with the assistance of only one government farmer—only rarely did the tribes raise enough food to feed themselves and thus were dependent upon the insufficient government rations just to make it through the year without starving. The reason for the continued failure of the Indians' crops was, of course, the natural dryness of the western plains, a condition the early agents mistakenly concluded was just a temporary drought. Since the goal of the federal government was to turn the Indian into a self-sufficient yeoman farmer, the agents pressured the tribes to grow crops on their small farms despite the lack of rainfall. The Wichitas and Caddos were inclined to do this anyway, since, in following the agent's desires, they were only continuing to practice the traditional agricultural methods they had developed in their ancestral homes in the more humid lands to the east.

This practice proved disastrous, since, as Agent Baldwin finally realized in 1897, "a favorable season . . . with abundant rainfall . . . could not be looked for, judging from the past, more often than once in six or seven years." Unfortunately, this statement was true; often, though, there would come one good year of rainfall after a few years of dryness, which would give the ever-optimistic agents (and the Indians) the belief that the "drought" had been temporary and the weather was bound to improve permanently. The corn crop on the reservation in 1879 was "almost a failure," but the following year it was "far better than has been grown for some years." This success gave Agent Hunt and the Wichitas and Caddos great hope, and in the spring of 1881 they were "unusually active, getting ready their plows and harnesses" for spring planting. Rain fell "at the proper intervals" throughout the spring; however, not a drop fell after May, and the entire crop was destroyed. Two years later, though, the rains came, and the crop yield was so great the members were able to sell a surplus to the traders. The weather reverted to form again in 1884 and remained dry until 1888 when the season was "propitious."[13]

By this time the agents and the government farmers had introduced more weather-resistant crops, such as kafir corn (to feed the stock), barley, oats, and sweet potatoes, to the receptive Wichitas and Caddos. Lack of government support, however, precluded the full-scale adoption of the one crop that could succeed on the plains, wheat. Although the two tribes raised small amounts of wheat, Congress refused to provide the money needed to build a flour mill, forcing Agent White to conclude in 1888 that "the wheat crop is almost valueless to them," despite a good yield. The weather remained sufficiently wet in 1889, but "excessive dryness" was the norm from 1890 through 1896. Despite two good years following the seven-year drought, Agent Baldwin admitted that the Indians should put less effort in agriculture and focus instead on stock raising, since the land was best suited for cattle, and "in most instances, [the Indians] are caring for their stock as well or better than the average white man."[14]

The idea to concentrate on stock raising finally came after two decades worth of failed attempts to raise crops. During many of those twenty years, the Wichitas and Caddos were weakened from lack of food and thus were susceptible to disease. During the first few years following the consolidation of the reservation, outbreaks of malaria were an annual occurrence; eventually, the Wichitas and Caddos learned to build their homes away from low-lying ground and incidents of "malarial fever" subsided. Throughout the period, though, the Indians continued to be plagued by whooping cough, measles, and influenza. In some years—1880, 1883, 1890—these diseases reached epidemic proportions. The worst outbreak of disease occurred in 1891 and 1892, when the Kiowa, Comanche, and Wichita reservations were struck by whooping cough, followed by measles and pneumonia. Nearly four hundred Indians (about 10 percent of the total population of both reservations) perished.[15]

Thus, for the first time in nearly half a century, despite having land it could securely call its own, the Wichita and Caddo population continued to decline on the reservation. The less prosperous Wichitas—who were also in the process of shifting from a mixed-farming and hunting economy—suffered the most. The total Wichita population hovered around 500 for the first five years following consolidation (see table). However, during the four-year drought which lasted until 1888, the Wichitas lost almost 100 people. The epidemics and drought of the 1890s continued to take their toll on the tribe, and by 1898 there were

Tribe Populations, 1879–1900

YEAR	CADDO	TAOVAYA	TAWAKONI	WACO	KICHAI	WICHITA
1879	543	209	155	49	75	488
1880	538	192	145	47	74	458
1881	552	206	151	49	77	483
1882	553	214	152	49	78	493
1883	535	216	162	51	77	506
1884	556	209	163	40	79	491
1885	570	199	162	39	74	474
1886	521	187	143	30	82	442
1887	525	192	157	37	72	458
1888	491	165	143	30	64	402
1889	512	164	145	29	62	400
1890	538	174	150	34	66	424
1891	545	175	150	35	66	426
1892	526	151	135	41	54	381
1893	507	153	126	37	52	368
1894	522	157	128	36	52	373
1895	498	—	—	—	—	—
1896	476	—	—	—	—	365
1897	494	—	—	—	—	364
1898	493	—	—	—	—	367
1899	—	—	—	—	—	—
1900	497	—	—	—	—	—

Sources: Annual Report of the Commissioner of Indian Affairs, except 1894, 1897, 1898, each from KAL 1.

only 367 Wichitas left. This 27 percent population decline over two decades was equally destructive to all four Wichita tribes: the Taovayas experienced a 25 percent population loss, the Tawakonis a 19 percent loss, the Wacos a 26 percent loss, and the Kichais a 30 percent decline.[16] Life on the reservation in the last quarter of the nineteenth century, then, proved to be only marginally better for the Wichitas' overall health than during the miserable Civil War years, when the tribal numbers fell from about 1,100 to 700, or a decline of 36 percent.

By remaining relatively healthy, the more prosperous Caddos—who were, for the most part, carrying out their traditional farming methods—actually had more people than the declining Wichitas (for the first time since the European intrusion) by the end of the century. The Caddo population hovered around 550 until the 1890s when hunger and disease caused a 15 percent decline to 493 in 1898 (table 1). Although this decline was a bit better than the 20 percent population loss the Caddos had experienced during the Civil War, the decrease did nothing to make the members satisfied with their situation on the reservation.

Although the Caddos and Wichitas modified their political systems, settlement patterns, and agricultural practices during the final two decades of the nineteenth century, these reforms were the tribes' natural responses to the new realities that confronted them on the reservation. For the most part, the Caddos and Wichitas made these changes on their own, with only little interference from the agents. The agents and the federal government, however, did take a great interest in providing the tribal children with an education, either at the Riverside Indian School on the reservation or at various Indian schools located around the country. Almost all whites accepted as gospel the idea that the education of Indian youth would successfully break tribal ties, resulting in the graduation of a "civilized" adult who would turn his back on his "savage" past and eagerly enter the Euro-American world. All the agents shared Agent Williams's belief that "there can be no question that a properly conducted school for educating the children of Indian parents is the main element in the great work of civilizing and Christianizing the Indians, and if continued under proper influences will ultimately accomplish that end." W. T. Calmes, who held the position of superintendent of Riverside from 1879 to 1884, stated bluntly that "school is among the most powerful agencies employed to improve these people [the Wichitas and Caddos], to change them from barbarians . . . to a civilized, and consequently, self-supporting people." Ultimately, this accepted truth proved to be wholly false; although most Wichita and Caddo children attended schools in the late nineteenth century, few were transformed into facsimiles of whites or had any inclination to abandon their tribe.[17]

Just as with other practices introduced to the Indians, the federal government put great stock in the idea that education would "civilize" the tribes, but it often did not follow up its claim with the funding necessary to complete the task. Agent Hunt's first order of educational business following the consolidation of the agency was to construct a school building to replace the one that had burned down in the spring of 1878. After discovering that all the bids to build a schoolhouse were above the sums Congress had appropriated, Hunt had an eight-room building constructed at minimum expense by the agency carpenter. It was not completed until October, 1879, and the school session began on the twentieth. This frame building lasted for two terms until it, and the adjoining dwelling house, burned to the ground on December 15, 1881. School was resumed a few days later in an unoccupied trader's store-house; this "temporary" move lasted four years, until 1885 when Congress finally appropriated enough money to construct a new school made of brick. Unfortunately, this new building, in addition to being far too small to accommodate all the Wichita and Caddo students who wished to attend, was also "a frail structure and a fraud upon the government, and would be unsafe in any severe windstorm." Despite the constant complaints of the agents and school superintendents, no money was forthcoming, and sleeping quarters for the children had to be impro-vised. The pupils were often forced to sleep three to a bed or in tents made of torn canvas, which allowed the rain to seep in. Not until 1899 did the government get around to constructing adequate dormitories and a mess hall for the children.[18]

Because of inadequate facilities, attendance at Riverside was un-even during the first decade or so following the consolidation of the reservation. In the first years of the new school's existence, Wichita parents eagerly enrolled their children; in 1880, even after sickness kept many students away, forty-seven of the seventy school-age Wichita children attended daily. The Caddos were less enthusiastic, as only twenty-eight of sixty school-age children attended daily. Although Wichita and Caddo boys outnumbered the girls almost two to one, the boys ran away much more often, preferring the relative freedom of their parents' homes over the stifling atmosphere of the boarding school. Hardly any students of either sex attended Riverside during the four years classes were held in the "temporary" school in the trader's store-house; only twenty Wichitas and eleven Caddos were regular pupils in 1884. However, students of both sexes and tribes flocked to the new brick schoolhouse which opened in 1885. Although the school officially had room enough for only sixty-five boarders, ninety or so Wichita and Caddo boys and girls regularly attended Riverside—without running away—throughout the 1890s. Although this number accounted for only about half of the school-age children, the rest of the Caddo and Wichita children either attended religiously affiliated mission schools, which opened on the reservation in the last decade of the nineteenth century, or went to nonreservation schools. By 1900, then, the Caddos and Wichitas had completely accepted mandatory school attendance for their children.[19]

The curriculum at Riverside—and at the mission schools—resembled that of any other public boarding school in the United States. Strict procedures were followed; students wore uniforms and were instructed to form precise lines for drill and to march to school and to meetings. Half the day was spent in the classroom where the children of both sexes learned math, history, geography, and the reading and writing of English. The boys and girls then split up for the rest of the day and were given instructions in the practical arts, which reflected the Victorian expectations of the era. The boys cut wood, hauled water, and tended to the animals and the fields of the school farm. The girls remained inside where they learned how to cook, sew, wash, iron, and do "general housework." To some extent, these practices reversed traditional Caddo and Wichita sex roles and reinforced the Euro-American roles both tribes were in the process of adopting; in the past both Caddo men and women had worked together in the fields, but only the Wichita women had engaged in agriculture.[20]

Although the curriculum at Riverside taught the Indian children how to be farmers or housewives, it did not succeed in breaking tribal ties. In fact, the focus on agricultural instruction—Congress refused to appropriate funds for an industrial arts building, which would have given the boys training in manual skills—only reinforced the Wichita and Caddo boys' disposition to stay on the reservation and take up farming, like their elders. Frank Thackeray, who assumed the position of Riverside's superintendent in 1899, complained that the Wichitas and Caddos lacked "the ambition to rise or to do anything further than to satisfy their natural and inherited appetites."[21]

Agent Hunt had realized the shortcomings of Riverside as early as 1881, and he heartily endorsed the idea of educating the Indian children at government-run boarding schools off the reservation. Hunt, like many educators of his era, believed that the nonreservation schools had the advantage of keeping the Indian child "from the influences of the camp [and] . . . deprived [him] entirely of any participation in the Indian savage customs and rites for a period of years, probably long enough to fairly establish him in the ways of civilized life."[22]

This view was fully shared by an officer in the U.S. Army, Richard Henry Pratt, who, with full government support, opened Carlisle Indian Industrial School in 1879.[23] Pratt firmly believed that Indians should be completely integrated into white society and thus combined education—with an emphasis on manual and industrial labor—with the "outing system," which placed students during the summer with rural families in the vicinity of Carlisle, Pennsylvania. A group of eight Wichitas (four boys and four girls) were among the first students from the Kiowa, Comanche, and Wichita Agency to attend a nonreservation school when they arrived at Carlisle in 1880 for the standard three-year term. The first Caddo student enrolled at Carlisle two years later was followed by only twelve fellow Caddos (nine boys and three girls) over the next twenty years. However, three more Wichitas attended Carlisle after the initial eight pupils.[24]

This was the result of Pratt's own success; he was a master of self-promotion, and he made Carlisle the prototype of the government-sponsored nonreservation schools that proliferated in the late nineteenth century. One of these schools, Chilocco Indian Agricultural School, founded in north-central Oklahoma in 1882, attracted many more Wichita and Caddo students than distant Carlisle. Between 1884 and 1900, 102 Caddos (71 boys and 31 girls) and 73 Wichitas (60 boys and 13 girls) enrolled for a three-year term at Chilocco. A small number of Wichitas and Caddos also attended the Haskell Institute, a government nonreservation school founded in Lawrence, Kansas, in 1884. Even fewer attended private schools, such as the Hampton Normal and Agricultural Institute in Virginia and White's Manual Labor Institute in Indiana, which received support from the federal government for providing instruction to Indian children, in addition to their regular students.[25]

Whereas almost all the Wichita and Caddo children attended Chilocco at some point in their educational career—usually after a stint at Riverside—only the children of the elite families, for the most part, traveled to the distant nonreservation schools. For example, Percy, son of Taovaya chief Tsodiako, was among the first Wichitas to attend Carlisle. He was followed two years later by the children of Waco chief Buffalo Good and of headman Long Soldier. Among the Caddo pupils who attended Carlisle were the mixed-blood children of Trader William Shirley and Farmer J. J. Sturm, both of whom were eventually adopted by the tribe. Tawakoni Jim, the most important leader of the Wichitas, sent his son, Charley Swift, to White's Institute.[26]

Whether the students were from elite families or not, or whether they attended Carlisle, Chilocco, or White's Institute, Wichita and Caddo children received basically the same instruction at all the nonreservation schools. Just as at Riverside, the students were instilled with military discipline, and manual training was divided by sex. However, federal government money flowed more freely to the nonreservation schools, and the Wichita and Caddo boys also received instruction in industrial arts such as blacksmithing, tinsmithing, shoemaking, printing, and carpentry. Although the Wichita and Caddo children often ran away from the nonreservation schools for short periods of time (especially from nearby Chilocco), most seemed to enjoy the experience, and it was common for some to stay on for a second three-year term before returning to the reservation. Very few children, though, shared the views of Minnie Finley, from the family of Caddo headman John Wilson, who spent nine years at Carlisle. Looking forward to her impending graduation in 1899, she informed Agent Baldwin that she was "very thankful that I was so richly blessed by being sent . . . to the grand school with all its advantages, privileges, and happiness. I wish . . . that other children of our tribe might have the chance that I have had, but I am sorry to say they seem to have no care to develop themselves for a higher, better life. I have seen their condition and have studied the way of my people, and I have no desire to return to live with them, but for myself I prefer living in a civilized community."[27]

Unlike Minnie Finley, most Wichitas and Caddos did not fulfill the government's desire that they eagerly enter white society following their experience at the nonreservation schools. Instead, they returned to their tribes armed with their new skills only to find them of no use on the reservation. As early as 1885, Agent Hunt regretted that he could give the returning students "no employment, nor have any funds out of which they can be paid for labor; so they must go to the camps and live with their people." A decade later, Agent Baldwin complained that "it is a notorious fact that graduates from nonreservation schools are sent back to the reservation without a cent in their pockets . . . and with little or no disposition to go to work at farming or stock raising, absolutely dependent upon the government or friends for their living." Thus, instead of "lifting" the Indian children into white society, often the nonreservation education made them unfit even for traditional agricultural work with their fellow tribespeople. By the turn of the century, then, the federal government returned its focus to schools located on the reservation.[28]

Educational options available to Wichita and Caddo schoolchildren on the reservation increased in the 1890s with the founding of several mission schools by various religious groups who sought to convert the Indians to Christianity. Christianity, like education, had always been considered by most reformers as a key element in the assimilation of Indians into white society. Although the Peace Policy had turned the administration of the Wichita Reservation over to the Quakers, it was the Baptists who had the most success in gaining converts. These conversions may have been the result, in part, of the fact that two of the first Baptist missionaries who arrived among the Wichitas, Caddos, and Delawares in 1878 were Tulsey Minco, a Seminole, and John McIntosh, a Creek. These two succeeded in winning the favor of the headmen of the various tribes, most importantly Delaware chief Black Beaver, who died in May, 1880, and was given a Christian burial, presided over by Reverend Minco. This incident drew only more support from the tribespeople, and by the end of the year the two Baptists had attracted enough followers to build a church—called Rock Springs— about five miles north of Anadarko, in which they held weekly meetings. Throughout the rest of the century, Rock Springs Baptist Church—often presided over by Indian preachers—continually drew great numbers of Wichita and Caddo followers.[29]

In the late 1880s representatives of other Christian denominations arrived on the reservation and began to compete with the Baptists for Wichita and Caddo members. To gain followers and to fulfill their evangelical duties, these missionaries also opened schools known as "contract schools" because they received financial support from the federal government. Since the facilities at Riverside could not accommodate all the Wichita and Caddo children who desired an education, the mission schools experienced some degree of success in the last decade of the nineteenth century. The missionaries themselves, however, were less successful in persuading the adults to become members of their particular church.[30]

Methodist missionary John Jasper Methvin arrived at the Kiowa, Comanche, and Wichita Agency in 1887 and within three years had constructed a church and school near Anadarko. Although Methvin made the rounds and preached at the various Wichita and Caddo settlements north of the Washita River, only a few children (three Caddos and two Wichitas) responded to his call, and the Methvin Institute School was peopled mainly with Kiowa and Comanche students. The Presbyterians who opened Mary Gregory Memorial School about four miles east of Anadarko in 1894 did not fare any better than the Methodists, for only eight Caddos (as well as eight Delawares) attended the school before the turn of the century. In response to the efforts of their Protestant brethren, the Baptists opened the Wichita Baptist Mission School near Rock Springs Baptist Church in 1891. Predictably, it did better than the upstart Methodists and Presbyterians and attracted thirty-eight students—mainly Wichitas—in 1896, the last year the federal government gave money to the mission schools.[31]

The contract school of the Catholic Church proved to be more successful in attracting students—especially Caddos—than the Protestant schools. Father Isidore Richlin, with financial support from Philadelphia philanthropist Katherine Drexel, opened Saint Patrick's Mission just west of Anadarko in 1892. Although the Caddos had rejected Spanish Catholic missionaries two centuries before, priests had lived in their midst for another one hundred years or so, and the tribe was very familiar with its teachings. As a result, Caddo children flocked to Saint Patrick's—thirty-nine in 1894—throughout the 1890s. Father Isidore had a lot to do with the success of the mission, since he seemed to possess a much warmer personality than the relatively stern Protestants. The fact that the Catholics allowed the pupils to speak Caddo—which was strictly forbidden at Riverside and the other schools—made it easier for Saint Patrick's to attract students. In addition, many Caddo adults abandoned Rock Springs Baptist Church and were baptized at Saint Patrick's.[32]

Although most Caddos and Wichitas were members of some sort of Christian church by the 1890s, their affiliation did not mean that they had fully adopted the whites' religion any more than other adaptations

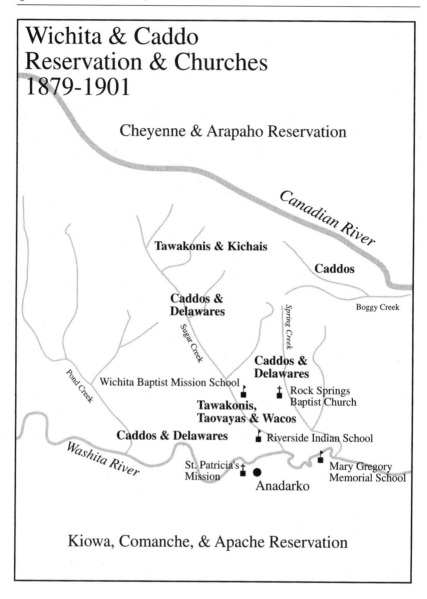

Wichita & Caddo
Reservation & Churches
1879-1901

Cheyenne & Arapaho Reservation

Canadian River

Tawakonis & Kichais

Caddos

Caddos &
Delawares

Boggy Creek

Spring Creek

Sugar Creek

Caddos &
Delawares

Pond Creek

Wichita Baptist Mission School

Rock Springs
Baptist Church

Tawakonis,
Taovayas & Wacos

Caddos & Delawares

Riverside Indian School

Washita River

St. Patricia's
Mission

Mary Gregory
Memorial School

Anadarko

Kiowa, Comanche, & Apache Reservation

they made on the reservation meant they had turned their backs on
their tribal ways. Their loyalty is made most evident by both tribes'
eager acceptance of the two native religious movements which rapidly
swept through the West in the decade: the Ghost Dance and peyotism.
Although a few tribes adopted these religions as an explicit rejection of

Euro-American values, the Caddos and Wichitas embraced them as a means of making sense of their new world, one in which they remained Indians, even though they were forced to accept the whites' ways in a necessary attempt to make a useful new life on the reservation.

The Ghost Dance religion was begun by Wovoka, a Paiute shaman in Nevada, who began preaching his message to his fellow tribesmen in the late 1880s. Combining Christian doctrines and native mysticism, the messiah promised that if all Indians would remain at peace, live honest and industrious lives, and perform the Ghost Dance, the "time will come when the whole Indian race, living and dead, will be reunited upon a regenerated earth, to live a life of aboriginal happiness, forever free from death, disease, and misery." Wovoka's uplifting and hopeful message was eagerly received by many western tribes, which had been reduced to a relatively miserable existence on their reservations by 1890. Some tribes—the Sioux, in particular—modified Wovoka's nonviolent peace message and made it into one of antagonism toward whites. The agents caused great turmoil on the various Sioux reservations in 1890 by attempting to suppress the new religion. As a result, by the end of the year, Sitting Bull, the famous Sioux religious leader and Ghost Dance proponent, had been killed by Indian police, and the U.S. Army had massacred 150 Sioux men, women, and children at Wounded Knee. The white response was different in the Indian Territory; in late 1890 Lt. Hugh L. Scott was ordered to investigate the religion among the tribes of Oklahoma, and he reported that there was no danger, since no tribe there had expressed explicitly antiwhite religious teachings, and he advised the government to follow a policy of noninterference. Thus, the Ghost Dance religion was able to flourish peacefully among the tribes of the Indian Territory.[33]

The tribes of the western portion of the Indian Territory were introduced to the Ghost Dance religion by a Northern Arapaho, also named Sitting Bull, who had traveled to Nevada in late 1889 with a delegation of Sioux and Northern Cheyennes to meet with Wovoka personally. In September, 1890, Sitting Bull held a meeting for the Southern Cheyennes and Arapahos on the north bank of the South Canadian River, just across the river from the Wichita Reservation. This meeting, in which Sitting Bull explained and performed the Ghost Dance for his audience, was attended by a large number of Caddos, Wichitas, and Kiowas. One of the Caddo headmen, John Wilson, joined in the ceremony with Sitting Bull and fell into a trance—the desired result of the Ghost Dance—in which he claimed to have visited the spirit world and saw "just what heaven is like."[34]

Wilson then returned to his reservation and exuberantly spread the word to the receptive Caddos and Wichitas. Both tribes fervently took up the Ghost Dance and refused to abandon it like the Kiowas did when one of their members, Apiatan, labeled the religion a hoax in February, 1891, after meeting with Wovoka. Instead, the Caddos and Wichitas sent their own delegation to meet with the messiah in the fall of 1891, and they returned to the reservation with increased reverence for Wovoka and, in accordance with his instructions, new times and methods of dancing. The Caddos usually danced with the Delawares—the leader, John Wilson, was half Delaware, one-fourth Caddo, and one-fourth French—near Caddo Jake's on Boggy Creek, but the Wichitas held their dances on Sugar Creek among Niastor's band of Tawakonis. The dances took place every six weeks and continued for five consecutive days, often beginning in the middle of the afternoon and lasting until daybreak. The dance was conducted around a pole and was set to various songs that were either borrowed from the Arapahos or made up by tribal members during visions. During the ceremony many dancers would fall into a trance that sometimes lasted up to half an hour.[35]

Despite the fervor with which the Caddos and Wichitas took up the Ghost Dance, the longed-for millennium never occurred, and within a few years the dance was discontinued, except for occasional social, instead of religious, gatherings. It was at this point, however, that John Wilson began spreading a new religion called peyotism, based upon the ingestion of the "buttons" of the peyote plant, a cactus of northern Mexico. When eaten, the dried peyote buttons produce a "warm and pleasant euphoria, an agreeable point of view, relaxation, colorful visual distortions, and a sense of timelessness." Natives had been using peyote ceremonially long before the arrival of Europeans, and by the early nineteenth century most of the tribes of Texas, including the Caddos and Wichitas, were familiar with the plant. It was not until the spread of the Ghost Dance religion, however, that Wilson popularized a ritual to be followed when ingesting peyote which gained great acceptance among many western Indians and continues to be a key ceremony of the Native American Church today.[36]

Wilson, also known as Nishkuntu, or Moon Head, became familiar with peyote in 1880 when he ate eight to fifteen buttons a night several times during a two-week period while "learning from the peyote" how to direct a peyote ritual. Although Wilson claimed to have learned the ceremony through divine revelation, a similar ceremony was also being developed among the Comanches called the Half Moon. Wilson's ritual was called the Big Moon or Moonhead ceremony and differed from the Half Moon in the shape of the altar that was used. Both preached the idea that peyote teaches one to think good thoughts and to discern between good and evil. The user should learn from peyote, for it comes from God and is therefore good. Although both ceremonies preached against the use of alcohol, Wilson's Big Moon was heavily influenced by Christianity and incorporated such familiar icons as Jesus, the crucifix, and the Bible. Wilson himself exhorted his followers to practice sexual restraint and marital fidelity, in addition to refraining from violence.[37]

Wilson's blending of the Half Moon and Christianity proved popular among the Wichitas and Caddos as well as to people from other tribes, especially in the wake of the fervor caused by the Ghost Dance. By 1895 Wilson was characterized as a missionary for peyotism, and he spread his ritual eastward to the reservations of the Osages and the Quapaws, who then influenced other tribes in the area. Among the Caddos, headman Enoch Hoag—descendant of Nadaco caddi Iesh—developed his own variation of the Big Moon ceremony, which also drew many followers. Although Wilson died in 1901, after having been struck by a train while returning from the Quapaw Reservation, peyotism continued to spread among the western tribes, and in 1918 the Native American Church was founded for the express purpose of keeping their peyote use from being outlawed by the federal government.[38]

The eagerness with which the Caddos and Wichitas took up both the Ghost Dance and peyotism, despite the millennial connotations of the former, did not represent an outright rejection of the new life they were in the process of adopting on the reservation. In fact, even as John Wilson—a Caddo headman who lived in a log house on a thirteen-acre farm that contained twenty horses, forty hogs, and fifty head of cattle—was leading his members in the Ghost Dance and the Big Moon ritual, he wrote a letter in 1893 in which he appealed to the commissioner of Indian affairs to permit the Caddos to send their children to Saint Patrick's Mission School since most "of us Caddos Indian Believe [sic] in the

John Wilson (seated), *along with a Delaware or Caddo man, 1893. Wilson, or Moon Head, introduced his peyote ritual to many tribes in Indian territory. Courtesy Smithsonian Institution, National Anthropological Archives*

Catholic Church."[39] Obviously, most Caddos and Wichitas had accepted their fate on the reservation and realized that it was the best they could hope for in the face of the powers of the federal government.

Rather than reject this reality, the Ghost Dance and peyotism represented an attempt by the Wichitas and Caddos to understand and bring order to their new world. Euro-American Christianity was insufficient for such a task, so, the members modified Christianity to meet their own distinct needs. Both movements preached peace and harmony among Indians as well as whites, but peyotism also stressed knowledge, truth, and understanding. Both the Ghost Dance and peyotism also called for temperance, and the latter preached sexual restraint. Both movements were attempts to provide a path to follow in this new, unfamiliar life on the reservation, a path proscribed by Indians, not handed down by alien whites. Although the Ghost Dance craze passed quickly, peyotism only gained strength over the years, and those Caddos and Wichitas who did not join the Native American Church and who continued to practice either Catholicism or the Baptist faith did so in a manner that incorporated their native beliefs instead of rejecting them.

Thus, the Ghost Dance religion and peyotism represented an acceptance by the Caddos and Wichitas of the realities of the reservation experience. This acceptance did not mean, though, that the members were ready to give up their tribal identities and embrace the Euro-American world; instead they had only reordered their Native American identity to fit their new situation, something the Wichitas and Caddos had been doing for over two centuries. Unfortunately, this effort did not satisfy federal government officers, who felt that all the Indians should completely give up their Indian ways and become whites. Thus, just as the Wichitas and Caddos (and other Indians) were becoming used to life on the reservation, the federal government decided that the only way to completely transform the Indians and break tribal ties was to dissolve the reservations altogether.

Chapter Seven

Dissolution of the Wichita Reservation

We beg to assure our Great Father that we are doing our best, we are trying to teach our young men and children the way of the white man, and we believe if not too much hurried, that in a few years we will be able to make our own selections, if we have granted to us a country of our own, where we can build cabins, clear our grounds, make our homes, and raise our children. Then we will be glad to say to our Father your children have traveled the white man's road awhile, he finds it good, and we want you to allot to us our homes. My people have instructed me to say to you that they hope you will set aside the order designating . . . when allotments should be made.

—Caddo chief White Bread, February 3, 1888

Even as the Wichitas and Caddos were making improvements on their reservation and incorporating items of Euro-American culture into their own life-styles, the federal government was taking steps, yet again, to undermine their efforts. Despite the continued attempts of reformers to introduce "civilization" to the Indians on the reservations, Native Americans throughout the United States clung tenaciously to their old ways and remained devoted to the integrity of their tribes. Reformers believed that tribalism was the greatest barrier to the assimilation of individual Indians into white society, and many of their programs—education, agriculture, and Christianity—were designed to break the bonds of the tribe. Although many tribes, such as the Wichitas and Caddos, accepted these innovations, tribalism had not been eradicated, much to the reformers' dismay.

In response to the persistence of tribalism, in 1887 Congress passed the Dawes General Allotment Act, a bill designed to break the Indians' ties to the tribe and put them on equal footing with white citizens by teaching them the value of private property. The Dawes Act authorized the president to allot small plots of reservation land—in keeping with the republican ideal of the yeoman farmer—to individual Indians: one hundred sixty acres to each family head, eighty acres to each single person over eighteen and each orphan under eighteen, and forty acres to other single persons under eighteen. Once an Indian received his allotment, he would become a citizen of the United States. The government would hold the allotted land in trust for twenty-five years to protect the allottee and his heirs while they learned the skills of managing a private farm. Then the government would issue a fee patent— a deed of unrestricted ownership—and the supposedly wiser allottee would be free, just like any other citizen, to dispose of his land in any way he wished.[1]

Although the Dawes Act was promoted as a humanitarian measure—it was believed that the Indians' survival depended upon their assimilation into white society—it also satisfied the demands of a land-hungry white populace. For, after the reservation lands had been allotted, the government would purchase the surplus lands and sell them to white homesteaders; the money paid to the Indians for the surplus reservation lands would be held in the U.S. Treasury for the sole use of the tribe. Although the humanitarian part of the Dawes Act failed miserably in achieving its goals—ultimately the Indians did not assimilate and actually became more dependent upon the federal government—the disposal of reservation lands was a complete success as whites gained 86 million of 138 million acres of Indian land between 1887 and 1934.[2]

Even though Wichita and Caddo members had already constructed individual family farms, they were unanimously opposed to allotment. Not only did they remain tied to the integrity of their tribes they also realized that allotment would cause them to lose most of the land of their reservation, the boundaries of which had yet to be satisfactorily defined. Thus, the Wichitas and Caddos were forced to fight a two-pronged legal battle with the federal government in the last decades of the nineteenth century: one, which opposed the allotment of their lands, and a second, which sought to extend the boundaries of their reservation. As was usually the case in their struggles with the federal government, the Wichitas and Caddos lost on both issues.

The debate over the Wichita Reservation boundary dated back to the decade prior to the passage of the Dawes Act. The Wichitas and Caddos had immediately disavowed the Wichita Agreement of October 19, 1872, upon the return of their members from Washington later that year. To make their protests official, on September 17, 1877, the Wichitas, Caddos, and Delawares met in council and reestablished their claim to the lands west of the boundary that Commissioner Walker had set in 1872. They now claimed that the south boundary of the reservation should be run up the Washita River from the 98th meridian to a point thirty miles west of Fort Cobb, then due west to the North Fork of the Red River to the 100th meridian. The western boundary would be the 100th meridian north to the Canadian River, which formed the northern boundary back down to the 98th meridian, the eastern boundary. Not only did this new boundary double the size of the Wichita Reservation by extending the western boundary by approximately eighty miles, it also encroached upon lands south of the Canadian River that the Cheyennes and Arapahos had received from the federal government in 1869.[3]

The boundary issue became a pressing concern for the Wichitas and Caddos in 1882 when the Cheyennes and Arapahos leased the disputed territory to white cattlemen. In order to force federal officials to hear their case, Caddo chief Winasaw and Tawakoni chief Niastor traveled to Washington in the spring of 1882. Winasaw and Niastor were accompanied on this trip by Joseph Leonard, a white man who had come with General Hazen to Fort Cobb in 1868 and had married a Caddo woman. Leonard acted as the chiefs' interpreter and helped them prepare a petition and protest which they delivered on April 1, 1882, to Hiram Price, commissioner of Indian affairs. As a result, a bill was introduced in Congress nine days later which recognized the enlarged Wichita Reservation boundary and appropriated twenty million dollars to the Wichitas and Caddos as payment for relinquishing the rights to the lands south of the Washita that had been given to the Kiowas and Comanches in 1867. To the disappointment of Winasaw and Niastor, Congress took no action on the bill.[4]

Leonard then hired Luther H. Pike to act as legal counsel for the Wichitas and Caddos. Pike was the son of Albert Pike, who had first visited the Wichitas in 1832, and had negotiated the treaty with them in 1861 as Confederate agent for the tribes of the Indian Territory. Pike set about preparing a legal brief that fully explained the history and claims of the Wichitas and Caddos, which was ultimately presented to the commissioner of Indian affairs on March 29, 1883.[5]

In the meantime, on January 20, 1883, Commissioner Price instructed Special Agent E. B. Townsend to visit the Wichita and Cheyenne and Arapaho reservations and investigate the conflicting land claims of the various tribes. Two days later Townsend held a council at the Wichita Agency in which Caddo and Wichita headmen testified that the Fort Arbuckle Agreement of July 1, 1859, had granted them all the land between the Canadian and Red Rivers and the 98th and 100th meridians. They also reiterated—and were backed up by Farmer Sturm and Trader Shirley—that they had been pressured into signing the Wichita Agreement of October 19, 1872, and had repudiated it upon their return to the reservation. Despite holding a second council at the Wichita Agency in May, 1883, Townsend recommended in his official report, dated July 26, 1883, that the smaller Wichita Reservation boundary determined in 1872 should be confirmed by Congress and that the western lands should remain in the hands of the Cheyennes and Arapahos. He justified this decision by characterizing the Fort Arbuckle Agreement as "simply a preliminary talk" that carried "no legal obligation." On the other hand, he argued that Caddo and Wichita headmen had actually signed the Wichita Agreement of October 19, 1872, and Townsend could find no proof to back up their claims of coercion. Besides, Townsend felt the Wichitas and Caddos already possessed "more land . . . than their actual needs require, and far more than either of them will cultivate or utilize through the peaceful arts of civilization." Although Congress, once again, did not act upon Townsend's recommendation to ratify the Wichita Agreement of October 19, 1872, the federal government continued to act as if the matter had officially been settled.[6]

Leonard and Pike returned to the Wichita Reservation with the bad news in September, 1883. They held a series of councils with Caddo and Wichita headmen in which they suggested that Townsend's decision in favor of the Cheyennes and Arapahos should not be accepted without a fight by the tribe members. They planned to set fire to the grass and destroy any fences that were established on the land they claimed south of the Canadian River. Upon hearing of these inflammatory councils, Agent Hunt ordered Leonard and Pike off the reservation on September 21. The two retired eastward, just across the boundary line into the Chickasaw Reservation, where they held yet another council on September 26. In response, Agent Hunt was granted permission by Secretary of the Interior Henry Teller, to arrest Pike. To add insult to injury, the following year Secretary Teller—in spite of Pike's lawsuit filed against Hunt for false imprisonment—denied Pike's request to be allowed to go upon the reservation as the attorney of the Wichitas and Caddos. Obviously, the agents of the federal government looked with extreme disfavor upon any white man who challenged their authority on the Wichita Reservation.[7]

Four years after losing the battle over the reservation's boundary, the Wichitas and Caddos were forced to deal with the issue of allotment, for on February 8, 1887, the Dawes General Allotment Act became law. Caddo Jake met with Commissioner of Indian Affairs L. Q. C. Lamar in Washington soon after the bill's passage and returned to the reservation where he told his fellow members that he had "got there just in time to save their land." Caddo Jake convinced the Wichitas and Caddos to raise money to hire lawyers to fight allotment. In response, Agent Hall threatened to throw any lawyer they hired off the reservation. Despite this threat, in December, 1887, the Wichitas and Caddos hired Texas lawyer J. W. Throckmorton to be represent them in the fight against allotment.[8]

Throckmorton, however, died before he could take up the tribes' cause. The tribes that resided in the Indian Territory immediately voiced their opposition to allotment and thus caused the struggle to be delayed. As a result of the Indians' intransigence, on March 2, 1889, Congress authorized the president to appoint three commissioners to negotiate with the Indian Territory tribes for the cession of their lands to the United States. President Harrison appointed David Jerome as chairman of the so-called Cherokee Commission, which began its work in May, 1890. Concerning the Wichita Reservation, the Cherokee Commission was instructed to negotiate with the tribes for the cession of the 743,610 acres occupied by them under the unratified agreement of 1872, while also taking into consideration their claim to lands included in the Fort Arbuckle Agreement of 1859.[9]

The Cherokee Commission negotiated settlements with other tribes—including one with the Cheyennes and Arapahos in which the

Indians received about fifty cents per acre for the three million acres they ceded to the United States—before meeting with the Wichitas, Caddos, and Delawares at Anadarko on May 9, 1891. Jerome opened the council by explaining the allotment plan "which if you will adopt and try your best to live up to, will give you more comforts and better living to you, and your families, than you have ever had before." Tawakoni Jim responded by insisting that the tribes be allowed to call for their attorneys, for without them "there is no use talking." Jerome assured the members that lawyers "would do you no good," for the commissioners could "explain it to you," and thus save the tribes a good deal of money. Nonetheless, the council came to a close without any decisions being made.[10]

Two days later the commissioners submitted an official offer to the tribes of the Wichita Reservation which would pay them $286,000—about fifty cents per acre—for the lands left over after allotment. The headmen refused to even consider the offer and continued to insist upon having legal counsel present before they entered into a contract. An additional two weeks of fruitless meetings passed before Luther Pike finally arrived at Anadarko on May 26 to take up the cause of his old friends.[11]

The Wichitas, Caddos, and Delawares consulted with Pike over the next four days and on May 30 met with the commissioners and submitted a counter offer to the May 13 proposal. The new proposal raised the price of the surplus land to $715,000—about $1.25 per acre—the payments to be made to the Indians directly and distributed among them per capita. They also came up with the novel idea of having the land allotted to them in common rather than individually. This proposal would keep the reservation intact, while allowing whites to settle on the excess lands west of this smaller reservation.[12]

Not surprisingly, the commissioners dismissed the idea of common allotment out of hand, while at the same time claiming that Congress would never approve the payment of $1.25 per acre for the surplus lands. Pike responded by preparing a paper on June 2 which stated that Congress had not forbidden the Cherokee Commission from offering $1.25, if such were a just and fair price, and that ultimately Congress would determine the price anyway. The tribes of the Wichita Reservation refused to budge from this stance, and thus on June 4 an agreement was reached between the parties in which the Wichitas, Caddos, and Delawares submitted to having their lands allotted individually, with Congress being the final arbiter of the price to be paid for the surplus lands.[13]

Although it had taken the Wichita Reservation tribes only a week after Pike's arrival to agree to have their lands allotted, it took Congress four years to ratify the agreement. One reason for the delay was the opposition of cattlemen who had been granted grazing leases on the reservation. They understood that allotment would deprive them of access to the grass their cattle grazed on so cheaply. Another reason for the delay was a claim put forth by the Choctaws and Chickasaws which argued that they had never fully relinquished their rights to the lands of the Leased District, and thus they, not the Wichitas, Caddos, and Delawares, should receive payment for the surplus lands of the Wichita Reservation. However, white homesteaders in the Indian Territory, known as "boomers," pressured Congress to ratify the agreement and open up the reservation to settlement. When Congress finally ratified the Wichita Agreement of June 4, 1891, on March 2, 1895, it provided for the sale of surplus lands not to exceed $1.25 per acre, and passed the Choctaw and Chickasaw claim to the Court of Claims with provision for appeal to the Supreme Court of the United States. Congress also stated that the surplus lands should be opened to settlement within one year after the allotments were made.[14]

Almost immediately after the ratification of the agreement, the Wichita Reservation tribes began the fight to delay the allotment of their lands for as long as possible. Delaware chief Jim Bobb informed the commissioner of Indian affairs in early 1896 that the Indians did not understand allotment and had no desire to take it, adding that Commissioner Jerome had "fooled us, pretty bad." The tribes found themselves an ally in Agent Baldwin, who had assumed his position in late 1894. In 1896 he counseled against opening the reservation for settlement for at least five years. As a result of the protests, allotment was temporarily delayed.[15]

In March, 1897, however, two special agents arrived on the Wichita Reservation with instructions to begin the allotment process. By April 17 the agents had made fifteen allotments, despite finding "great opposition among the Indians." This opposition was voiced in a series of councils held by the Wichitas, Caddos, and Delawares almost immediately after the allotting agents arrived in Anadarko. As a result of the councils, the Wichita Reservation tribes addressed a memorial to Congress, dated June 3 and 4, 1897, requesting that allotment be delayed until the legal dispute with the Choctaws and Chickasaws had been adjudicated. They also proposed that the allotments be increased to 640 acres, arguing that 160 acres was not enough land for profitable grazing purposes. Tawakoni Jim traveled to Washington to plead the Indians' case in person to the commissioner of Indian affairs and the secretary of the Interior. He was assisted by Josiah M. Vale, the attorney the Wichita Reservation tribes had hired (following Pike's death in 1894) to represent them in their dispute with the Choctaws and Chickasaws. As a result of the memorial and Tawakoni Jim's visit, Secretary of the Interior C. N. Bliss suspended the allotment process and determined that the reservation should not be opened without further legislation.[16]

The suspension of the allotments enraged the boomers who had been eagerly awaiting the opening of the Wichita Reservation's surplus lands. They accused Agent Baldwin of manipulating the Indians to oppose allotment in order to keep his cattlemen allies from having to give up their grazing leases. The Spanish-American War rescued Baldwin from the factional dispute when he was relieved of duty as Kiowa, Comanche, and Wichita agent on May 16, 1898, and ordered into active service in the military. His civilian replacement William Walker, did nothing to end the dispute in his one year of tenure, but his successor, Col. James F. Randlett, was able to rise above the factions and do the best job he could in presiding over the final dissolution of the reservations.[17]

By the turn of the century it became obvious that the Wichitas and Caddos would be unable to delay the allotment process any longer. On January 9, 1899, the Court of Claims ruled against the Wichitas and Caddos and stated that the Choctaws and Chickasaws were entitled to the money earned from the sale of the surplus lands of the Wichita Reservation. The decision was appealed and on December 10, 1900, the U.S. Supreme Court overturned the lower court's determination and ruled in favor of the Wichitas and Caddos. On January 12, 1901, the Supreme Court mandated that a decree should be made in behalf of the Wichita Reservation tribes fixing the amount of compensation to be made to them for the surplus lands. Three weeks later the Court of Claims decreed that the tribes should receive $1.25 per acre for lands reserved for schools, colleges, and public buildings. For the rest of their lands, the tribes were to be paid whatever amount, not exceeding $1.25, the United States sold the land to the homesteaders. The decree also stated that the tribes were only entitled to allotments of 160 acres per individual.[18]

The legal victory for the Wichitas and Caddos was hollow at best. Although they won the right to be paid for the surplus lands of their reservation, the court ruling set the allotment process in motion. On February 15, 1901, the Department of the Interior ordered the allotting agents to resume their work on the Wichita Reservation with instructions to complete the allotment process by July 1 so that the surplus lands might be opened at the same time as those of the Kiowa-Comanche Reservation. This order caused the allotment of the Wichita Reservation to be a rushed and confused affair, resulting in a situation that dissatisfied the Wichitas and Caddos.[19]

Upon their arrival at the Wichita Reservation in mid-March, the allotting agents, with Agent Randlett's assistance, instructed the Indians to go upon the lands they desired to select and remain there until the agents visited them. Two weeks later this plan was scratched, and the Indians were instructed instead to travel to Anadarko and make an application for a survey of their proposed allotment. Only a few members responded favorably to the new plan; most remained on their chosen parcels of land. The work of surveying the reservation was begun on April 11, and by the beginning of June almost half of the Indians had received allotments.[20]

Caddo and Wichita headmen, however, refused to take allotments, believing that the process might still be delayed. In May White Bread and Tawakoni Jim traveled to Washington to register their protests in person to the commissioner of Indian affairs. While in Washington, the two headmen met with an unnamed lawyer who told them that if they paid him fifteen thousand dollars he could get a court to issue an injunction against allotment and the opening of their reservation. White Bread and Tawakoni Jim returned to the reservation and spread the news among their fellow tribe members. According to Agent Randlett, their report of a possible injunction "induced a large number of the Indians to hold back in selecting their lands for allotment."[21]

In an effort to dissuade the tribes from pursuing their attempt to fight allotment, Agent Randlett held a council in Anadarko on May 29. Various headmen spoke out against the Wichita Agreement of June 4, 1891, and claimed that the agreement as ratified by Congress in 1895 was different than the one they had signed four years before. Therefore, Tawakoni Jim suggested that another treaty should be worked out between the federal government and the tribes, adding that he did "not know any danger for the Secretary [of the Interior] to wait awhile." Agent Randlett responded that the law had been made and the allotment would be carried out; if members felt that "injustice has been done" following the allotment and the opening up of the reservation, they should take the matter up with Congress then.[22]

True to Agent Randlett's word, the allotment process continued, and the only protest the Wichitas and Caddos could make was to refuse to select their lands. This form of protest was in vain, for those members who held out only had their allotment chosen for them by the allotting agents, who estimated they were forced to make arbitrary allotments for about two hundred tribe members. By June 25 the allotment process had been completed, and on July 4, 1901, President William McKinley issued a proclamation opening the Wichita and the Kiowa-Comanche reservations to white settlement on August 6. Ultimately, 957 Wichitas, Caddos, and Delawares received allotments, including 27 whites who had been officially adopted by the tribes. The land allotted to the Indians amounted to 152,714 acres, while 586,468 acres of surplus land was opened to white settlement. The Wichitas, Caddos, and Delawares ultimately received $675,371.91—$1.25 per acre—for their surplus lands, of which $43,332.93 was used for legal fees. Thus, each man, woman, and child of the Wichita Reservation received about $700 to become individual citizens of the United States. The reservation experiment, which had lasted forty-seven years, was now over for the Wichitas and Caddos.[23]

Epilogue

Despite having their reservation broken up and being forced to accept individual allotments of land, the Wichitas and Caddos continued to resist assimilation, retaining their identities to the present. For the first three decades of the twentieth century, members of both tribes struggled as best they could to survive on their parcels of land. The acreage was generally too small for successful cattle raising, and the weather was too dry for productive agriculture. Most Wichita and Caddo children continued to attend federal boarding schools, only to return to their homes in southwestern Oklahoma following graduation. Almost all learned English, and most attended one of the many Christian churches in the area.

Despite constant federal pressure to suppress their traditional cultures, the Wichitas and the Caddos resisted. Members of the two tribes continued to perform their traditional dances—sometimes in secret—while many Wichitas and Caddos, young and old, continued to practice the peyote ritual and participated in the formation of the Native American Church. Other tribal customs and rituals were kept alive by elders and handed down orally to the next generation.

Finally, in the 1930s, Franklin Delano Roosevelt and his New Dealers radically changed federal Indian policy for the first time since the founding of the United States. The Indian New Deal, as embodied in the Indian Reorganization Act of 1934 and the Oklahoma Indian Welfare Act of 1936, sought to promote Native American self-determination, the preservation of tribal cultures, and the retention of Indian-owned land. These acts included provisions which allowed each tribe to write a constitution and bylaws in order to organize as a whole for the benefit of tribal members. A federal charter provided that the tribe could administer credit, operate production marketing efforts, and provide consumer protection as well as land management.[1]

The Caddos and Wichitas both took advantage of the shift in federal Indian policy to reassert control over their own lives, albeit using different methods. In 1938 the federal government issued a corporate charter to the Kadohadachos, Hasinais, and Nadacos as the Caddo Indian tribe of Oklahoma, and the tribe adopted a constitution and bylaws. By the 1970s the Caddos recognized that this constitution had become obsolete, and in 1976 a new constitution was written and ratified. Today the three thousand Caddos maintain a tribal complex located on thirty-seven acres of tribal-controlled land about seven miles north of Gracemont in Caddo County, Oklahoma. In addition to promoting self-government, the Caddos created the Whitebead Hasinai Cultural Center in 1975 in an effort to retain their cultural identity through the preservation of "tribal values and traditions."[2]

Unlike the Caddos, the Wichitas did not organize under the Oklahoma Indian Welfare Act and chose instead to govern themselves through traditional means on an unwritten constitutional basis. In 1961 its governing rules were approved by resolution and adopted by the tribe and the 1,500 Wichitas—most of whom also live in Caddo County—continue to be governed by these means. Like the Caddos, the Wichitas have taken active measures to preserve their culture; the tribe has created a complex on ten acres of land once controlled by the Riverside Indian School on which dances are held and tribal songs recorded. Together, the Wichitas and Caddos—as well as the Delawares—put together WCD Enterprise Corporation to promote economic development.[3] Obviously, while much has changed in the Wichita and Caddo cultures over the past half millennium, the assimilationist policies of the U.S. government did not completely succeed, and the Wichitas and Caddos of today continue to exist with their Native American identities intact.

Notes

Works frequently cited have been identified by the following abbreviations:

Co	*Chronicles of Oklahoma*
DDOIHC	Doris Duke Oral Indian History Collection. Western History Collections. University of Oklahoma, Norman.
HED	U.S. Congress. House of Representatives. *Executive Documents.*
HR	U.S. Congress. *House Reports.*
KAF	Kiowa Agency Files. Microfilm Copies. Indian Archives. Oklahoma Historical Society, Oklahoma City.
SED	U.S. Congress. Senate. *Executive Documents.*
SR	U.S. Congress. Senate. *Reports.*
SWHQ	*Southwestern History Quarterly* (from July, 1897, to April, 1912, this publication appeared as the *Texas State Historical Association Quarterly*)
TAL	Letters received by the Office of Indian Affairs from the Texas Agency. Photostatic copy. Eugene C. Barker Library, University of Texas, Austin.
TIP	Winfrey, Dorman, ed. *The Indian Papers of Texas and the Southwest, 1825–1916.* 5 vols. Austin: Texas State Library, 1959–61.
WAL	Letters received by the Office of Indian Affairs. Wichita Agency, 1857–1878. National Archives Microfilm Publications M-234, Rolls 928–33.
WBSP	Wichita Boarding School Papers. Microfilm Copies. Indian Archives. Oklahoma Historical Society. Oklahoma City.
WTHAYB	*West Texas Historical Association Year Book*

Introduction

1. The best introduction to the long history of federal Indian policy is Francis Paul Prucha, *The Great Father: The United States Government and the American Indians*, 2 vols.

2. For an excellent historiography of Native American history over the past century, see R. David Edmunds, "Native Americans, New Voices: American Indian History, 1895–1995," *American Historical Review* 100 (June, 1995): 717–40.

3. Most important among these histories are James M. Merrell, *The Indians' New World: Catawbas and Their Neighbors from European Contact through the Era of Removal*; Neal Salisbury, *Manitou and Providence: Indians, Europeans, and the Making of New England, 1500–1643*; William Cronon, *Changes in the Land: Indians, Colonists, and the Ecology of New England*; Daniel H. Usner, Jr., *Indians, Settlers, and Slaves in a Frontier Exchange Economy: The Lower Mississippi Valley before 1783*.

4. Elizabeth A. H. John's *Storms Brewed in Other Men's Worlds: The Confrontation of Indians, Spanish, and French in the Southwest, 1540–1795* expertly traces the history of the Wichitas and Caddos (among others) up to the eve of the American period. Her three-part study of the Taovayas traces one branch of the Wichitas up to the point they established a formal relationship with the United States in 1835. See Elizabeth Ann Harper [John], "The Taovayas Indians in Frontier Trade and Diplomacy, 1719–1768," *CO* 31 (Autumn, 1953):268–89; "The Taovayas Indians in Frontier Trade and Diplomacy, 1769–1779," *SWHQ* 57 (Oct., 1953): 181–201; "The Taovayas Indians in Frontier Trade and Diplomacy, 1779–1835," *Panhandle-Plains Historical Review* 26 (1953): 40–72. The same ground is traversed by Ralph Smith, "The Tawehash (Taovayas) in French, Spanish, English, and American Imperial Affairs," *WTHAYB* 28 (Oct., 1952): 18–49. A study that traces the Wichitas to the point they permanently settle on a reservation is Earl Henry Elam, "The History of the Wichita Indian Confederacy to 1868" (Ph.D diss., Texas Tech University, 1971). Only W. W. Newcomb's short, general survey, *A People Called Wichita*, looks at the tribe beyond 1868. Works on the Caddos that focus on their early interaction with the French and the Spanish include William Joyce Griffith, *The Hasinai Indians of East Texas as Seen by Europeans, 1687–1772*; Herbert Eugene Bolton, *The Hasinais: Southern Caddoans as Seen by the Earliest Europeans*, ed. Russell M. Magnaghi; Timothy K. Perttula, *The Caddo Nation: Archaeological and Ethnohistoric Perspectives*. The one study that does focus on the Caddos' relations with the United States before the reservation period is William B. Glover, "A History of the Caddo Indians," *Louisiana Historical Quarterly* 18 (Oct., 1935): 872–946. The two works by Caddo tribal members are Vynola Beaver Newkumet and Howard L. Meredith, *Hasinai: A Traditional History of the Caddo Confederacy*, and Cecile Elkins Carter, *The Caddo Indians: Where We Come From*.

5. F. Todd Smith, *The Caddo Indians: Tribes at the Convergence of Empires, 1542–1854*.

Chapter One: Through the Treaty of Council Springs

1. Henry C. Armbruster, "Torrey's Trading Post," *Texana* 2 (Summer, 1964): 113–31.
2. David J. Weber, *The Spanish Frontier in North America*, 45–55.
3. The Caddos call themselves Hasinai, meaning "our people." The term *Caddo* derives from the French, and then the Anglo-American, abbreviation of *Kadohadacho*, the name of the Caddo confederacy located on the Red River near the Great Bend. At the time of first relations with the United States, the Kadohadachos were the most powerful of the Caddo confederacies; thus, as the various Caddo tribes gradually bonded together during the nineteenth century, they became collectively known as the Caddos. Since one of the confederacies is also known as the Hasinai, I have chosen to use the term Caddo to designate all the tribes of the three confederacies. See James Mooney, *The Ghost Dance Religion and the Sioux Outbreak of 1890*, 1092–93; and Newkumet and Meredith, *Hasinai*, 117.
4. Smith, *The Caddo Indians*, 8.
5. Bolton, *The Hasinais*, 82–86, 138–55.
6. Bolton, *The Hasinais*, 74–81; Newkumet and Meredith, *Hasinai*, 56–57.
7. Newkumet and Meredith, *Hasinai*, 13–34; Bolton, *The Hasinais*, 92–110.
8. Bolton, *The Hasinais*, 86–91, 111–15; Newkumet and Meredith, *Hasinai*, 35–40, 46–50; Father Anastasius Douay, "Narrative of La Salle's Attempt to Ascend the Mississippi in 1687," *The Journeys of René-Robert Cavelier, Sieur de la Salle*, ed. Isaac Joslin Cox, 1: 232.
9. Newkumet and Meredith, *Hasinai*, 41–45; Fray Francisco Casañas de Jesús María to the Viceroy of Mexico, Aug. 15, 1691, in Mattie Austin Hatcher, ed. and trans., "Descriptions of the Tejas or Asinai Indians, 1691–1722," *SWHQ* 30 (Jan., 1927): 213–14, 285; Fray Isidro Felís de Espinosa on the Asinai and their Allies in Hatcher, ed. and trans., "Descriptions of the Tejas or Asinai Indians, 1691–1722," *SWHQ* 31 (Oct., 1927): 175–77.
10. Bolton, *The Hasinais*, 170–80.
11. The Wichitas call themselves the Kitikitish. The name *Wichita* comes from a small tribal group that was associated with the Taovayas, the largest of the Wichita tribes. Officials of the United States mistakenly designated the Taovayas as "Witchetaws" in the first treaty signed by the two parties in 1835. From that point on, the Taovayas were known as the Wichitas, a term which came to include the related tribes—the Wacos, Tawakonis, and Kichais—that bonded together with them. I have chosen to use the term Wichita to indicate the confederacy as a whole; individual tribes will be called by their accepted names. See Mooney, *The Ghost Dance Religion*, 1095; Elam, "History of the Wichita Confederacy," 22–31.
12. Jack T. Hughes, "Prehistory of the Caddoan-Speaking Tribes," *Caddoan Indians*, 3: 325–26.
13. Mildred Mott Wedel, *The Wichita Indians, 1541–1750*, 16–27.
14. Wedel, *The Wichita Indians*, 18–19; Robert E. Bell, Edward B. Jelks, and W. W. Newcomb, *Wichita Indian Archaeology and Ethnology*, 327, 341–42; George A. Dorsey, *The Mythology of the Wichita*, 53–55.

15. Dorsey, *The Mythology of the Wichita*, 16–20; Newcomb, *The Indians of Texas: From Prehistoric to Modern Times*, 270–76.
16. Bell, Jelks, and Newcomb, *Wichita Indian Archaeology*, 310–15.
17. Bell, Jelks, and Newcomb, *Wichita Indian Archaeology*, 319–21, 340–41; Karl Schmitt and Iva Osanai Schmitt, *Wichita Kinship: Past and Present*, 11–30.
18. Newcomb, *Indians of Texas*, 250–53; Elam, "History of the Wichita Confederacy," 35–40.
19. Smith, *The Caddo Indians*, 36–50.
20. Bell, Jelks, and Newcomb, *Wichita Indian Archaeology*, 328, 349–50; Elam, "History of the Wichita Confederacy," 30–31.
21. John, *Storms Brewed*, 338–42.
22. The most detailed list of gifts and trade goods the Wichitas and Caddos received comes from the period just after the transfer of Louisiana to Spain. However, the list was drawn up by Athanase de Mézières, a French soldier who had been in Louisiana since 1733. See Alejandro O'Reilly to Athanase de Mézières, Jan. 22, 1770, in Bolton, ed., *Athanase de Mézières and the Louisiana-Texas Frontier, 1768–1780*, 1: 132–33.
23. See also Contract of Juan Pisneros with de Mézières, Feb. 3, 1770, in Bolton, ed., *Athanase de Mézières*, 143–46.
24. Smith, *The Caddo Indians*, 51–62; Robert M. Weddle, *The San Sabá Mission: Spanish Pivot in Texas*, 72–133.
25. Smith, *The Caddo Indians*, 63–75.
26. Smith, *The Caddo Indians*, 30–31, 54; John C. Ewers, "The Influence of Epidemics on the Indian Populations and Cultures of Texas," *Plains Anthropologist* 18: 104–15.
27. Smith, *The Caddo Indians*, 85–102; F. Todd Smith, "The Kadohadacho Indians and the Louisiana-Texas Frontier, 1803–1815," *SWHQ* 94 (Oct., 1991): 200–21; Harper [John], "Frontier Trade and Diplomacy, 1779–1835" 40–58; Bell, Jelks, and Newcomb, *Wichita Indian Archaeology*, 351.
28. Smith, *The Caddo Indians*, 103–26.
29. Elam, "History of the Wichita Confederacy," 212–22.
30. Elam, "History of the Wichita Confederacy," 231–46; Harper [John], "Frontier Trade and Diplomacy, 1779–1835" 61–68; "Treaty with the Comanche and Witchetaw Indians and their Associated Bands," in Charles J. Kappler, ed., *Indian Affairs: Laws and Treaties*, 2: 435–39.
31. Smith, *The Caddo Indians*, 125–42.
32. Elam, "History of the Wichita Confederacy," 215–22.
33. Smith, *The Caddo Indians*, 143–48.
34. Minutes of an Indian Council at Tehuacana Creek, Mar. 28, 1843, in Dorman Winfrey, ed., *TIP* 1: 149–62.
35. A. M. Upshaw to William Armstrong, Aug. 15, 1845, *SED*, 29 Cong., 1 sess., doc. 1, 525; testimony of J. B. Thoburn, Sept. 22, 1928, C. Ross Hume Collection, Western History Collections, University of Oklahoma, Norman, Oklahoma.
36. Ferdinand Roemer, *Texas, with Particular Reference to German Immigration and the Physical Appearance of the Country*, 200–201; Grant Foreman, ed., "The Journal of Elijah Hicks," *CO* 13 (Mar., 1935): 93; Robert S. Neighbors

to Col. William Medill, June 22, 1847, *HED,* 30 Cong., 1 sess., doc. 8, 894; L. H. Williams to Thomas G. Western, July 16, 1845, *TIP* 2: 292.

37. Minutes of Final Day of Council at Tehuacana Creek, May 15, 1844, *TIP,* 55; Minutes of a Council held at Tehuacana Creek, Sept. 21, 1845, *TIP,* 341.

38. Kenneth P. Neighbours, "José María: Anadarko Chief," *CO* 44 (Autumn, 1966): 254–74; Neighbors to Medill, June 22, 1847, *HED,* 30 Cong., 1 sess., doc. 8, 894.

39. Minutes of an Indian Council at Tehuacana Creek, Mar. 28, 1843, *TIP* 1: 160; Neighbors to Medill, Aug. 10, 1848, *HED,* 30 Cong., 2 sess., doc. 1, 593; G. W. Hill to Neighbors, Aug. 10, 1853, TAL.

40. H. Allen Anderson, "The Delaware and Shawnee Indians and the Republic of Texas, 1820–1845," *SWHQ* 94 (Oct., 1990): 231–60.

41. Proclamation by Sam Houston, Sept. 29, 1843, *TIP* 1: 241–46; Minutes of a Council at Tehuacana Creek, May 12–15, 1844, *TIP* 2: 31–56; Treaty Signed in Council at Tehuacana Creek, Oct. 9, 1845, *TIP* 2: 114–19.

42. Letter to Sam Houston from J. C. Eldredge, Dec. 8, 1843, *TIP* 1: 257; Report from Benjamin Sloat to Thomas G. Western, Nov. 13, 1844, *TIP* 2: 143.

43. Statement of Utstutskins to William Shirley, 1882, *SR,* 49 Cong., 1 sess., doc. 1278, 126; Capt. Randolph B. Marcy, "Exploration of the Red River of Louisiana in the Year 1852," *SED,* 33 Cong., 1 sess., doc. 54, 78.

44. Elam, "History of the Wichita Confederacy," 286–87.

45. Jodye Lynn Dickson Schilz and Thomas F. Schilz, *Buffalo Hump and the Penateka Comanches,* 25–29.

46. Minutes of a Treaty Council with the Waco, Tawakoni, Keechi, and Wichita Indians, Nov. 13–16, 1845, *TIP* 2: 399–405.

47. Grant Foreman, "The Texas Comanche Treaty of 1846," *SWHQ* 51 (Apr., 1948): 313–25; Foreman, "Journal of Elijah Hicks," 68–82.

48. Foreman, "Journal of Elijah Hicks," 86–87.

49. Foreman, "Journal of Elijah Hicks," 89–91; Elam, "History of the Wichita Confederacy," 271–72.

50. Treaty with the Comanche and Other Tribes, May 15, 1846, *TIP* 3: 43–52.

Chapter Two: Searching for a Home, 1846-53

1. Three studies include information on the unique situation in Texas. The two best are George D. Harmon, "The United States Indian Policy in Texas, 1845–1860," *Mississippi Valley Historical Review* 17 (Dec., 1930): 377–403; Robert A. Trennert, Jr., *Alternative to Extinction: Federal Indian Policy and the Beginnings of the Reservation System, 1846–1851.* Of lesser quality is Lena Clara Koch, "The Federal Indian Policy in Texas, 1845–1860," *SWHQ* 28 (Jan., 1925): 223–34; 28 (Apr., 1925): 259–86; 29 (July, 1925): 19–35; 29 (Oct., 1925): 98–127.

2. Quoted in Harmon, "United States Indian Policy in Texas," 381.

3. Butler and Lewis to Medill, Aug. 8, 1846, *HED,* 29 Cong., 2 sess., doc. 76, 8–9; Treaty between U.S. and José María and the Anadarko Indians, July 25, 1846, *TIP* 3: 68; Neighbours, "José María: Anadarko Chief," 264; G. W. Hill to Robert S. Neighbors, Oct. 1, 1853, TAL; Elam, "History of the Wichita Confederacy," 274–76.

4. Elam, "History of the Wichita Confederacy," 278–80.
5. Neighbors to Medill, Jan. 6, 1847, *HED*, 29 Cong., 2 sess., doc. 100, 3–4.
6. Neighbors to Medill, Jan. 6, 1847, *HED*, 29 Cong., 2 sess., doc. 100, 3.
7. Neighbors to Medill, June 22, 1847, *HED*, 30 Cong., 1 sess., doc. 8, 894.
8. Neighbors to Medill, June 22, 1847, *HED*, 30 Cong., 1 sess., doc. 8, 894–96.
9. Neighbors to Medill, Aug. 5, 1847, *HED*, 30 Cong., 1 sess., doc. 8, 897; Governor J. P. Henderson to William Marcy, Aug. 22, 1847, TAL; Henderson to Neighbors, Aug. 23, 1847, *TIP* 3: 83. Neighbors had helped negotiate a treaty between the Germans and the Penateka Comanches in March, 1847, in which the Indians gave the Germans the right to survey land between the Llano and the San Saba. See R. L. Biesele, "The Relations between the German Settlers and the Indians in Texas, 1844–1860," *SWHQ* 31 (1927): 124–25; and Karl A. Hoerig, "The Relationship between German Immigrants and the Native Peoples in Western Texas," *SWHQ* 97 (Jan., 1994): 431–32.
10. Neighbors to Medill, Sept. 14, 1847, *HED*, 30 Cong., 1 sess., doc. 8, 899–901; Neighbors to Medill, Oct. 12, 1847, *HED*, 30 Cong., 1 sess., doc. 8, 905.
11. Neighbors to Medill, Sept. 14, 1847, *HED*, 30 Cong., 1 sess., doc. 8, 899–901.
12. Neighbors to Medill, Oct. 12, 1847, *HED*, 30 Cong., 1 sess., doc. 8, 903–906; Neighbors to Medill, Mar. 2, 1848, *HED*, 30 Cong., 2 sess., doc. 1, 583–85.
13. Neighbors to Medill, Oct. 12, 1847, *HED*, 30 Cong., 1 sess., doc. 8, 904–906.
14. Neighbors to Medill, June 15, 1848, *HED*, 30 Cong., 2 sess., doc. 1, 592; Neighbors to Medill, Aug. 14, 1848, *HED*, 30 Cong., 2 sess., doc. 1, 594.
15. Capt. M. T. Johnson to Mr. Spencer, Jan. 4, 1848, TAL; Neighbors to Medill, Mar. 2, 1848, *HED*, 30 Cong., 2 sess., doc. 1, 581–85.
16. Neighbors to Medill, Mar. 2, 1848, *HED*, 30 Cong., 2 sess., doc. 1, 581; E. B. Ritchie, ed., "Copy of Report of Colonel Samuel Cooper, Assistant Adjutant General of the United States, of Inspection Trip from Fort Graham to the Indian Villages on the Upper Brazos Made in June, 1851," *SWHQ* 42 (Apr., 1939): 329–30; Jesse Stem to Luke Lea, n.d., *SED*, 32 Cong., 1 sess., doc. 1, 522–23.
17. Neighbors to Medill, Mar. 2, 1848, *HED*, 30 Cong., 2 sess., doc. 1, 581–83.
18. Captain Highsmith to the editors of the *Texas Democrat*, Mar. 30, 1848, *SR*, 30 Cong. 1 sess., doc. 171, 51–52; Neighbors to Medill, Apr. 28, 1848, *HED*, 30 Cong., 1 sess., doc. 1, 587; Henry O. Hedgcoxe to Neighbors, Feb. 18, 1848, *HED*, 30 Cong., 1 sess., doc. 1, 575–76; Elam, "History of the Wichita Confederacy," 291. The surveyors were engaged in running the line on the southwest boundary of a large tract granted to W. S. Peters by the Republic of Texas, commonly called the Peters Colony. The line stretched about one hundred thirty miles west of the newly founded city of Dallas on the Trinity River well into territory claimed by the Wichitas.
19. C. E. Barnard to Neighbors, n.d., *HED*, 30 Cong., 2 sess., doc. 1, 588–89.
20. C. E. Barnard to Neighbors, n.d., *HED*, 30 Cong., 2 sess., doc. 1, 589; Neighbors to Medill, Apr. 28, 1848, TAL.
21. H. G. Catlett to Medill, May 12, 1849, *SED*, 31 Cong., 1 sess., doc. 1, 969–70.
22. Neighbors to Medill, June 15, 1848, *HED*, 30 Cong., 2 sess., doc. 1, 591.
23. Neighbors to Medill, Aug. 10, 1848, *HED*, 30 Cong., 2 sess., doc. 1, 593–95; Agreement between R. S. Neighbors and Colonel P. H. Bell and principal

chiefs of the Caddo, José María, Toweash, and Haddabah, Sept. 14, 1848, TAL. No charges were brought against any Rangers, but the Caddos were finally paid the five hundred dollars on February 27, 1849. Neighbors to Medill, June 18, 1849, TAL.

24. Neighbors to Medill, June 15, 1848, *HED*, 30 Cong., 2 sess., doc. 1, 591; Neighbors to Medill, Aug. 10, 1848, *HED*, 30 Cong., 2 sess., doc. 1, 593; Neighbors to Medill, Sept. 14, 1848, *HED*, 30 Cong., 2 sess., doc. 1, 594–95; A. Williams to Captain Highsmith, Aug. 20, 1848, *HED*, 30 Cong., 2 sess., doc. 1, 596–97; Neighbors to Medill, Oct. 23, 1848, *HED*, 30 Cong., 2 sess., doc. 1, 597.

25. Neighbors to Medill, Oct. 23, 1848, *HED*, 30 Cong., 2 sess., doc. 1, 597; Neighbors to Medill, Feb. 15, 1849, TAL; Jesse Stem to Luke Lea, summer, 1851, *SED*, 32 Cong., 1 sess., doc. 1, 522; Ritchie, "Report of Colonel Samuel Cooper," 331.

26. Neighbors to Worth, Mar. 7, 1849, *SED*, 31 Cong., 1 sess., doc. 1, 963–65.

27. Neighbors to Medill, June 18, 1849, TAL; Trennert, *Alternative to Extinction*, 77–78, 81–82.

28. John Conner to Gen. George M. Brooke, Aug. 30, 1849, TAL; L. W. Williams to Neighbors, Oct. 9, 1849, TAL.

29. Trennert, *Alternative to Extinction*, 84–87; Harmon, "United States Indian Policy in Texas," 384.

30. Capt. Randolph B. Marcy, "Exploration of the Red River of Louisiana in the Year 1852," *SED*, 33rd Cong, 1 sess., doc. 54, 101.

31. Capt. W. R. Montgomery to Maj. George Deas, June 27, 1850, *SED*, 31 Cong., 2 sess., doc. 1, 45–46; Captain Blake to Major Deas, Aug. 28, 1850, *SED*, 31 Cong., 2 sess., doc. 1, 60.

32. Extract of a letter from John H. Rollins, Nov. 2, 1850, *SED*, 31 Cong., 2 sess., doc. 1, 143–45; Treaty between United States and the Comanche, Caddo, Lipan, Quapaw, Tawakoni, and Waco Tribes of Indians, Dec. 10, 1850, *TIP* 3: 130–37.

33. Treaty between United States and the Comanche, Caddo, Lipan, Quapaw, Tawakoni, and Waco Tribes of Indians, Dec. 10, 1850, *TIP* 3: 130–37. At the same time Agent Rollins was putting together the council, Congress appropriated money for a three-man commission to investigate the Indian problem in Texas. Although the commissioners eventually realized the need for the reservation system to be implemented in Texas, no immediate results were forthcoming. See Trennert, *Alternative to Extinction*, 88–91.

34. Ritchie, "Report of Colonel Samuel Cooper," 328; Stem to Lea, summer, 1851, *SED*, 32 Cong., 1 sess., doc. 1, 521; Koch, "Federal Indian Policy," (Apr., 1925), 262.

35. Ritchie, "Report of Colonel Samuel Cooper," 330; Stem to Lea, n.d., *SED*, 32 Cong., 1 sess., doc. 1, 522; Stem to Lea, Feb. 20, 1852, TAL.

36. Ritchie, "Report of Colonel Samuel Cooper," 331; Stem to Lea, n.d., *SED*, 32 Cong., 1 sess., doc. 1, 522.

37. Stem to Lea, n.d., *SED*, 32 Cong., 1 sess., doc. 1, 523.

38. Marcy, "Exploration of the Red River," 83–87.

39. Earl Buck Braly, "Fort Belknap," *WTHAYB* 30 (Oct., 1954): 84; Stem to Lea, Nov. 1, 1851, *SED*, 32 Cong., 1 sess., doc. 1, 525.

40. Stem to Lea, Oct. 8, 1852, *HED*, 32 Cong., 2 sess., doc. 1, 435; G. W. Hill to Neighbors, Aug. 10, 1853, TAL.
41. Stem to Lea, Oct. 8, 1852, *HED*, 32 Cong., 2 sess., doc. 1, 436; Stem to H. G. Loomis, Mar. 30, 1853, TAL.
42. Stem to Lea, Oct. 8, 1852, *HED*, 32 Cong., 2 sess., doc. 1, 434.
43. Stem to Loomis, Jan. 9, 1853, TAL; Stem Talk with Koweaka, Wichita Chief, Feb. 22, 1853, TAL; Stem to Loomis, Mar. 30, 1853, TAL.
44. Stem to Loomis, Mar. 30, 1853, TAL.
45. Stem to Loomis, Mar. 30, 1853, TAL.
46. Hill to Neighbors, Aug. 10, 1853, TAL.
47. Hill to Neighbors, Oct. 1, 1853, TAL.
48. Hill to Neighbors, Oct. 1, 1853, TAL.
49. Harmon, "United States Indian Policy in Texas," 392–93.

Chapter Three: The Brazos Reserve, 1854-59

1. See Trennert, *Alternative to Extinction*, for the development of this policy.
2. Neighbors to Mix, Sept. 10, 1855, *HED*, 34 Cong., 1 sess., doc. 1, 501.
3. Neighbors to Manypenny, Sept. 16, 1854, *SED*, 33 Cong., 1 sess., doc. 1, 367; Hill to Neighbors, Sept. 20, 1854, *SED*, 33 Cong., 1 sess., doc. 1, 372; Hill to Neighbors, Aug. 31, 1855, *HED*, 34 Cong., 1st dess., doc. 1, 504; Elias Rector to A. B. Greenwood, July 2, 1859, *SED*, 36 Cong., 1 sess., doc. 2, 673.
4. Hill to Neighbors, Mar. 26, 1854, TAL; Hill to Neighbors, Sept. 20, 1854, *SED*, 33 Cong., 1 sess., doc. 1, 372; Hill to Neighbors, Dec. 15, 1854, TAL.
5. Report of an expedition to the sources of the Brazos and Big Wichita rivers, during the summer of 1854, by Captain R. B. Marcy, Seventh Infantry, *SED*, 34 Cong., 1 sess., doc. 60, 2–3; Report of Marcy and Neighbors to Governor P. H. Bell, Sept. 30, 1854, *TIP* 3: 188.
6. Report of Marcy and Neighbors to Governor P. H. Bell, Sept. 30, 1854, *TIP* 3: 188; Report of an expedition to the sources of the Brazos and Big Wichita rivers, *SED*, 34 Cong., 1 sess., doc. 60, 22–23.
7. "Treaty with the Choctaw and Chickasaw, 1855," in Kappler, *Indian Affairs* 2: 706–14.
8. Neighbors to Mix, Oct. 30, 1854, TAL; Hill to Neighbors, Dec. 15, 1854, TAL; Neighbors to Manypenny, Jan. 8, 1855, TAL.
9. Hill to Neighbors, Apr. 3, 1855, TAL.
10. Newcomb, *Indians of Texas*, 133–41; Thomas Frank Schilz, "People of the Cross Timbers: A History of the Tonkawa Indians" (Ph.D. diss., Texas Christian University, 1983), 152–66.
11. Kenneth H. Neighbours, "Chapters from the History of Texas Indian Reservations," *WTHAYB* 33 (Oct., 1957): 6–9.
12. Shapley P. Ross to Neighbors, Sept. 30, 1856, *SED*, 34 Cong., 3 sess., doc. 5, 730–31; Samuel Church to Ross, Sept. 9, 1857, *SED*, 35 Cong., 1 sess., doc. 2, 559; Jonathan Murray to Ross, Sept. 10, 1857, *SED*, 35 Cong., 1 sess., doc. 2, 562; General Statement of houses formerly occupied by each of the several tribes at Brazos Agency, Texas, July 30, 1859, TAL.
13. Hill to Neighbors, Aug. 31, 1855, *HED*, 34 Cong., 1 sess., doc. 1, 504–505.
14. Neighbors to Mix, Sept. 10, 1855, *HED*, 34 Cong., 1 sess., doc. 1, 500;

Neighbors to Manypenny, Sept. 18, 1856, *SED*, 34 Cong., 3 sess., doc. 5, 724, 727; Ross to Neighbors, Sept. 30, 1856, *SED*, 34 Cong., 3 sess., doc. 5, 730–31.

15. Ross to Neighbors, Sept. 11, 1857, *SED*, 35 Cong., 1 sess., doc. 2, 557–58; Church to Ross, Sept. 9, 1857, *SED*, 35 Cong., 1 sess., doc. 2, 558–59; Neighbors to J. W. Denver, Sept. 16, 1857, *SED*, 35 Cong., 1 sess., doc. 2, 550–51; Murray to Ross, Sept. 10, 1857, *SED*, 35 Cong., 1 sess., doc. 2, 559–60.

16. Ross to Neighbors, Sept. 6, 1858, *SED*, 35 Cong., 2 sess., doc. 1, 533; Neighbors to Mix, Sept. 16, 1858, *SED*, 35 Cong., 2 sess., doc. 1, 525.

17. Invoice of hogs sold for Brazos Reserve Indians, July 27, 1859, TAL; invoice of property belonging to the tribes of the Brazos Reserve, July 30, 1859, TAL.

18. Census Roll of Indians, March 31, 1855, TAL; Hill to Neighbors, Sept. 20, 1854, *SED*, 33 Cong., 1 sess., doc. 1, 372.

19. Census Roll of Indians, Mar. 31, 1855, TAL; Neighbors to Gen. D. E. Twiggs, July 17, 1857, *SED*, 35 Cong., 1 sess., doc. 2, 552; Census Roll of Indians, Aug. 1, 1859, TAL.

20. Census Roll of Indians, Mar. 31, 1855, TAL; Census Roll of Indians, Dec. 31, 1857, TAL.

21. Neighbors to Manypenny, Sept. 18, 1856, *SED*, 34 Cong., 3 Sess., doc. 5, 724.

22. Neighbors to Mix, Sept. 10, 1855, *HED*, 34 Cong., 1 sess., doc. 1, 501.

23. Murl L. Webb, "Religious and Educational Efforts among Texas Indians in the 1850's," *SWHQ* 69 (July, 1965): 25; Neighbors to John W. Phillips, Sept. 10, 1855, TAL; Neighbors to Mix, Sept. 10, 1855, *HED*, 34 Cong., 1 sess., doc. 1, 501.

24. Ross to Neighbors, Sept. 30, 1856, *SED*, 34 Cong., 3 sess., doc. 5, 730–31.

25. Webb, "Religious and Educational Efforts," 26; Ross to Neighbors, Sept. 11, 1857, *SED*, 35 Cong. 1 sess., doc. 2, 558.

26. Webb, "Religious and Educational Efforts," 27.

27. Z. E. Coombes to Ross, Sept. 7, 1858, *SED*, 35 Cong., 2 sess., doc. 1, 535; Barbara Ledbetter, "Zachariah Ellis Coombes, the Samuel Pepys of the Texas Frontier," *WTHAYB* 44 (Oct., 1968): 68–77.

28. Coombes to Ross, Sept. 7, 1858, *SED*, 35 Cong., 2 sess., doc. 1, 535; Coombes, *Diary of a Frontiersman, 1858–1859*, 14–15.

29. Coombes to Ross, Nov. 30, 1858, TAL.

30. Coombes, *Diary of a Frontiersman*, 34; Coombes to Ross, Feb. 28, 1859, *SED*, 36 Cong., 1 sess., doc. 2, 627–28.

31. Coombes to Ross, Mar. 30, 1859, TAL; Coombes to Ross, Apr. 30, 1859, TAL; Webb, "Religious and Educational Efforts," 34.

32. Rupert N. Richardson, *The Comanche Barrier to South Plains Settlement*, 183–92; Schilz and Schilz, *Buffalo Hump*, 40–44.

33. Ross to Neighbors, Sept. 30, 1855, *HED*, 34 Cong., 1 sess., doc. 1, 505–506.

34. Ross to Neighbors, Sept. 30, 1855, *HED*, 34 Cong., 1 sess., doc. 1, 506; Ross to Neighbors, Oct. 7, 1855, TAL.

35. Neighbors to Manypenny, Sept. 18, 1856, *SED*, 34 Cong., 3 sess., doc. 5, 725; R. C. Crane, "Robert E. Lee's Expedition in the Upper Brazos and Colorado Country," *WTHAYB* 13 (Oct., 1937): 54; Ross to Neighbors, June 30, 1856, TAL.

36. Crane, "Lee's Expedition," 58; Baylor to Neighbors, July 12, 1856, TAL.

37. Ross to Neighbors, July 23, 1856, TAL.
38. Ross to Neighbors, July 23, 1856, TAL.
39. Ross to Neighbors, Oct. 31, 1856, TAL; Neighbors to Manypenny, Nov. 8, 1856, TAL.
40. Ross to Neighbors, Nov. 30, 1856, TAL; Ross to Neighbors, Apr. 26, 1858, TAL; Ross to Neighbors, Jan. 10, 1857, TAL. For the most recent study on white attitudes toward the two reserves, see George Klos, "'Our people could not distinguish one tribe from another': The 1859 Expulsion of the Reserve Indians from Texas," *SWHQ* 97 (Apr., 1994): 598–619.
41. Neighbors to Mix, Apr., 2, 1858, TAL; quoted in Averam B. Bender, *The March of Empire: Frontier Defense in the Southwest, 1848–1860*, 213–14.
42. Ross to Neighbors, Mar. 31, 1857, TAL; Ross to Neighbors, July 30, 1857, TAL.
43. Neighbors to Denver, Dec. 8, 1857, TAL; Neighbors to Mix, Jan. 17, 1858, TAL.
44. Petitions from Williamson and Lampasas Counties, Dec. 15, 1857, TAL.
45. Capt. W. G. Evans to Capt. Joseph Withers, Jan. 14, 1858, TAL.
46. Neighbors to Mix, Jan. 17, 1858, TAL.
47. Ross to Neighbors, Feb. 17, 1858, TAL.
48. John Salmon Ford, *Rip Ford's Texas*, 223–25; Brad Agnew, "The 1858 War against the Comanches," *CO* 49 (Summer, 1971): 214–15.
49. Ross to Neighbors, Mar. 31, 1858, TAL; Ford, List of Indians, actual settlers of Brazos Agency of Texas engaged April 23 to May 22, 1858, July 15, 1858, TAL.
50. W. J. Hughes, "'Rip' Ford's Indian Fight on the Canadian," *Panhandle-Plains Historical Review* 30 (1957): 12–19; Agnew, "The 1858 War," 214–15; Ford, *Rip Ford's Texas*, 229–33; Ross to Neighbors, June 30, TAL.
51. Ford, *Rip Ford's Texas*, 233–36; Hughes, "'Rip' Ford's Indian Fight," 19–25; Agnew, "The 1858 War," 216–18.
52. Quoted in Ford, *Rip Ford's Texas*, 238; Address by H. R. Runnels to Captain Ford's Company of Texas Rangers, May 28, 1858, *TIP* 3: 287.
53. Ford, *Rip Ford's Texas*, 237–38; Ross to Neighbors, Apr. 26, 1858, TAL; Ross to Neighbors, June 30, 1858, TAL.
54. Quoted in Bender, *The March of Empire*, 214.
55. Bender, *The March of Empire*, 214; Affidavit of John S. Ford, Nov. 22, 1858, TAL.
56. Ross to Neighbors, Sept. 30, 1858, TAL.
57. Agnew, "The 1858 War," 225–26; Harold B. Simpson, *Cry Comanche: The Second United States Cavalry in Texas, 1855–1861*, 108–10; William Y. Chalfant, *Without Quarter: The Wichita Expedition and the Fight on Crooked Creek*, 37–40; Ross to Neighbors, Sept. 30, 1858, TAL.
58. Grant Foreman, ed., "A Journal Kept by Douglas Cooper," *CO* 5 (Sept., 1927): 388–90; Lt. J. E. Powell to Second Lieutenant Offley, Aug. 26, 1858, *SED*, 35 Cong., 2 sess., doc. 1, 421–23.
59. Agnew, "The 1858 War," 227–28; Simpson, *Cry Comanche*, 113–14; Chalfant, *Without Quarter*, 41–44; Coombes, *Diary of a Frontiersman*, 7–8.
60. Elias Rector to Mix, Oct. 22, 1858, *SED*, 36 Cong., 1 sess., doc. 2, 583–84; Rector to Mix, Oct. 23, 1858, *SED*, 36 Cong., 1 sess., doc. 2, 585–86; Census Rolls of Wichita Camp on Caddo Creek, Jan. 30, 1859, WAL; Elam, "History of the Wichita Confederacy," 334–39.
61. Ross to Neighbors, Jan. 26, 1859, *SED*, 36 Cong., 1 sess., doc. 2, 596.

62. J. J. Sturm to Ross, Jan. 15, 1859, *SED*, 36 Cong., 1 sess., doc. 2, 599; Letter to the People of Texas, Jan. 4, 1859, *SED*, 36 Cong., 1 sess., doc. 2, 607.

63. Sturm to Ross, Jan. 15, 1859, *SED*, 36 Cong., 1 sess., doc. 2, 599.

64. Sturm to Ross, Dec. 30, 1858, *SED*, 36 Cong., 1 sess., doc. 2, 589–90.

65. Sturm to Ross, Jan. 15, 1859, *SED*, 36 Cong., 1 sess., doc. 2, 599; Sturm to Ross, Dec. 28, 1858, *SED*, 36 Cong., 1 sess., doc. 2, 589.

66. Sturm to Ross, Dec. 30, 1858, *SED*, 36 Cong., 1 sess., doc. 2, 589–90; Sturm to Ross, Jan. 15, 1859, *SED*, 36 Cong., 1 sess., doc. 2, 599–600.

67. Sturm to Ross, Jan. 15, 1859, *SED*, 36 Cong., 1 sess., doc. 2, 600.

68. Palo Pinto Citizens Committee to Neighbors and Ross, Dec. 27, 1858, *SED*, 36 Cong., 1 sess., doc. 2, 602–603; Sturm to Ross, Jan. 15, 1859, *SED*, 36 Cong., 1 sess., doc. 2, 600.

69. Ross to Neighbors, Jan. 26, 1859, *SED*, 36 Cong., 1 sess., doc. 2, 596–97.

70. Capt. T. N. Palmer to Lt. W. W. Lowe, Jan. 10, 1859, *SED*, 36 Cong., 1 sess., doc. 2, 601–602.

71. Letter to the People of Texas, Jan. 4, 1859, *SED*, 36 Cong., 1 sess., doc. 2, 606–609; Minutes of Assembly, Jan. 6, 1859, *SED*, 36 Cong., 1 sess., doc. 2, 613–14.

72. Report of the Commissioners, Jan. 12, 1859, *SED*, 36 Cong., 1 sess., doc. 2, 614–15.

73. Proclamation by H. R. Runnels, Jan. 10, 1859, *TIP* 3: 312–13.

74. Neighbors to Denver, Jan. 15, 1859, *SED*, 36 Cong., 1 sess., doc. 2, 590–91; *HR*, 44 Cong., 1 sess., doc. 804, 1.

75. Neighbors to Denver, Jan. 30, 1859, *SED*, 36 Cong., 1 sess., doc. 2, 594–95; Ross to Neighbors, Jan. 26, 1859, *SED*, 36 Cong., 1 sess., doc. 2, 596–97.

76. Ford to E. J. Gurley, Jan. 22, 1859, *SED*, 36 Cong., 1 sess., doc. 2, 606; Neighbors to Denver, Feb. 14, 1859, *SED*, 36 Cong., 1 sess., doc. 2, 603–604; *HR*, 44 Cong., 1 sess., doc. 804, 1.

77. Ross to Neighbors, Feb. 12, 1859, *SED*, 36 Cong., 1 sess., doc. 2, 621–22; Neighbors to Denver, Feb. 22, 1859, *SED*, 36 Cong., 1 sess., doc. 2, 620–21.

78. Ross to Neighbors, Feb. 12, 1859, *SED*, 36 Cong., 1 sess., doc. 2, 621–22; Ross to Neighbors, Feb. 24, 1859, *SED*, 36 Cong., 1 sess., doc. 2, 625–26; Sturm to Ross, Feb. 28, 1859, *SED*, 36 Cong., 1 sess., doc. 2, 627.

79. Ross to Neighbors, Feb. 24, 1859, *SED*, 36 Cong., 1 sess., doc. 2, 625–26; Coombes, *Diary of a Frontiersman*, 49.

80. F. M. Harris to Ross, Mar. 1, 1859, *SED*, 36 Cong., 1 sess., doc. 2, 629; Ross to Neighbors, Mar. 2, 1859, *SED*, 36 Cong., 1 sess., doc. 2, 628; Ross to Runnels, Mar. 4, 1859, *SED*, 36 Cong., 1 sess., doc. 2, 630–31; Coombes, *Diary of a Frontiersman*, 53.

81. Ross to Runnels, Mar. 4, 1859, *SED*, 36 Cong., 1 sess., doc. 2, 630; Ross to Neighbors, Mar. 25, 1859, TAL; Coombes, *Diary of a Frontiersman*, 56.

82. Ross to Neighbors, Mar. 25, 1859, TAL; Neighbors to Denver, Mar. 25, 1859, TAL; Coombes, *Diary of a Frontiersman*, 59.

83. Mix to Neighbors, Mar. 30, 1859, *SED*, 36 Cong., 1 sess., doc. 2, 631–32; Mix to Elias Rector, Mar. 30, 1859, *SED*, 36 Cong., 1 sess., doc. 2, 632–34.

84. Neighbors to Mix, May 12, 1859, *SED*, 36 Cong., 1 sess., doc. 2, 636–37; Ross to Neighbors, May 1, 1859, *SED*, 36 Cong., 1 sess., doc. 2, 639; Gurley to Neighbors, May 5, 1859, *SED*, 36 Cong., 1 sess., doc. 2, 642–43.

85. Petition of Citizens, Apr. 25, 1859, *SED*, 36 Cong., 1 sess., doc. 2, 641–42; Ross to Neighbors, May 1, 1859, *SED*, 36 Cong., 1 sess., doc. 2, 639.

86. Ross to Neighbors, May 1, 1859, *SED*, 36 Cong., 1 sess., doc. 2, 640; Simpson, *Cry Comanche*, 126.

87. Simpson, *Cry Comanche*, 126–29; Chalfant, *Without Quarter*, 64–95; Richardson, *Comanche Barrier*, 242.

88. Sturm to Ross, May 8, 1859, TAL; Raymond Estep, ed., *The Removal of the Texas Indians and the Founding of Fort Cobb: Lieutenant William E. Burnet Letters*, 27–28.

89. Estep, *Burnet Letters*, 28.

90. Estep, *Burnet Letters*, 28; Sturm to Ross, May 8, 1859, TAL.

91. Sturm to Ross, May 8, 1859, TAL; Estep, *Burnet Letters*, 30.

92. Estep, *Burnet Letters*, 31.

93. Estep, *Burnet Letters*, 31.

94. Estep, *Burnet Letters*, 33–34; Ross to Neighbors, May 23, 1859, *SED*, 36 Cong., 1 sess., doc. 2, 645; J. B. Plummer to the Assistant Adjutant General, May 23, 1859, *SED*, 36 Cong., 1 sess., doc. 2, 644.

95. J. B. Plummer to the Assistant Adjutant General, May 23, 1859, *SED*, 36 Cong., 1 sess., doc. 2, 644, 644; Estep, *Burnet Letters*, 34.

96. Plummer to the Assistant Adjutant General, May 23, 1859, *SED*, 36 Cong., 1 sess., doc. 2, 645; Ross to Neighbors, May 26, 1859, *SED*, 36 Cong., 1 sess., doc. 2, 645; Estep, *Burnet Letters*, 34–35.

97. Plummer to the Assistant Adjutant General, May 23, 1859, *SED*, 36 Cong., 1 sess., doc. 2, 645; Ross to Neighbors, May 26, 1859, *SED*, 36 Cong., 1 sess., doc. 2, 645–46; Estep, *Burnet Letters*, 34–35.

98. Ross to Neighbors, May 30, 1859, TAL; Estep, *Burnet Letters*, 36–37.

99. Estep, *Burnet Letters*, 37; Neighbors to A. B. Greenwood, June 10, 1859, *SED*, 36 Cong., 1 sess., doc. 2, 648–49; Charles Barnard to Neighbors, May 30, 1859, TAL.

100. Neighbors to A. B. Greenwood, June 10, 1859, *SED*, 36 Cong., 1 sess., doc. 2, 649–50; Greenwood to Neighbors, June 11, 1859, *SED*, 36 Cong., 1 sess., doc. 2, 650–51.

Chapter Four: The Civil War Era, 1859-67

1. Instructions to peace commissioners, June 6, 1859, *SED*, 36 Cong., 1 sess., doc. 2, 657–58; Runnels to Allison Nelson, June 6, 1859, *SED*, 36 Cong., 1 sess., doc. 2, 655–56.

2. Report of the peace commission, June 27, 1859, *SED*, 36 Cong., 1 sess., doc. 2, 665; G. B. Erath to Neighbors and Ross, June 20, 1859, *SED*, 36 Cong., 1 sess., doc. 2, 663.

3. Meeting of the citizens of Parker County, June 24, 1859, *SED*, 36 Cong., 1 sess., doc. 2, 684–85; To the citizens and friends of the frontier counties of the State of Texas, June 24, 1859, *SED*, 36 Cong., 1 sess., doc. 2, 685–86; Neighbors to Greenwood, July 10, 1859, *SED*, 36 Cong., 1 sess., doc. 2, 686–87.

4. Rector to Greenwood, July 2, 1859, *SED*, 36 Cong., 1 sess., doc. 2, 673–77; Mark Keller and Thomas A. Belser, Jr., eds., "Albert Pike's Contribution to the *Spirit of the Times*, Including His 'Letter from the Far, Far West,'" *Arkansas Historical Quarterly* 37 (Winter, 1978): 339–47; Muriel H. Wright,

"A History of Fort Cobb," *CO* 34 (Spring, 1956): 55; Berlin B. Chapman, "Establishment of the Wichita Reservation," *CO* 3 (Summer, 1955): 1047.

5. This council, which would come to be known as the Fort Arbuckle Agreement of July 1, 1859, would prove to be a major point of contention between the federal government and the Wichitas and Caddos in the future struggle over the precise definition of their lands. See Rector to Greenwood, July 2, 1859, *SED*, 36 Cong., 1 sess., doc. 2, 678; Neighbors to Greenwood, July 4, 1859, *SED*, 36 Cong., 1 sess., doc. 2, 683; Keller and Belser, "Albert Pike's Contributions," 349–50; Testimony of Niastor and George Washington, Jan. 22, 1883, *SED*, 49 Cong., 1 sess., doc. 13, 119–20, 123–24. Despite the promises of indemnity, the reserve tribes were never repaid by the United States. For an example of one of the many pleas for repayment on the part of the Indians see Milo Gookins to D. N. Cooley, May 18, 1866, WAL.

6. General statement of houses formerly occupied by each of the several tribes at Brazos Agency, Texas, July 30, 1859, TAL; Invoice of Indian hogs sold, July 27, 1859, TAL.

7. Ross to Greenwood, May 30, 1860, WAL; Ross to Neighbors, Aug. 25, 1859, TAL.

8. John Henry Brown to Neighbors, July 14, 1859, *SED*, 36 Cong., 1 sess., doc. 2, 689; Neighbors to Greenwood, July 25, 1859, *SED*, 36 Cong., 1 sess., doc. 2, 688.

9. Neighbors to Greenwood, July 25, 1859, *SED*, 36 Cong., 1 sess., doc. 2, 688; Matthew Leeper to Neighbors, July 24, 1859, *SED*, 36 Cong., 1 sess., doc. 2, 692–93.

10. Kenneth F. Neighbours, "Indian Exodus out of Texas in 1859," *WTHAYB* 36 (Oct., 1960): 82–84.

11. Census Roll of Indians, July 28, 1859, TAL; Abstract of articles for Indians of Texas issued as presents, July 31, 1859, TAL; Memorandum of travel from Brazos Agency, Texas to False Washita Agency, July 31, 1859, TAL; Invoice of property belonging to the Brazos Reserve tribes on their removal, July 30, 1859, TAL.

12. Memorandum of travel, Aug. 1, 1859, TAL; Estep, *Burnet Letters*, 49.

13. Memorandum of travel, Aug 1–7, 1859, TAL; Neighbours, "Indian Exodus out of Texas," 85–87.

14. Neighbours, "Indian Exodus out of Texas," 87.

15. Memorandum of travel, Aug. 8, 1859, TAL; quoted in Neighbours, "Indian Exodus out of Texas," 80.

16. Neighbours, "Indian Exodus out of Texas," 88.

17. Memorandum of travel, Aug. 9–13, 1859, TAL.

18. Neighbors to Greenwood, Aug. 18, 1859, *SED*, 36 Cong., 1 sess., doc. 2, 697; Blain to Rector, Aug. 12, 1859, *SED*, 36 Cong., 1 sess., doc. 2, 698; Blain to Rector, Aug. 15, 1589, *SED*, 36 Cong., 1 sess., doc. 2, 699.

19. Memorandum of travel, Aug. 14–15, 1859, TAL; Neighbors to Greenwood, Aug. 18, 1859, *SED*, 36 Cong., 1 sess., doc. 2, 697; Neighbours, "Indian Exodus out of Texas," 94.

20. Memorandum of travel, Aug. 16–17, 1859, TAL; Neighbors to Greenwood, Aug. 18, 1859, *SED*, 36 Cong., 1 sess., doc. 2, 697.

21. Neighbors to Greenwood, Sept. 3, 1859, *SED*, 36 Cong., 1 sess., doc. 2, 700.

22. Neighbors to Greenwood, Sept. 3, 1859, *SED*, 36 Cong., 1 sess., doc. 2, 700–701; quotes from Neighbours, "Indian Exodus out of Texas," 94–96.

23. Statement of Leeper, Sept. 15, 1859, *SED*, 36 Cong., 1 sess., doc. 2, 701–702; Neighbours, "The Assassination of Robert S. Neighbors," *WTHAYB* 34 (Oct., 1958): 47–49. Cornett was not indicted for murder until May, 1860, but he did not appear for trial. Later that fall a contingent of Texas Rangers found Cornett where he was hiding in the hills around Belknap and killed him.

24. Greenwood to Jacob Thompson, *SED*, 36 Cong., 1 sess., doc. 2, 383.

25. Wright, "A History of Fort Cobb," 55–56; Neighbors to Greenwood, Sept. 3, 1859, *SED*, 36 Cong., 1 sess., doc. 2, 700; William S. Nye, *Carbine and Lance: The Story of Old Fort Sill*, 28.

26. Neighbors to Greenwood, Sept. 3, 1859, *SED*, 36 Cong., 1 sess., doc. 2, 700; Blain to Greenwood, Jan. 25, 1860, WAL; Leeper to Rector, Sept. 26, 1860, WAL; Leeper to Rector, Jan. 13, 1862, in Annie Heloise Abel, *The American Indian as Slaveholder and Secessionist*, 339–41.

27. Rector to Greenwood, Feb. 15, 1859, WAL; Blain to Greenwood, Mar. 31, 1859, WAL.

28. Blain to Greenwood, Mar. 31, 1859, WAL.

29. Leeper to Rector, Sept. 26, 1860, WAL; Rector to Greenwood, Aug. 9, 1860, WAL; Rector to Mix, Sept. 10, 1860, WAL.

30. Milton Jacks to President James Buchanan, Feb. 7, 1860, WAL.

31. Jacks to Buchanan, Feb. 7, 1860, WAL; J. B. Standifer to Buchanan, Mar. 4, 1860, WAL; Blain to Governor Sam Houston, Apr. 15, 1860, WAL.

32. Blain to Houston, Apr. 23, 1860, *TIP* 3: 31–33.

33. Blain to Houston, Apr. 23, 1860, *TIP* 3: 31–33.

34. Rector to Greenwood, May 3, 1860, WAL; Blain to Houston, May 10, 1860, *TIP* 3: 3–34.

35. Nye, *Carbine and Lance*, 28.

36. Rector to Greenwood, Aug. 23, 1860, WAL.

37. Leeper to Rector, Oct. 12, 1860, WAL.

38. Nye, *Carbine and Lance*, 32; John Shirley to Captain Gilbert, Dec. 22, 1860, WAL; Shirley to Gilbert, Dec. 28, 1860, WAL.

39. Leeper to Greenwood, Jan. 19, 1861, WAL.

40. E. D. Townsend to Lt. Col. William H. Emory, Mar. 18, 1861, *The War of the Rebellion: A Compilation of the Official Records of the Union and Confederate Armies*, 1st ser., 1: 658; Wright, "A History of Fort Cobb," 57.

41. Emory to Townsend, Apr. 13, 1861, *War of the Rebellion*, 1st ser., 1: 665; Emory to the commanding officer at Fort Cobb, Apr. 10, 1861, *War of the Rebellion*, 1st ser., 1: 663; Leeper to Emory, Mar. 31, 1861, WAL.

42. Emory to Townsend, May 19, 1861, *War of the Rebellion*, 1st ser., 1: 648; Wright, "A History of Fort Cobb," 57–59.

43. Wright, "A History of Fort Cobb," 59; Ariel Gibson, "Confederates on the Plains: The Pike Mission to the Wichita Agency," *Great Plains Journal* 4 (Fall, 1964): 9, 14.

44. Albert Pike to Robert Toombs, May 29, 1861, *War of the Rebellion*, 4th ser., 1: 359–61; Pike to Leeper, May 26, 1861, WAL.

45. Gibson, "Confederates on the Plains," 9–10.

46. Gibson, "Confederates on the Plains," 10; Articles of a Convention, Aug. 12, 1861, *War of the Rebellion*, 4th ser., 1: 542–46.

47. Gibson, "Confederates on the Plains," 14; J. J. Hooper to President Jefferson Davis, Dec. 24, 1861, *War of the Rebellion*, 4th ser., 1: 813.

48. Wright, "A History of Fort Cobb," 59; John Reed Swanton, *Source Material on the History and Ethnology of the Caddo Indians*, 116, claims that according to the *Jackson Catalogue of Photographic Prints*, George Washington was "captain during the rebellion of a company of Indian scouts and rangers in the service of the Confederate States army."

49. George W. Collamore to William P. Dole, Apr. 21, 1862, *SED*, 37 Cong., 3 sess., doc. 1, 301; E. H. Carruth to Dole, Apr. 10, 1862, WAL; Wright, "A History of Fort Cobb," 59.

50. Neighbours, "José María: Anadarko Chief," 274.

51. S. S. Scott to James A. Seddon, Jan. 12, 1863, *War of the Rebellion*, 4th ser., 2: 354–56; Wright, "A History of Fort Cobb," 59; Nye, *Carbine and Lance*, 29.

52. Scott to Seddon, Jan. 12, 1863, *War of the Rebellion*, 4th ser., 2: 354–55; Jeanne V. Harmon, "Matthew Leeper, Confederate Agent at the Wichita Agency, Indian Territory," *CO* 47 (Fall, 1967): 249.

53. Wright, "A History of Fort Cobb," 61; Nye, *Carbine and Lance*, 28.

54. Scott to Seddon, Jan. 12, 1863, *War of the Rebellion*, 4th ser., 2: 355.

55. Carruth to W. G. Coffin, Sept. 6, 1863, *HED*, 38 Cong., 1 sess., doc. 1, 304; Coffin to Dole, Sept. 24, 1863, *HED*, 38 Cong., 1 sess., doc. 1, 295.

56. Carruth to Coffin, June 14, 1863, *HED*, 38 Cong., 1 sess., doc. 1, 326.

57. Milo Gookins to Coffin, Oct. 20, 1864, *HED*, 38 Cong., 2 sess., doc. 1, 465.

58. Gookins to Coffin, Oct. 11, 1864, WAL; Coffin to Dole, Sept. 24, 1864, *HED*, 38 Cong., 2 sess., doc. 1, 449; A. V. Coffin to W. G. Coffin, Aug. 25, 1864, *HED*, 38 Cong., 2 sess., doc. 1, 451–52.

59. Coffin to Dole, Sept. 24, 1864, *HED*, 38 Cong., 2 sess., doc. 1, 449; Allan C. Ashcraft, ed., "Confederate Indian Department Conditions in August 1864," *CO* 41 (Autumn, 1963): 280.

60. Gookins to Coffin, Oct. 20, 1864, *HED*, 38 Cong., 2 sess., doc. 1, 463–64; Coffin to Dole, Sept. 24, 1864, *HED*, 38 Cong., 2 sess., doc. 1, 449.

61. Gookins to Coffin, Oct. 20, 1864, *HED*, 38 Cong., 2 sess., doc. 1, 463; Gookins to Coffin, Oct. 17, 1864, WAL.

62. Gookins to Coffin, Oct. 17, 1864, WAL; Memorial of the Chiefs and Headmen, Oct. 14, 1864, WAL.

63. Coffin to Gookins, Oct. 27, 1864, WAL.

64. Gookins to Elijah Sells, Sept. 18, 1865, *HED*, 39 Cong., 1 sess., doc. 1, 473–74; Gookins to D. N. Cooley, Dec. 18, 1865, WAL.

65. Gookins to Dole, Apr. 24, 1865, WAL; Gookins to Sells, Sept. 18, 1865, *HED*, 39 Cong., 1 sess., doc. 1, 473.

66. Gookins to Dole, Apr. 24, 1865, WAL; Gookins to Sells, Sept. 18, 1865, *HED*, 39 Cong., 1 sess., doc. 1, 472–73.

67. Gookins to Sells, Sept. 18, 1865, *HED*, 39 Cong., 1 sess., doc. 1, 472–73; Sells to Cooley, n.d., *HED*, 39 Cong., 1 sess., doc. 1, 443–44. The census showed 392 Taovayas, 135 Wacos, 151 Tawakonis, and 144 Kichais. Henry Shanklin to Sells, Sept. 29, 1866, *HED*, 39 Cong., 2 sess., doc. 1, 322.

68. Gookins to Cooley, Mar. 29, 1866, WAL; Gookins to Cooley, May 2, 1866, WAL.

69. Gookins to Cooley, June 2, 1866, WAL; Gookins to Cooley, May 10, 1866, WAL.

70. Gookins to Cooley, June 2, 1866, WAL; Henry Shanklin to Sells, July 6, 1866, WAL; Shanklin to Sells, July 13, 1866, WAL; Shanklin to Sells, Sept. 29, 1866, *HED*, 39 Cong., 2 sess., doc. 1, 322.

71. Shanklin to Sells, July 6, 1866, WAL; Shanklin to Sells, July 23, 1866, WAL; Sells to Cooley, Sept. 30, 1866, *HED*, 39 Cong., 2 sess., doc. 1, 282.

72. Statement of provisions, Aug. 3, 1866, WAL; Statement of provisions, July 31, 1867, WAL; James McCullough to Cooley, Sept. 21, 1866, WAL; Shanklin to William Byers, Nov. 12, 1866, WAL; Byers to William Bogy, Dec. 7, 1866, WAL.

73. Byers to Bogy, Dec. 21, 1866, WAL; Shanklin to Col. James Wortham, July 5, 1867, WAL.

74. Wortham to N. G. Taylor, Oct. 21, 1867, *HED*, 40 Cong., 2 sess., doc. 1, 316; Shanklin to Taylor, May 21, 1867, WAL; E. G. Ross to Taylor, May 28, 1867, WAL.

75. Shanklin to Wortham, July 5, 1867, WAL; Shanklin to Wortham, Sept. 1, 1867, *HED*, 40 Cong., 2 sess., doc. 1, 322.

76. Shanklin to Wortham, Sept. 1, 1867, *HED*, 40 Cong., 2 sess., doc. 1, 322.

77. Shanklin to Wortham, Sept. 1, 1867, *HED*, 40 Cong., 2 sess., doc. 1, 322; Statement of provisions issued to Indians from July 1–31, July 31, 1867, WAL; Shanklin to Wortham, Sept. 1, 1867, *HED*, 40 Cong., 2 sess., doc. 1, 322; J. J. Chollar to Wortham, Oct. 19, 1867, WAL.

78. Shanklin to Wortham, Oct. 24, 1867, WAL; Philip McCaskin to Col. Thomas Murphy, Nov. 15, 1867, WAL; Shanklin to Col. James Hotchiss, Nov. 17, 1867, WAL.

Chapter Five: Reestablishment of the Wichita Agency, 1868-78

1. For an overview of the Peace Policy see Prucha, *The Great Father*, 1: 479–519.

2. Kappler, *Indian Affairs: Laws and Treaties*, 2: 977–82.

3. Kappler, *Indian Affairs: Laws and Treaties*, 1: 839–41.

4. C. F. Garrett to J. B. Henderson, Dec. 24, 1867, WAL; Garrett to N. G. Taylor, Feb. 7, 1868, WAL; Shanklin to Wortham, June 6, 1868, WAL; List of Indians at the Wichita Agency, November 30, 1869, KAF 2.

5. Shanklin to Taylor, May 30, 1868, WAL; Shanklin to Wortham, June 6, 1868, WAL; Shanklin to Taylor, June 15, 1868, WAL; Shanklin to S. N. Robinson, Oct. 1, 1868, *HED*, 40 Cong., 3 sess., doc. 1, 747.

6. Shanklin to Wortham, June 6, 1868, WAL; Shanklin to Taylor, June 15, 1868, WAL; Robinson to Taylor, Nov. 16, 1868, WAL.

7. Robinson to Taylor, Nov. 16, 1868, WAL; Gen. W. B. Hazen to Philip McCusker, Jan. 20, 1869, WAL; Nye, *Carbine and Lance*, 84–88.

8. Jonathan Richards to Enoch Hoag, Oct. 26, 1870, WAL.

9. Statistical Return of Farming at the Wichita Agency, 1869, WAL.

10. Report of Vincent Colyer, 1869, *HED*, 41 Cong., 2 sess., doc. 1, 526–27; Views of a delegation of Friends, Sept. 22, 1869, *HED*, 41 Cong., 2 sess., doc. 1, 526–27.

11. Aubrey L. Steele, "The Beginning of Quaker Administration of Indian Affairs in Oklahoma," *CO* 17 (Dec., 1939): 366–71; Hoag to Hazen, Apr. 11, 1870, WAL.

12. Richards to Hoag, Oct. 26, 1870, *HED*, 41 Cong., 3 sess., doc. 1, 857–58; Chapman, "Establishment of the Wichita Reservation," 1052–53.

13. Richards to Hoag, Aug. 21, 1871, *HED*, no. 1, 42 Cong., 2 sess., 892–95; Richards to Ely S. Parker, Jan. 30, 1871, WAL; Richards to Hoag, Sept. 1, 1872, *HED*, 43 Cong., 3 sess., doc. 1, 636–37.

14. Ration amounts listed in Richards to Hoag, Nov. 13, 1872, WAL; Richards to Hoag, Aug. 30, 1870, WAL; Richards to Hoag, Oct. 26, 1870, *HED*, 41 Cong., 3 sess., doc. 1, 858; Richards to Hoag, Sept. 1, 1872, *HED*, 42 Cong., 3 sess., doc. 1, 638; Richards to Hoag, Jan. 10, 1873, WAL. Four years later the new agent was making the same request for monthly rations. See A. C. Williams to William Nicholson, Feb. 17, 1877, WAL.

15. Richards to Hoag, Feb. 7, 1871, WAL; Statistical return of farming, 1871, *HED*, 42 Cong., 2 sess., doc. 1, 1048; Richards to Hoag, Sept. 1, 1872, *HED*, 42 Cong., 3 sess., doc. 1, 636–37; Richards to Hoag, Sept. 1, 1873, *HED*, 43 Cong., 1 sess., doc. 1, 591–92; Statistical Returns by Tribe and Band, 1873, WAL.

16. Statistical returns by tribe and band, 1873, WAL; Richards to Hoag, Sept. 1, 1872, *HED*, 42 Cong., 3 sess., doc. 1, 636; Table showing the number of acres in Indian reservations & c., 1872, *HED*, 42 Cong., 3 sess., doc. 1, 788–89.

17. Richards to Hoag, Sept. 1, 1872, *HED*, 42 Cong., 3 sess., doc. 1, 636–37; Richards to Hoag, Sept. 1, 1873, *HED*, 43 Cong., 1 sess., doc. 1, 591–92; Statistical returns by tribe and band, 1873, WAL.

18. Richards to Hoag, Sept. 1, 1874, *HED*, 43 Cong., 2 sess., doc. 1, 545.

19. Josiah Butler, "Pioneer School Teaching at the Comanche-Kiowa Agency School, 1870–1873: Being the Reminiscences of the First Teacher," *Co* 6 (Dec., 1928): 499–507; Richards to Hoag, Aug. 28, 1871, *HED*, 42 Cong., 2 sess., doc. 1, 894.

20. Thomas C. Battey, *The Life and Adventures of a Quaker among the Indians*, 27–75; Standing to Richards, June 5, 1873, WBSP.

21. Richards to Hoag, Sept. 1, 1872, *HED*, 42 Cong., 3 sess., doc. 1, 637; Standing to Richards, June 5, 1873, WBSP; Richards to Hoag, Sept. 1, 1873, *HED*, 43 Cong., 1 sess., doc. 1, 592; Richards to Longstreet, Nov. 20, 1873, WAL; Richards to Hoag, Sept. 1, 1874, *HED*, 43 Cong., 2 sess., doc. 1, 546.

22. Richards to Hoag, Aug. 28, 1871, *HED*, 42 Cong., 2 sess., doc. 1, 893; Richards to Hoag, Sept. 1, 1872, *HED*, 42 Cong., 3 sess, doc. 1, 636–38; Richards to Hoag, Sept. 1, 1873, *HED*, 43 Cong., 1 sess., doc. 1, 592; Statistical returns by tribe and band, 1873, WAL.

23. Richards to Hoag, Feb. 7, 1871, WAL; Richards to Hoag, Aug. 28, 1871, *HED*, 42 Cong., 2 sess., doc. 1, 894.

24. William T. Hagan, *United States–Comanche Relations: The Reservation Years*, 60–86.

25. Report of Capt. Henry E. Alvord, Oct. 10, 1872, *HED*, 42 Cong., 3 sess., doc. 1, 513–16; Richards to Hoag, Jan. 13, 1873, WAL.

26. Affidavit of J. J. Sturm, Feb. 24, 1883, *SR*, 49 Cong., 1 sess., doc. 1278, 127–28; Report of Alvord, Oct. 10, 1872, *HED*, 42 Cong., 3 sess., doc. 1, 525.

27. Affidavits of Sturm, Philip McCusker, and William Shirley, Feb. 22–26, 1883, *SR*, 49 Cong., 1 sess, doc. 1278, 127–29; General council of the Wichitas and Affiliated Tribes, May 15, 1883, KAF 48. Wichita, Caddo, Delaware, and Penateka Comanche headmen met in council in 1877 to protest the land settlement and officially claim all the land westward to the 100th meridian. See Petition of chiefs and headmen, Sept. 17, 1877, WAL.

28. Agreement with the Wichitas and other Indians, Oct. 19, 1872, *HED*, 42 Cong., 3 sess., doc. 65, 1–3; Chapman, "Establishment of the Wichita Reservation," 1053–55.

29. Richards to Hoag, Sept. 1, 1872, *HED*, 42 Cong., 3 sess., doc. 1, 637; Richards to Hoag, July 19, 1873, WAL; Beede to Edward P. Smith, July 28, 1873, WAL; Richards to Hoag, Feb. 19, 1874, WAL; Richards to Hoag, Sept. 1, 1874, *HED*, 43 Cong., 2 sess., doc. 1, 546.

30. Isaac Gibson to Hoag, May 21, 1873, WAL; Apology of chiefs and headmen of Osage tribe, May 31, 1873, WAL; Richards to Hoag, Sept. 1, 1873, *HED*, 43 Cong., 1 sess., doc. 1, 593.

31. Hagan, *United States–Comanche Relations*, 92–109; James L. Haley, *The Buffalo War: The History of the Red River Indian Uprising of 1874*, 95–106.

32. Haley, *The Buffalo War*, 114–16.

33. Haley, *The Buffalo War*, 116–23; J. Connell to Richards, Aug. 22, 1874, WAL; Lt. Col. J. W. Davidson to Assistant Adjutant General, Dept. of Texas, Aug. 27, 1874, WAL.

34. Richards to Hoag, Aug. 28, 1874, WAL; Richards to Hoag, Sept. 1, 1874, *HED*, 43 Cong., 2 sess., doc. 1, 546; Hagan, *United States–Comanche Relations*, 119; Richard Henry Pratt, *Battlefield and Classroom: Four Decades with the American Indian, 1867–1904*, ed. Robert M. Utley, 67.

35. In his annual report Richards states that "a band of Tooc-a-nie Kiowas (part Wichita and part Kiowa) who had for several years lived with the Wichitas and Wacoes went to the Kiowas of the Kiowa agency." This statement flies in the face of the historical enmity between the tribes and seems unlikely. However, there is no doubt that the Wichitas went somewhere; their population totals which had been consistently near 700 since 1868, dropped to 486 in 1875 and would stay near that level for the rest of the century. Here are the census returns for 1874 and 1875, respectively: 300/228 Taovayas, 140/66 Wacos, 125/102 Tawakonis, and 106/90 Kichais. Since the Kiowas and Pawnees were in such a state of flux, their census returns are inconclusive. Richards to Smith, Sept. 1, 1875, *HED*, 44 Cong., 1 sess., doc. 1, 791; Williams to the CIA, *HED*, 45 Cong., 2 sess., doc. 1, 508; Martha Royce Blaine, *Pawnee Passage: 1870–1875*, 269–92; Karl Schmitt, "Wichita-Kiowa Relations and the 1874 Outbreak," CO 28 (Summer, 1950): 154–60.

36. Richards to Hoag, Nov. 28, 1878, WAL; Richards to Hoag, Mar. 12, 1875, WAL; Richards to Hoag, Sept. 1, 1875, *HED*, no. 1, 44 Cong., 1 sess., 790.

37. Richards to Hoag, Sept. 1, 1875, *HED*, 44 Cong., 1 sess., doc. 1, 790–91.

38. Williams to the CIA, Aug. 21, 1876, *HED*, 44 Cong., 2 sess., doc. 1, 468; Table showing agricultural improvements . . . 1876, *HED*, 44 Cong., 2 sess., doc. 1, 632–33; Table showing agricultural improvements . . . 1877, *HED*, 45

Cong., 2 sess., doc. 1, 706–707; Table showing agricultural improvements . . .
1878, *HED*, 45 Cong., 3 sess., doc. 1, 798–99.

39. Table showing agricultural improvements . . . 1875, *HED*, 44 Cong., 1 sess.,
doc. 1, 626–27; Table showing agricultural improvements . . . 1876, *HED*, 44
Cong., 2 sess., doc. 1, 632–33; Williams to CIA, Dec. 1, 1876, KAF 6; Table
showing agricultural improvements . . . 1877, *HED*, 45 Cong., 2 sess., doc. 1,
706–707; Williams to Ezra Hayt, Dec. 1, 1877, KAF 7; Table showing agricultural improvements . . . 1878, *HED*, 45 Cong. 3 sess., doc. 1, 798–99;
Statistics of stock owned . . . 1882, *HED*, 47 Cong., 2 sess., doc. 1, 412–13.

40. Williams to the CIA, Aug. 20, 1877, *HED*, 45 Cong., 2 sess., doc. 1, 508.

41. Henry Dawes, Annual Report, July 1, 1876, WBSP; Dawes, Monthly
Report, Dec. 31, 1877; Williams to the CIA, Aug. 31, 1878, *HED*, 45 Cong., 3
sess., doc. 1, 566; Charles Campbell to Hoag, Mar. 29, 1878, WAL.

42. Appointment of Andrew Williams, Feb. 8, 1876, WAL; Williams to the
CIA, Apr. 2, 1877, KAF 6.

43. Hagan, *United States–Comanche Relations*, 135–38; Davidson to the Assistant Adjutant General, July 24, 1878, WAL.

44. Williams to CIA, July 2, 1878, WAL; Davidson to the Assistant Adjutant
General, July 24, 1878, WAL.

Chapter Six: Life on the Wichita Reservation, 1879–1901

1. J. Lee Hall to CIA, Aug. 26, 1886, *HED*, 49 Cong., 2 sess., doc. 1, 346–47;
P. B. Hunt to CIA, Aug. 30, 1879, *HED*, 46 Cong., 2 sess, doc. 1, 169; Hunt,
Monthly Report, July 3, 1879, KAF 9; Hunt to CIA, Jan. 7, 1880, KAF 9.

2. Hunt to CIA, Aug. 30, 1879, *HED*, 46 Cong., 2 sess., doc. 1, 170; E. E.
White to CIA, Aug. 18, 1888, *HED*, 50 Cong., 2 sess., doc. 1, 95; George
Day to CIA, Aug. 30, 1892, *HED*, 52 Cong., 2 sess., doc. 1, 387; List of
persons employed in the Indian Agency service on June 30, 1901, *HED*, 57
Cong., 1 sess., doc. 5, 770; Hagan, *United States–Comanche Relations*, 141.

3. Hagan, *United States–Comanche Relations*, 166–70.

4. Hagan, *United States–Comanche Relations*, 216–19.

5. Hunt to CIA, Aug. 30, 1879, *HED*, 46 Cong., 2 sess., doc. 1, 170.

6. J. Lee Hall to CIA, Sept. 29, 1886, *HED*, 49 Cong., 2 sess., doc. 1, 346–47;
Journal of Webb Meridaux, 1885, KAF 99.

7. List of Farms on the Wichita Agency, June 30, 1890, KAF 99; Journal of
Webb Meridaux, 1885, KAF 99; E. E. White, *Experiences of a Special Indian
Agent*, 242.

8. Bessie Hunter Snake Interview, DDOIHC; Journal of Webb Meridaux,
1885, KAF 99; List of Farms on the Wichita Agency, June 30, 1890, KAF 99.

9. Wichita Agency Census, 1883, KAF 2; Wichita and Affiliated Bands
Census, 1894, KAF 4; List of Indians at the Kiowa, Comanche, and
Wichita Agency, Jan. 20, 1898, KAF 29. For a Caddo genealogy, see Elsie
Clews Parsons, "Notes on the Caddo," *Memoirs of the American Anthropo-
logical Association* 57 (1941): 14–21.

10. Wichita Agency Census, 1883, KAF 2; Wichita Census, June 30, 1889, KAF
2; Wichita and Affiliated Bands Census, 1894, KAF 4; List of Indians at the
Kiowa, Comanche, and Wichita Agency, Jan. 20, 1898, KAF 29.

11. Hunt to CIA, July 3, 1879, KAF 9; Hunt to CIA, Aug. 10, 1879, KAF 9; Hunt to CIA, Aug. 30, 1879, *HED*, 46 Cong., 2 sess., doc. 1, 172; Hunt to CIA, Sept. 1, 1880, *HED*, 46 Cong., 3 sess., doc. 1, 197; Hunt to CIA, Sept. 1, 1881, *HED*, 47 Cong., 1 sess., doc. 1, 139; Hunt to CIA, Aug. 31, 1885, *HED*, 49 Cong., 1 sess., doc. 1, 313; E. E. White to CIA, *HED*, 50 Cong., 2 sess., doc. 1, 97; W. D. Myers to CIA, Aug. 27, 1889, *HED*, 51 Cong., 1 sess., doc. 1, 190.

12. Hunt to CIA, Sept. 1, 1880, *HED*, 46 Cong., 3 sess., doc. 1, 197–98; Frank Baldwin to the secretary of the interior, Feb. 20, 1895, KAL 22; Report of CIA, 1898, *HED*, 55 Cong., 3 sess., doc. 5, 56.

13. Baldwin to CIA, Aug. 28, 1897, *HED*, 55 Cong., 2 sess., doc. 5, 231; Hunt to CIA, Nov. 11, 1879, KAF 9; Hunt to CIA, Sept. 1, 1881, *HED*, 47 Cong., 1 sess., doc. 1, 136–37; Hunt to CIA, Aug. 17, 1883, *HED*, 48 Cong., 1 sess., doc. 1, 129; White to CIA, Aug. 18, 1888, *HED*, 50 Cong., 1 sess., doc. 1, 96–97.

14. White to CIA, Aug. 18, 1888, *HED*, 50 Cong., 1 sess., doc. 1, 96–97; Baldwin to CIA, *HED*, 54 Cong., 1 sess., doc. 5, 251; Baldwin to CIA, *HED*, 55 Cong., 2 sess., doc. 5, 231.

15. Hunt to CIA, Aug. 30, 1879, *HED*, 46 Cong., 2 sess., doc. 1, 174; Hunt to CIA, Feb. 5, 1880, KAF 9; Hunt to CIA, Sept. 1, 1881, *HED*, 47 Cong., 1 sess., doc. 1, 140; Hunt to CIA, Aug. 17, 1883, *HED*, 48 Cong., 1 sess., doc. 1, 128; Adams to CIA, Sept. 16, 1890, *HED*, 51 Cong., 2 sess., doc. 1, 186–87; Day to CIA, Aug. 30, 1892, *HED*, 52 Cong., 2 sess., doc. 1, 387.

16. The Taovaya population dropped from 209 in 1879 to 157 in 1894, the last time the Wichitas were accurately enumerated by tribe. The Tawakonis dropped from 155 to 128, the Wacos from 49 to 36, and the Kichais from 75 to 52.

17. Williams to CIA, Aug. 21, 1876, *HED*, 44 Cong., 2 sess., doc. 1, 470; Calmes to Hunt, Aug. 30, 1879, WBSP. For background on federal policy regarding education for Indians, see Francis Paul Prucha, *American Indian Policy in Crisis: Christian Reformers and the Indian, 1865–1900*, 265–327.

18. Ruby W. Shannon, *"Friends" For the Indians: One Hundred Years of Education at Riverside Indian School, Anadarko, Oklahoma*, 24–28; Hunt to CIA, Nov. 1, 1879, KAF 9; Statement of Calmes, Dec. 24, 1881, WBSP; Hunt to CIA, Aug. 31, 1885, *HED*, 49 Cong., 1 sess., doc. 1, 311–12; Hall to CIA, Aug. 26, 1886, *HED*, 49 Cong., 2 sess., doc. 1, 347; George Pigg to CIA, June 30, 1897, *HED*, 55 Cong., 2 sess., doc. 5, 234; Randlett to CIA, Sept. 1, 1899, *HED*, 56 Cong., 1 sess., doc. 5, 287.

19. Calmes, Monthly Report, Jan. 31, 1880, WBSP; Calmes to Hunt, Sept. 6, 1881, *HED*, 47 Cong., 1 sess., doc. 1, 143; J. W. Hadden, Monthly Report, Jan. 1, 1884, *HED*, 47 Cong., 1 sess., doc. 1, 143; Statistics as to Indian schools during the year ended June 30, 1898, *HED*, 55 Cong., 3 sess., doc. 5, 588–89.

20. Andrew Dunlap Interview, DDOIHC; Calmes to Hunt, Aug. 18, 1883, KAF 12; George Pigg to CIA, June 30, 1897, *HED*, 55 Cong., 2 sess., doc. 5, 234. For an overview of the curriculum at Indian schools throughout the country, see Michael C. Coleman, *American Indian Children at School, 1850–1930*, 105–26.

21. Thackeray to CIA, July 5, 1900, *HED*, 56 Cong., 2 sess., doc. 5, 335. For the failure of boarding schools to destroy tribal identity, see Sally J. McBeth,

Ethnic Identity and the Boarding School Experience of West-Central Oklahoma American Indians.

22. Hunt to CIA, Sept. 1, 1881, *HED*, 47 Cong., 1 sess., doc. 1, 140.

23. Pratt had commanded Wichita and Caddo scouts in the final campaigns against the Comanches. See Pratt, *Battlefield and Classroom*, 67.

24. Prucha, *American Indian Policy in Crisis*, 271–80; Carlisle Indian School Statement of Attendance, Nov. 25, 1900, KAF 90.

25. Coleman, *American Indian Children at School*, 41–50; K. Tsianina Lomawaima, *They Called It Prairie Light: The Story of Chilocco Indian School*, 1–6; List of Pupils from Kiowa and Comanche Agency enrolled at Chilocco, from 1884 to 1900, inclusive, KAF 91; Donald F. Lindsey, *Indians at Hampton Institute, 1877–1923*, 40–44.

26. Pratt to Hunt, Aug. 27, 1881, KAF 89; List of Indian Children selected from the several tribes at the Kiowa, Comanche, and Wichita Agency sent to Carlisle, Penn., Aug. 20, 1882, KAF 12; O. K. Bales to U.S. Indian Agent, Anadarko, July 5, 1892, KAF 93.

27. Lomawaima, *They Called It Prairie Light*, 20–21; Coleman, *American Indian Children at School*, 112–15; Finley to Baldwin, Feb. 10, 1898, KAF 89.

28. Hunt to CIA, Aug. 31, 1885, *HED*, 49 Cong., 1 sess., doc. 1, 311–12; Baldwin to CIA, Aug. 28, 1896, *HED*, 54 Cong., 2 sess., doc. 5, 256; Prucha, *American Indian Policy in Crisis*, 279–83.

29. Williams to CIA, Aug. 31, 1878, *HED*, 45 Cong., 3 sess., doc. 1, 566; Hunt to CIA, Aug. 30, 1879, *HED*, 46 Cong., 2 sess., doc. 1, 174; Hunt to CIA, June 2, 1880, KAF 10; Hunt to CIA, Sept. 1, 1881, *HED*, 47 Cong., 1 sess., doc. 1, 140; Adams to CIA, Sept. 16, 1890, *HED*, 51 Cong., 2 sess., doc. 1, 188.

30. Prucha, *American Indian Policy in Crisis*, 290–91.

31. Bruce David Forbes, "John Jasper Methvin, Methodist 'Missionary to the Western Tribes'" in *Churchmen and the Western Tribes, 1820–1920*, ed. Clyde A. Milner II and Floyd A. O'Neill, 48–56; Methvin Mission Standard Report, June 30, 1890, and Mar. 31, 1893, KAF 96; Mary Gregory Memorial School Report of Pupils, Mar., 1897, and Dec. 31, 1897, KAF 96; Statistics as to Indian schools during the year ended June 30, 1896, *HED*, 54 Cong., 2 sess., doc. 5, 510–11.

32. St. Patrick's Quarterly Report, Dec. 25, 1894, KAF 93; Sadie Weller Interview and Andrew Dunlap Interview, DDOIHC.

33. Mooney, *The Ghost Dance Religion*, 772–91; Prucha, *The Great Father*, 2: 726–30.

34. Mooney, *The Ghost Dance Religion*, 900–905; Parsons, "Notes on the Caddo," 47–50.

35. Mooney, *The Ghost Dance Religion*, 900–905; Parsons, "Notes on the Caddo," 47–50; Newkumet and Meredith, *Hasinai*, 68–69; Sadie Weller, Lillie Hoag Whitehorn, and Frank Miller Interviews, DDOIHC; Carter, *Caddo Indians*, 91–97.

36. Omer C. Stewart, *Peyote Religion: A History*, 3–67.

37. Stewart, *Peyote Religion*, 86–92; Weston La Barre, *The Peyote Cult*, 151–58; Parsons, "Notes on the Caddo," 50–53.

38. Stewart, *Peyote Religion*, 92–127, 222–26; Sadie Weller and Lillie Hoag Whitehorn Interviews, DDOIC.

39. Quoted in Melburn D. Thurman, "Supplementary Material on the Life of John Wilson, 'The Revealer of Peyote,'" *Ethnohistory* 20 (Summer, 1973): 282.

Chapter Seven: Dissoluton of the Wichita Reservation

1. The Dawes Act, related documents, and commentary have been collected in Wilcomb E. Washburn, *The Assault on Indian Tribalism: The General Allotment Law (Dawes Act) of 1887*.
2. Janet A. McDonnell, *The Dispossession of the American Indian, 1887–1934*, 121–25.
3. Petition of Chiefs and Headmen of Wichitas and Affiliated Tribes, Sept. 17, 1877, WAL.
4. Hunt to CIA, Mar. 3, 1882, KAF 10; R. A. Sneed, "Reminiscences of an Indian Trader," CO 14 (June, 1936): 145; Petition of Wichitas and Caddos, Apr. 1, 1882, SR, 48 Cong., 1 sess., doc. 13, 117; A Bill for the relief of the Wichitas, Caddoes, and Affiliated bands of Indians, Apr. 10, 1882, SR, 48 Cong., 1 sess., doc. 13, 117.
5. Hiram Price to the secretary of the Interior, Oct. 9, 1883, SR, 48 Cong., 1 sess., doc. 13, 95.
6. Proceedings of council held Jan., 22, 1883, SR, 48 Cong., 1 sess., doc. 13, 119–29; Report of E. B. Townsend, July 26, 1883, SR, 48 Cong., 1 sess., doc. 13, 131–38; Proceedings of council held May 15–21, 1883, KAF 48.
7. Hunt to CIA, Sept. 22, 1883, KAF 12; Statements of Left Hand and Tawakoni Jim, Sept. 17, 1883, KAF 13; Chapman, "Dissolution of the Wichita Reservation, Part I," 199.
8. Hall to CIA, Mar. 9, 1877, KAF 15; White to George Grayson, Dec. 19, 1887, KAF 16.
9. Prucha, *The Great Father*, 2: 746–47; Chapman, "Dissolution of the Wichita Reservation, Part I," 193.
10. Chapman, "Dissolution of the Wichita Reservation, Part I," 194.
11. Chapman, "Dissolution of the Wichita Reservation, Part I," 200; SED, 52 Cong., 1 sess., doc. 46, 21.
12. SED, 52 Cong., 1 sess., doc. 46, 22.
13. SED, 52 Cong., 1 sess., doc. 46, 22–23; SED, 52 Cong., 1 sess., doc. 14, 9–11.
14. Chapman, "Dissolution of the Wichita Reservation, Part I," 206–207.
15. Chapman, "Dissolution of the Wichita Reservation, Part I," 208–209; Baldwin to CIA, Aug. 28, 1896, HED, 54 Cong., 2 sess., doc. 5, 255–56.
16. Chapman, "Dissolution of the Wichita Reservation, Part II," 300–304; Council Proceedings, Mar. 23 and 24, 1897, SED, 55 Cong., 1 sess., doc. 53, 3–14; Memorial of the Wichita and Affiliated Bands of Indians, June 3 and 4, 1897, HED, 55 Cong., 1 sess., doc. 74, 2–10; Contract between the Wichita and Affiliated bands of Indians and Josiah M. Vale, May 1, 1895, HED, 54 Cong., 1 sess., doc. 97, 11–13.
17. Chapman, "Dissolution of the Wichita Reservation, Part II," 304–305; Hagan, *United States–Comanche Relations*, 231–49.
18. Chapman, "Dissolution of the Wichita Reservation, Part II," 305–306; Payment Under Decree of Court of Claims, etc., SED, 56 Cong., 2 sess., doc. 191, 4–5.
19. Chapman, "Dissolution of the Wichita Reservation, Part II," 307.

20. Chapman, "Dissolution of the Wichita Reservation, Part II," 308–309.
21. Randlett to CIA, May 25, 1901, KAF 61.
22. Council Proceedings, May 29, 1901, KAF 61.
23. Randlett to CIA, Sept. 1, 1901, *HED*, 57 Cong., 1 sess., doc. 5, 320; Frank Miller and Bertha Prevost Interviews, DDOIHC; Chapman, "Dissolution of the Wichita Reservation, Part II, 310–14.

Epilogue

1. Newkumet and Meredith, *Hasinai*, 51–52; Howard Meredith, *Dancing on Common Ground: Tribal Cultures and Alliances on the Southern Plains*, 115.
2. Newkumet and Meredith, *Hasinai*, 77–78, 90–101; Carter, *Caddo Indians*, 194–96; Meredith, *Dancing on Common Ground*, 134–35.
3. Newcomb, *A People Called Wichita*, 92–94; Meredith, *Dancing on Common Ground*, 116–21, 134.

Bibliography

Manuscript Collections

Duke, Doris, Oral Indian History Collection. Western History Collections. University of Oklahoma. Norman, Oklahoma.

Hume, C. Ross, Collection. Western History Collections. University of Oklahoma. Norman, Oklahoma.

Kiowa Agency Files. Microfilm copies. Indian Archives. Oklahoma Historical Society. Oklahoma City.

Records of the Bureau of Indian Affairs. Letters received by the Office of Indian Affairs from the Texas Agency. Photostat copy. Eugene C. Barker Library, University of Texas, Austin.

————. Letters received by the Office of Indian Affairs from the Wichita Agency. National Archives Microfilm Publication M234, Rolls 928–30 (1857–78).

Wichita Boarding School Papers. Microfilm copies. Indian Archives. Oklahoma Historical Society. Oklahoma City.

Government Documents

U.S. Congress. House of Representatives. *Executive Documents.* 29 Cong., 2 sess., Doc. 76; 29 Cong., 2 sess., Doc. 100; 30 Cong., 1 sess., Doc. 8; 30 Cong., 2 sess., Doc. 1; 32 Cong., 2 sess., Doc. 1; 34 Cong., 1 sess., Doc. 1; 38 Cong., 1 sess., Doc. 1; 38 Cong., 2 sess., Doc. 1; 39 Cong., 1 sess., Doc. 1; 39 Cong., 2 sess., Doc. 1; 40 Cong., 2 sess., Doc. 1; 40 Cong., 3 sess., Doc. 1; 41 Cong., 2 sess., Doc. 1; 41 Cong., 3 sess., Doc. 1; 42 Cong., 2 sess., Doc. 1; 42 Cong., 3 sess., Doc. 1; 42 Cong., 3 sess., Doc. 65; 43 Cong., 1 sess., Doc. 1; 43 Cong., 2 sess., Doc. 1; 44 Cong., 1 sess., Doc. 1; 44 Cong., 2 sess., Doc. 1; 45 Cong., 2 sess., Doc. 1; 45 Cong., 3 sess., Doc. 1; 46 Cong., 2 sess., Doc. 1; 46 Cong., 3 sess., Doc. 1; 47 Cong., 1 sess., Doc. 1; 47 Cong., 2 sess., Doc. 1; 48 Cong., 1 sess., Doc. 1; 49 Cong., 1 sess., Doc. 1; 49 Cong., 2 sess., Doc. 1; 50 Cong., 1 sess., Doc. 1; 50 Cong., 2 sess., Doc. 1; 51 Cong., 1 sess., Doc. 1; 51 Cong., 2 sess., Doc. 1; 52 Cong.,

2 sess., Doc. 1; 54 Cong., 1 sess., Doc. 5; 54 Cong., 1 sess., Doc. 97; 54 Cong., 2 sess., Doc. 5; 55 Cong., 1 sess., Doc. 74; 55 Cong., 2 sess., Doc. 5; 55 Cong., 3 sess., Doc. 5; 56 Cong., 1 sess., Doc. 5; 56 Cong., 2 sess., Doc. 5; 57 Cong., 1 sess., Doc. 5.

———. Senate. *Executive Documents.* 29 Cong., 1 sess., Doc. 1; 31 Cong., 1 sess., Doc. 1; 31 Cong., 2 sess., Doc. 1; 32 Cong., 1 sess., Doc. 1; 33 Cong., 1 sess., Doc. 1; 33 Cong., 1 sess., Doc. 54; 34 Cong., 1 sess., Doc. 60; 34 Cong., 3 sess., Doc. 5; 35 Cong., 1 sess., Doc. 2; 35 Cong., 2 sess., Doc 1; 36 Cong., 1 sess., Doc. 2; 52 Cong., 1 sess., Doc. 14; 52 Cong., 1 sess., Doc. 46; 55 Cong., 1 sess., Doc. 53; 56 Cong., 2 sess., Doc. 191.

———. *Reports.* 30 Cong., 1 sess., Doc. 171; 44 Cong., 1 sess., Doc. 804; 48 Cong., 1 sess., Doc. 13; 49 Cong., 1 sess., Doc. 1278.

Other Sources

Abel, Annie Heloise. *The American Indian as Slaveholder and Secessionist.* Reprint. Lincoln: University of Nebraska, 1992.

Agnew, Brad. "The 1858 War against the Comanches." *Chronicles of Oklahoma* 49 (Summer, 1971): 211–29.

Anderson, H. Allen. "The Delaware and Shawnee Indians and the Republic of Texas, 1820–1845." *Southwestern Historical Quarterly* 94 (October, 1990): 231–60.

Armbruster, Henry C. "Torrey's Trading Post." *Texana* 2 (Summer, 1964): 113–31.

Ashcraft, Allan C., ed. "Confederate Indian Department Conditions in August 1864." *Chronicles of Oklahoma* 41 (Autumn, 1963): 270–85.

Battey, Thomas C. *The Life and Adventures of a Quaker among the Indians.* Williamstown, Mass.: Corner House Publishers, 1972.

Bell, Robert E., Edward B. Jelks, and W. W. Newcomb. *Wichita Indian Archaeology and Ethnology.* New York: Garland Publishing, 1974.

Bender, Averam B. *The March of Empire: Frontier Defense in the Southwest, 1848–1860.* Lawrence: University of Kansas Press, 1952.

Biesele, R. L. "The Relations between the German Settlers and the Indians in Texas, 1844–1860." *Southwestern Historical Quarterly* 31 (1927): 116–29.

Blaine, Martha Royce. *Pawnee Passage: 1870–1875.* Norman: University of Oklahoma Press, 1990.

Bolton, Herbert Eugene, ed. *Athanase de Mézières and the Louisiana-Texas Frontier, 1768–1780.* 2 vols. Cleveland: Arthur H. Clark Company, 1914.

———. *The Hasinais: Southern Caddoans as Seen by the Earliest Europeans.* Edited by Russell M. Magnaghi. Norman: University of Oklahoma Press, 1987.

Braly, Earl Buck. "Fort Belknap." *West Texas Historical Association Year Book* 30 (October, 1954): 83–114.

Butler, Josiah. "Pioneer School Teaching at the Comanche-Kiowa Agency School, 1870–1873: Being the Reminiscences of the First Teacher." *Chronicles of Oklahoma* 6 (December, 1928): 482–528.

Carter, Cecile Elkins. *Caddo Indians: Where We Come From.* Norman: University of Oklahoma Press, 1995.

Chalfant, William Y. *Without Quarter: The Wichita Expedition and the Fight on Crooked Creek.* Norman: University of Oklahoma Press, 1991.

Chapman, Berlin B. "Establishment of the Wichita Reservation." *Chronicles of Oklahoma* 11 (December, 1933): 1044–55.

———. "Dissolution of the Wichita Reservation," *Chronicles of Oklahoma* 22 (Summer, 1944): 192–209; 22 (Autumn, 1944): 300–14.

Coleman, Michael C. *American Indian Children at School, 1850–1930.* Jackson: University Press of Mississippi, 1993.

Coombes, Zachariah E. *Diary of a Frontiersman, 1858–1859.* Edited by Barbara Ledbetter. Newcastle, Tex.: n.p., 1961.

Crane, R. C. "Robert E. Lee's Expedition in the Upper Brazos and Colorado Country." *West Texas Historical Association Year Book* 13 (October, 1937): 53–63.

Cronon, William. *Changes in the Land: Indians, Colonists, and the Ecology of New England.* New York: Oxford University Press, 1983.

Dorsey, George A. *The Mythology of the Wichita.* Washington, D.C.: Carnegie Institution, 1904.

Douay, Father Anastasius. "Narrative of La Salle's Attempt to Ascend the Mississippi in 1687." In vol. 1, *The Journeys of René Robert Cavelier, Sieur de La Salle.* Edited by Isaac J. Cox. 2 vols. New York: A. S. Barnes and Co., 1905.

Edmunds, R. David. "Native Americans, New Voices: American Indian History, 1895–1995." *American Historical Review* 100 (June, 1995): 717–40.

Elam, Earl Henry. "The History of the Wichita Indian Confederacy to 1868." Ph.D. diss., Texas Tech University, 1971.

Estep, Raymond, ed. *The Removal of the Texas Indians and the Founding of Fort Cobb: Lieutenant William E. Burnet Letters.* Oklahoma City: Oklahoma Historical Society, 1961.

Ewers, John C. "The Influence of Epidemics on the Indian Populations and Cultures of Texas." *Plains Anthropologist* 18 (1973): 104–18.

Forbes, Bruce David. "John Jasper Methvin, Methodist 'Missionary to the Western Tribes.'" *Churchmen and the Western Tribes, 1820–1920.* Edited by Clyde A. Milner II and Floyd A. O'Neill. Norman: University of Oklahoma Press, 1985.

Ford, John Salmon. *Rip Ford's Texas.* Edited by Stephen B. Oates. Austin: University of Texas Press, 1963.

Foreman, Grant, ed. "A Journal Kept by Douglas Cooper." *Chronicles of Oklahoma* 5 (September, 1927): 381–90.

———. "The Journal of Elijah Hicks." *Chronicles of Oklahoma* 13 (March, 1935): 68–99.

———. "The Texas Comanche Treaty of 1846." *Southwestern Historical Quarterly* 51 (April, 1948): 314–32.

Gibson, Ariel. "Confederates on the Plains: The Pike Mission to the Wichita Agency." *Great Plains Journal* 4 (Fall, 1964): 7–16.

Glover, William B. "A History of the Caddo Indians." *Louisiana Historical Quarterly* 18 (October, 1935): 872–946.

Griffith, William Joyce. *The Hasinai Indians of East Texas as Seen by Europeans, 1687–1772.* Middle American Research Institute, Philological and Documentary Studies, vol. 2, no. 3. New Orleans: Tulane University Press, 1954.

Hagan, William T. *United States–Comanche Relations: The Reservation Years.* Norman: University of Oklahoma Press, 1990.

Haley, James L. *The Buffalo War: The History of the Red River Indian Uprising of 1874.* Norman: University of Oklahoma Press, 1976.

Harmon, George D. "The United States Indian Policy in Texas, 1845–1860." *Mississippi Valley Historical Review* 17 (December, 1930): 377–403.

Harmon, Jeanne V. "Matthew Leeper, Confederate Agent at the Wichita Agency, Indian Territory." *Chronicles of Oklahoma* 47 (Fall, 1967): 242–57.

Hatcher, Mattie Austin, ed. and trans. "Descriptions of the Tejas or Asinai Indians,

1691–1722." *Southwestern Historical Quarterly* 30 (January, 1927): 206–18; (April, 1927): 283–304; 31 (July, 1927): 50–62; (October, 1927): 150–80.

Hoerig, Karl. A. "The Relationship between German Immigrants and the Native Peoples in Western Texas." *Southwestern Historical Quarterly* 97 (January, 1994): 422–51.

Hughes, Jack T. "Prehistory of the Caddoan-Speaking Tribes." *Caddoan Indians*. Vol. 3. New York: Garland Publishing Company, 1974.

Hughes, W. J. "'Rip' Ford's Indian Fight on the Canadian." *Panhandle-Plains Historical Review* 30 (1957): 1–26.

John, Elizabeth A. H. *Storms Brewed in Other Men's Worlds: The Confrontation of Indians, Spanish, and French in the Southwest, 1540–1795*. College Station: Texas A&M University Press, 1975. Reprint, Lincoln: University of Nebraska Press, 1981.

———. "The Taovayas Indians in Frontier Trade and Diplomacy, 1719–1768." *Chronicles of Oklahoma* 31 (Autumn, 1953): 268–89.

———. "The Taovayas Indians in Frontier Trade and Diplomacy, 1769–1779." *Southwestern Historical Quarterly* 57 (October, 1953): 181–201.

———. "The Taovayas Indians in Frontier Trade and Diplomacy, 1779–1835." *Panhandle-Plains Historical Review* 26 (1953): 40–72.

Kappler, Charles J., ed. *Indian Affairs: Laws and Treaties*. 3 vols. Washington, D.C.: U.S. Government Printing Office, 1910–13.

Keller, Mark, and Thomas A. Belser, Jr., eds. "Albert Pike's Contribution to the *Spirit of the Times*, Including His 'Letter from the Far, Far West.'" *Arkansas Historical Quarterly* 37 (Winter, 1978): 318–53.

Klos, George. "'Our people could not distinguish one tribe from another': The 1859 Expulsion of the Reserve Indians from Texas." *Southwestern Historical Quarterly* 97 (April, 1994): 598–619.

Koch, Lena Clara. "The Federal Indian Policy in Texas, 1845–1860." *Southwestern Historical Quarterly* 28 (January, 1925): 223–34; 28 (April, 1925): 259–86; 29 (July, 1925): 19–35; 29 (October, 1925): 98–127.

La Barre, Weston. *The Peyote Cult*. Norman: University of Oklahoma Press, 1989.

Ledbetter, Barbara. "Zachariach Ellis Coombes, the Samuel Pepys of the Texas Frontier." *West Texas Historical Association Year Book* (October, 1968): 68–77.

Lindsey, Donald F. *Indians at Hampton Institute, 1877–1923*. Urbana: University of Illinois Press, 1995.

Lomawaima, Tsianina. *They Called It Prairie Light: The Story of Chilocco Indian School*. Lincoln: University of Nebraska Press, 1994.

McBeth, Sally J. *Ethnic Identity and the Boarding School Experience of West-Central Oklahoma American Indians*. Washington: University Press of America, 1983.

McDonnell, Janet A. *The Dispossession of the American Indian, 1887–1934*. Bloomington: University of Indiana Press, 1991.

Meredith, Howard. *Dancing on Common Ground: Tribal Cultures and Alliances on the Southern Plains*. Lawrence: University of Kansas Press, 1995.

Merrell, James M. *The Indians' New World: Catawbas and Their Neighbors from European Contact through the Era of Removal*. Chapel Hill: University of North Carolina Press, 1989.

Mooney, James. *The Ghost Dance Religion and the Sioux Outbreak of 1890*. Fourteenth Annual Report of the Bureau of Ethnology, 1892–93, pt. 2. Washington, D.C.: Government Printing Office, 1896.

Neighbours, Kenneth F. "Chapters from the History of Texas Indian Reservations." *West Texas Historical Association Year Book* 33 (October, 1957): 3–16.

———. "The Assassination of Robert S. Neighbors." *West Texas Historical Association Year Book* 34 (October, 1958): 38–49.

———. "Indian Exodus out of Texas in 1859." *West Texas Historical Association Year Book* 36 (October, 1960): 80–97.

———. "José María: Anadarko Chief." *Chronicles of Oklahoma* 44 (Autumn, 1966): 254–74.

Newcomb, W. W. *The Indians of Texas: From Prehistoric to Modern Times.* Austin: University of Texas Press, 1961.

———. *A People Called Wichita.* Phoenix: Indian Tribal Series, 1976.

Newkumet, Vynola Beaver, and Howard L. Meredith. *Hasinai: A Traditional History of the Caddo Confederacy.* College Station: Texas A&M University Press, 1988.

Nye, William S. *Carbine and Lance: The Story of Old Fort Sill.* Norman: University of Oklahoma Press, 1937.

Parsons, Elsie Clews. "Notes on the Caddo." *Memoirs of the American Anthropological Association* 57 (1941): 1–76.

Perttula, Timothy K. *The Caddo Nation: Archaeological and Ethnohistoric Perspectives.* Austin: University of Texas Press, 1992.

Pratt, Richard Henry. *Battlefield and Classroom: Four Decades with the American Indian, 1867–1904.* Edited by Robert M. Utley. New Haven: Yale University Press, 1964.

Prucha, Francis Paul. *American Indian Policy in Crisis: Christian Reformers and the Indian, 1865–1900.* Norman: University of Oklahoma Press, 1976.

———. *The Great Father: The United States Government and the American Indians.* 2 vols. Lincoln: University of Nebraska Press, 1984.

Richardson, Rupert N. *The Comanche Barrier to South Plains Settlement.* Glendale, Calif.: Arthur C. Clark Company, 1933.

Ritchie, E. B., ed. "Copy of Report of Colonel Samuel Cooper, Assistant Adjutant General of the United States, of Inspection Trip from Fort Graham to the Indian Villages on the Upper Brazos made in June, 1851." *Southwestern Historical Quarterly* 42 (April, 1939): 327–33.

Roemer, Ferdinand. *Texas, with Particular Reference to German Immigration and the Physical Appearance of the Country.* Translated by Oswald Mueller. San Antonio: Standard Printing Company, 1935.

Salisbury, Neal. *Manitou and Providence: Indians, Europeans, and the Making of New England, 1500–1643.* New York: Oxford University Press, 1982.

Schilz, Jodye Lynn, and Thomas F. Schilz. *Buffalo Hump and the Penateka Comanches.* El Paso: Texas Western Press, 1989.

Schilz, Thomas Frank. "People of the Cross Timbers: A History of the Tonkawa Indians." Ph.D. diss., Texas Christian University, 1983.

Schmitt, Karl. "Wichita-Kiowa Relations and the 1874 Outbreak." *Chronicles of Oklahoma* 28 (Summer, 1950): 154–60.

———, and Iva Osanai Schmitt. *Wichita Kinship: Past and Present.* Norman: University Book Exchange, 1952.

Shannon, Ruby W. *"Friends" for the Indians: One Hundred Years of Education at Riverside Indian School, Anadarko, Oklahoma.* Anadarko, Okla.: n.p., 1971.

Simpson, Harold B. *Cry Comanche: The Second United States Cavalry in Texas, 1855–1861.* Hillsboro, Tex.: Hill Junior College Press, 1979.

Smith, F. Todd. *The Caddo Indians: Tribes at the Convergence of Empires, 1542–1854.* College Station: Texas A&M University Press, 1995.

———. "The Kadohadacho Indians and the Louisiana-Texas Frontier, 1803–1815. *Southwestern Historical Quarterly* 94 (October, 1991): 172–201.

Smith, Ralph. "The Tawehash (Taovayas) in French, Spanish, English, and American Imperial Affairs." *West Texas Historical Association Year Book* 28 (October, 1952): 18–49.

Sneed, R. A. "Reminiscences of an Indian Trader." *Chronicles of Oklahoma* 14 (June, 1936): 135–55.

Steele, Aubrey. "The Beginning of Quaker Administration of Indian Affairs in Oklahoma." *Chronicles of Oklahoma* 17 (December, 1939): 364–92.

Stewart, Omer C. *Peyote Religion: A History.* Norman: University of Oklahoma Press, 1987.

Swanton, John Reed. *Source Material on the History and Ethnology of the Caddo Indians.* Bureau of American Ethnology Bulletin 132. Washington, D.C.: Government Printing Office, 1942.

Thurman, Melburn D. "Supplementary Material on the Life of John Wilson, 'The Revealer of Peyote.'" *Ethnohistory* 20 (Summer, 1973): 279–87.

Trennert, Robert A., Jr. *Alternative to Extinction: Federal Indian Policy and the Beginnings of the Reservation System, 1846–1851.* Philadelphia: Temple University Press, 1975.

Usner, Daniel H., Jr. *Indians, Settlers, and Slaves in a Frontier Exchange Economy: The Lower Mississippi Valley before 1783.* Chapel Hill: University of North Carolina Press, 1992.

The War of the Rebellion: A Compilation of the Official Records of the Union and Confederate Armies. 130 vols. Washington, D.C.: Government Printing Office, 1880.

Washburn, Wilcomb E. *The Assault on Indian Tribalism: The General Allotment Law (Dawes Act) of 1887.* Philadelphia: J. B. Lippincott Company, 1975.

Webb, Murl L. "Religious and Educational Efforts among Texas Indians in the 1850s." *Southwestern Historical Quarterly* 69 (July, 1965): 22–37.

Weber, David J. *The Spanish Frontier in North America.* New Haven: Yale University Press, 1992.

Weddle, Robert S. *The San Sabá Mission: Spanish Pivot in Texas.* Austin: University of Texas Press, 1964.

Wedel, Mildred Mott. *The Wichita Indians, 1541–1750.* Reprints in Anthropology, Volume 38. Lincoln, Neb.: J & L Reprint Company, 1988.

White, E. E. *Experiences of a Special Indian Agent.* Norman: University of Oklahoma Press, 1965.

Winfrey, Dorman, ed. *The Indian Papers of Texas and the Southwest, 1825–1916.* 5 vols. Austin: Texas State Library, 1959–61.

Wright, Muriel H. "A History of Fort Cobb." *Chronicles of Oklahoma.* 34 (Spring, 1956): 53–71.

Index